Hook to Heal!

100 Crochet Exercises For Health, Growth, Connection, Inspiration and Honoring Your Inner Artist

By Kathryn Vercillo

Copyright © 2015 by Kathryn Vercillo

All rights reserved. This book, or parts thereof, may not be reproduced or copied in any form without express permission of the author. The author is more than happy to consider such requests. You can contact the author through her website (www.crochetconcupiscence.com) to request such permission.

First Printing, November 2015

ISBN-13: 978-1519300447
ISBN-10: 1519300441

A Loving Note to My Readers

I am an indie DIY author and this is a self-published labor of love. If you believe in this work, you can support it. Each of the following things truly helps:

- Buy a copy of the book as a gift for someone else.
- Suggest the title to your local library; many library websites have a tool that makes this easy!
- Suggest the title to your local yarn stores, craft stores and small businesses; they can purchase it wholesale through Amazon.
- Write a positive review of the book for Amazon and/ or Goodreads.
- Blog about this book on your own site.
- Recommend the book to others through social media, forums, web groups, etc.
- Tell your friends what you liked about the book.
- Gift copies of the book to doctor's offices and other waiting rooms.
- Leave a copy of the book in a local Little Free Library bin. Or leave a random copy behind in a coffee shop or public space.

You are welcome to quote the book directly when you are sharing it as long as you refer to the book by title and author when you do so. You are also welcome to use any images of the book's cover. However, please do not copy and share any of the exercises without getting my express permission. Doing so violates terms of copyright. I'm happy to work with you! You can email me at kathryn.vercillo@gmail.com with any questions.

Whether or not you choose to share this book with others, I hope that you find it to be a useful tool. That you are even choosing to try it for yourself makes me endlessly happy. May you find peace, joy and growth in these pages.

Resources for Learning to Crochet

The exercises in *Hook to Heal* are designed to be adaptable to all different skill levels of crochet. However, this book does not teach you how to do the craft. Here are some of my favorite resources for learning how to crochet if you're a beginner. (These sources were relevant and active as of November 2015):

Online Crochet Lessons

You can gain a solid introduction to the basics of crochet from the following sources:

- Crochet School (23 Online Lessons) by Craftyminx: http://www.craftyminx.com/2011/11/crochet-school-.html/
- Learn How to Crochet (Beginner's Course) by Moogly: http://www.mooglyblog.com/learn-how-to-crochet/
- How to Crochet for Beginners (24 Courses) by The Crochet Crowd: https://www.youtube.com/playlist?list=PL69F5A7FE3F95232F
- Various Online Classes at Craftsy: http://www.craftsy.com

You can also find links to a variety of specific techniques and tutorials on Crochet Concupiscence at http://www.crochetconcupiscence.com/how-to-crochet-crochet-tutorials-roundup/.

"How to Crochet" Books

There are many, many great crochet books out there. Some of my favorites for beginners are:

- The Complete Photo Guide to Crochet by Margaret Hubert
- The Crochet Workshop: Learn to Crochet in Quick and Easy Steps by Emma Osmond
- Basic Crocheting and Projects by Sharon Hernes Silverman
- How to Crochet by Sara Delaney
- Donna Kooler's Encyclopedia of Crochet

You can also learn to crochet from in-person lessons, which are usually offered through local craft stores. Everyone learns differently, so find the learning style that works best for you!

TABLE OF CONTENTS

INTRODUCTION	9
HOW TO USE THIS BOOK	13
GATHERING THE TOOLS YOU NEED FOR THIS CREATIVE JOURNEY	17
TOOL #1: CROCHET JOURNAL	17
TOOL #2: MINDFULNESS	20
TOOL #3: YOUR CREATIVE COMMITMENT	21
MINDFULNESS CROCHET	23
MINDFULNESS CROCHET EXERCISE #1: BASIC PRACTICE	25
MINDFULNESS CROCHET EXERCISE #2: NOTICE EVERY ASPECT OF THE STITCH	25
MINDFULNESS CROCHET EXERCISE #3: MANTRA CROCHET	26
MINDFULNESS CROCHET EXERCISE #4: 60 SECOND OBSERVATION	27
MINDFULNESS CROCHET EXERCISE #5: INCREASED BREATHING TRIANGLE	28
MINDFULNESS CROCHET EXERCISE #6: NEVER-ENDING CIRCLE	29
MINDFULNESS CROCHET EXERCISE #7: CHOOSE A MINDFULNESS CUE	30
MINDFULNESS CROCHET EXERCISE #8: MICROMOMENTS OF CROCHET	31
LETTING GO, RELEASING, RELAXING	32
LETTING GO EXERCISE #1: THE "WRONG" MATERIALS	39
LETTING GO EXERCISE #2: BE A BEGINNER	41
LETTING GO EXERCISE #3: JOIN A MYSTERY CROCHET-A-LONG	43
LETTING GO EXERCISE #4: RIP IT, RIP IT, RIP IT	45
LETTING GO EXERCISE #5: TOSS YOUR WIPS	47
LETTING GO EXERCISE #6: INTENTIONAL MISTAKE	49
SELF-CARE AND SELF-ESTEEM BUILDING	53
AFFIRMATIONS EXERCISE #1: UNCOVER YOUR NEGATIVE CRAFTY SELF-TALK	58
AFFIRMATIONS EXERCISE #2: EXCAVATING THE NEGATIVE SOURCES	60
AFFIRMATIONS EXERCISE #3: FLIP IT AROUND	63
AFFIRMATIONS EXERCISE #4: UNCOVERING YOUR AFFIRMATIONS	65
AFFIRMATIONS EXERCISE #5: SIMPLE REPEAT AFFIRMATION	67
AFFIRMATIONS EXERCISE #6: END-OF-ROW AFFIRMATIONS	69
AFFIRMATIONS EXERCISE #7: SETTING INTENTIONS	70
SELF-CARE EXERCISE #8: CROCHET FOR DIET CRAVINGS AND ADDICTIONS	73
SELF-CARE EXERCISE #9: CROCHET AS PART OF YOUR SLEEP ROUTINE	76
SELF-CARE EXERCISE #10: DECLUTTERING YOUR MAKES	78
SELF-CARE EXERCISE #11: MAKE SOMETHING THAT YOU NEED	81

SELF-CARE EXERCISE #12: CROCHET A BASKET FOR ITEMS YOU LOVE	83
SELF-CARE EXERCISE #13: SET THE ENVIRONMENT	86
SELF-CARE EXERCISE #14: A LIST OF SAFE PROJECTS	90

EMBRACE A SENSE OF ADVENTURE — 94

ADVENTURE EXERCISE #1: RANDOM LINES PATTERN	97
ADVENTURE EXERCISE #2: FOUND LINES PATTERN	99
ADVENTURE EXERCISE #3: RESEARCH A CROCHET ARTIST	100
ADVENTURE EXERCISE #4: RESEARCH A PERIOD OF CROCHET HISTORY IN DEPTH	103
ADVENTURE EXERCISE #5: OTHER AREAS OF CROCHET RESEARCH	106
ADVENTURE EXERCISE #6: GO ON A CROCHET RETREAT	108
ADVENTURE EXERCISE #7: USE UNPREDICTABLE COLORS IN CROCHET	109
ADVENTURE EXERCISE #8: CROCHET IN AN UNEXPECTED PLACE	111
ADVENTURE EXERCISE #9: ORDER SURPRISE YARN!	112

FACING FEARS — 116

FACING FEARS EXERCISE #1: FEAR OF CHANGE	120
FACING FEARS EXERCISE #2: BUILDING BLOCKS OF GROWTH	121
FACING FEARS EXERCISE #3: FEAR OF TRYING NEW THINGS	123
FACING FEARS EXERCISE #4: FEAR OF NOT BEING PERFECT	125
FACING FEARS EXERCISE #5: FEAR OF THE UNKNOWN	127
FACING FEARS EXERCISE #6: MAKE A MAGIC BALL OF YARN	128
FACING FEARS EXERCISE #7: JEALOUSY & FEAR OF NOT BEING GOOD ENOUGH	130
FACING FEARS EXERCISE #8: FEAR OF REJECTION	132
FACING FEARS EXERCISE #9: ADDRESSING EXCUSES	133
FACING FEARS EXERCISE #10: THE VALUE OF CRAFT	135

CREATE ABUNDANCE — 139

ABUNDANCE EXERCISE #1: FEAR OF SCARCITY	141
ABUNDANCE EXERCISE #2: ABUNDANCE OF PROJECTS	142
ABUNDANCE EXERCISE #3: HAVE THE RIGHT TOOLS	144
ABUNDANCE EXERCISE #4: ENJOY YOUR YARN	146
ABUNDANCE EXERCISE #5: "NOT ENOUGH TIME"	147
ABUNDANCE EXERCISE #6: CROCHET IN EXCESS	149
ABUNDANCE EXERCISE #7: "NOT ENOUGH SPACE"	151
ABUNDANCE EXERCISE #8: "NOT ENOUGH ENERGY"	152
ABUNDANCE EXERCISE #9: THE STAGES OF HAPPINESS	154
ABUNDANCE EXERCISE #10: CROCHET FOR ALL FIVE SENSES	156
ABUNDANCE EXERCISE #11: CROCHET YOURSELF A SPECIAL GIFT	158

RELATIONSHIPS AND CONNECTING — 161

RELATIONSHIPS EXERCISE #1: SWAP CRAFT LOVE WITH YOUR PARTNER	162
RELATIONSHIPS EXERCISE #2: FAMILY CRAFT HOUR	164

Relationships Exercise #3: Appreciation Blanket	166
Relationships Exercise #4: Re-Create a Favorite Memory in Crochet	167
Relationships Exercise #5: Crochet a Gift with Intention	168
Relationships Exercise #6: Make Friends Through Crochet	169
Relationships Exercise #7: Create a Crochet Book Club	171
Relationships Exercise #8: Crafting Family Tree	174

GIVING BACK — 177

Giving Back Exercise #1: Crochet for a Charity	179
Giving Back Exercise #2: Teach Someone to Crochet	180
Giving Back Exercise #3: Donate Supplies	182
Giving Back Exercise #4: Yarnbombing to Raise Awareness	183
Giving Back Exercise #5: Charity Crochet Group	185
Giving Back Exercise #6: Slow Yarn!	186
Giving Back Exercise #7: Support Fair Trade Crochet	188

BALANCE — 191

Balance Exercise #1: Same Item, Different Yarn	192
Balance Exercise #2: Holding Your Hook	193
Balance Exercise #3: One Item, One Change	195
Balance Exercise #4: Four-Handed Crochet Project	196
Balance Exercise #5: Many Hands, One Project	197
Balance Exercise #6: Convertible Crochet	199
Balance Exercise #7: Reversible Crochet	200
Balance Exercise #8: Symmetrical Crochet	201
Balance Exercise #9: Crochet a Puzzle	202
Balance Exercise #10: Crochet The Missing Piece	203
Balance Exercise #11: The Opposite of What You Want to Make	205
Balance Exercise #12: Crochet a Stone Paperweight	206
Balance Crochet Exercise #13: Chakra Crochet	207

ARTISTIC DEVELOPMENT — 211

Art Exercise #1: Frame Your Crochet	212
Art Exercise #2: Crochet a Frame	214
Art Exercise #3: Crochet Collage on Canvas	215
Art Exercise #4: Crochet Painting on Canvas	215
Art Exercise #5: Crochet a 3 Dimensional Scene	216
Art Exercise #6: Crochet a Self Portrait	217
Art Exercise #7: Mixed Media Crochet Art	219
Art Exercise #8: Crochet a Color Wheel	220
Art Exercise #9: Crochet Inspiration Board	221
Art Exercise #10: Write a Story and Crochet the Characters	223
Art Exercise #11: Submit Your Work to an Art Exhibit	224

ART EXERCISE #12: CROCHET A DREAM CATCHER	225
CONCLUSION: BACK TO THE BEGINNING	227
REFERENCES AND RESOURCES	243
BOOKS	243
CHARITIES THAT ACCEPT CROCHET DONATIONS	246
FAIR TRADE CROCHET ORGANIZATIONS	248
SPECIAL THANKS	250

Introduction

I am an artist. So are you. Bear with me if you don't believe that yet, because by the end of your journey through this creativity workbook you'll understand exactly what I mean.

I was born into a home that was absent of religion. In the vacuum, I had to invent my own belief system. I had to seek and search and question and struggle. It is still difficult for me to comfortably say aloud that I am spiritual. And yet, it has never been difficult for me to say that I am creative. An artist? Yes, that was hard to learn to say and own. A writer, slightly less so but still difficult to claim. But creative? That was never tough to say. Creativity seems like the most natural way of life for me. And in learning to embrace that natural drive that is my creativity, I came to view creativity as the foundation of my own spiritual practice.

We all create. We do it in ways big and small every single day, intentionally and unintentionally. We create personal fashion styles through the clothes we select and combine and wear at different times in our lives. We create magical moments when we say the right word at the right time or allow the right space to happen when things need to pause. We create relationships with others. We create ourselves. Creation, creativity ... it's at the heart of all that we do. And yet there remain so many people who deny their creativity. I find this all too often in my life and it especially saddens me when I see it in the craft community where people are making something by hand every single day and yet hesitate to name themselves as creative, let alone as artists!

I am here to show you that you are creative. I am here to let you discover for yourself that you are an artist. And more than that, I am here to encourage you to own those names and honor them because in doing so you make more room for creativity and art in your life. In my opinion, the world thrives when each of us creates in the way that is truest to our hearts, when we do it often, when we do it daily, when we create in every single breath that we take and word choice that we make and stitch that we pull up onto a hook.

Anyone who follows my writing for any length of time will eventually come to hear me share my very favorite all-time quote. It is the quote from Martha Graham when she brilliantly said:

"There is a vitality, a life force, an energy, a quickening that is translated through you into action, and because there is only one of you in all of time, this expression is unique. And if you block it, it will

> *never exist through any other medium and it will be lost. The world will not have it. It is not your business to determine how good it is nor how valuable nor how it compares with other expressions. It is your business to keep it yours clearly and directly, to keep the channel open. You do not even have to believe in yourself or your work. You have to keep yourself open and aware to the urges that motivate you."*

I not only love the language of this quote but it remains my favorite quote over all the years and everything else I've read because it hits so close to the core of what I personally believe is true. I believe that we are each born with a unique self and this self gets information and input and influences all throughout the course of life. There is no one else in the entire history of the universe who has had the exact same combination of the original born self and those influences and experiences and therefore there is no one who is exactly like you. I believe that it adds value to the entire world when you share that unique self with others through your creativity. We are all connected, we are all contributing to a piece of a larger whole that is this world and this history that we both inherit and create, and we each have the responsibility to become our best, fullest, truest selves in order to give the most back to that bigger thing beyond us. How magical it is that in doing that we also get to be entirely self-focused in the sense that we get to turn deeply inwards and really hear and experience our own truths as valid. We get to have our own original unique experience and expression and simply by doing that we offer something to the world around us.

    I believe that this is a magical opportunity, a true gift, and also a responsibility. I believe that when we fail to become our fullest creative selves, the world loses out. And I believe that when we denigrate or dismiss our creative abilities, when we are too scared to call ourselves artists and too timid to carve out the time to intentionally create, that we are doing damage to the world around us because we are not giving it our maximum potential. Some have said that it is selfish to take time to create art. I know of people who crochet that hide their yarn stash and lie about the amount of time that they spend on their craft because they feel guilty, thinking that they are being selfish by indulging "wastefully" in this craft that no one else understands. I say that this way of thinking is a harmful lie. I say that it is the opposite that is the truth; it is when we don't create art and when we don't take time for craft that we are really being selfish because it is in the act of not owning our full creative potential that we do the most harm to others around us. I believe that the only way to be our best selves is to take the time to understand our own inner experience and then to express that through creativity.

And I believe that in doing that we heal ourselves. The best thing for the world is for the world to consist of healthy, happy people. When we each do our best to become our most well selves, we help make the world well again. I believe that through creativity, art and craft we are able to improve every aspect of our lives, from our own abilities in work and play to our relationships with others. I believe that this can be done through any form of creativity from dance to painting but here in this book I will look specifically, of course, at how it can be done through crochet. Although I dabble in other arts and crafts, crochet is my true medium and artistic love. As I shared in my previous book, *Crochet Saved My Life*, this craft pulled me out of a deep lifelong battle with depression. I have experienced it as healing for myself and seen it work miracles in healing so many others. I've created this book so that people of all levels in crochet can utilize the craft to heal their inner wounds, nurture their inner artist and bring the full flowering of their own creativity into the light for the world's benefit.

Listen to me carefully ... you are an artist. You with your hook and yarn are creating something that has never before existed in quite the same way as the way that you are making it. Yes, even if you are a beginner at crochet. Yes, even if you always follow patterns to the letter. Because every stitch is an act of creation, every choice you make in the selection of patterns adds up to a body of crafted work that is unique from any other that has been made by another crafter. It may not be comfortable yet to call yourself an artist. It may be scary to say that you are going to own your creativity and make it a priority. That's okay. It's okay to be scared. Do it anyway.

Yes, owning your own creativity can make huge changes in your life and even when you desire those changes it can be intimidating to actually take the steps forward into the new life that's waiting just beyond the bend. Another of my favorite quotes is one I learned years ago when doing my own early creativity work with Julia Cameron's books in The Artist's Way series. She reiterates several times, "leap and the net will appear". It is an idea I've lived by when creative work seems risky and frightening. I invite you to do it, too. I invite you to raise your hook high and jump, to claim that you are the artist that I know that you are even if you doubt it a little bit right now. I invite you to use the exercises and suggestions in the following pages to move deeper and deeper into yourself so that you can have a better life and bring more of your beauty to the world around you. I invite you to come on a journey with me, a journey where we will hook to heal.

How to Use this Book

I'm going to offer you a suggestion for how to use this book but I want you to know that there are many different ways that it can be beneficial to you and that in the end I fully respect, embrace and encourage your choice to use it in whatever way is absolutely best for you. This suggestion is just what I would do based on my knowledge of the materials I've created as well as my experience working with other creativity programs on my own over the years. That said, I'd encourage you to give my suggestion a try and see if it works for you, but to be open to the possibility that you may benefit from using the book in another way.

My best recommendation for you is to use this book in a structured way from start to finish. The reason for this is because what you have the opportunity to do here is to undertake an amazing transformational experience that will bring you to places of inner peace and outer creativity that you've probably been seeking for a really long time. To do that, you have to commit to it, and choosing to work with this book in a scheduled and structured way facilitates that commitment.

What do I mean by scheduled and structured? I think it's worth it to actually carve out specific amounts of scheduled time to work with the materials in this book. When you don't do that, it becomes easy to just let the work slide, especially when the going gets tough. The going can get tough in different ways when you take on a transformational project like this one. It can get tough when life itself gets tough, tempting you to decide that this isn't important enough right now because you need to do x, y or z first or instead. But it can also get tough because when you go through inner change there is something inside that can get scared and can cause you to want to run away. Change is a big deal and our minds are these tricky, slippery things that find innumerable ways to stop working towards change in order to keep us in what feels like a safe place. Let me tell you a secret; being stuck is not a safe place even when it feels familiar! By committing to a schedule of working with this book you give yourself an easy way to ignore the external and internal impulses to set aside the work. You just say to the world and to your own inner critic, "well, it's Tuesday at 11am, it's time to do this work, so too bad that you've got other plans" and you do the work. Eventually, by continuing this process week in and week out you will see changes take place. You will get stronger and stronger in your commitment until it becomes a part of your regular life that you can't imagine ever having lived without. At least, that's been my experience.

So what's the right schedule for working with this book? I'll give you an option but I strongly suggest that you take time to think about it and tweak it to whatever is going to be truly right for you. Ultimately what you want is a regularly scheduled period of working with this book each week, something that you can put on the calendar, but something that is going to be realistic for you to stick to over a period of months. One example is to set aside an hour per day, five days per week, to work with this material. You can do that as a single hour, two separate half hour periods or even three separate twenty-minute periods each day. Believe me, I know that in today's busy, overscheduled world it feels impossible to pull an hour out of each day, but for most of us it turns out not to be if we choose to make the commitment. And the difficulty of scheduling in those five hours per week reaps rewards that actually can make you feel like you have more time instead of less because you're feeling creatively fulfilled throughout the days. So sit down with a calendar and figure out if you can carve out that time. Here are some suggestions for how to find an extra hour in your already busy day:

- Order pizza (or some other delivery food) once a week instead of making dinner. Use the time when you would have made dinner as your creative crochet time.
- Wake up half an hour early and go to bed half an hour later, using that time to work on your crochet creativity.
- Pick a TV show that you watch regularly and commit to giving it up, using that time to crochet and create instead. You can always watch it online later if you feel like you missed out!
- Take public transportation instead of driving to your destinations. You can't crochet while driving but you can crochet on buses and trains!
- Arrive at all appointments twenty minutes early. Whether it's the doctor's office or the school pickup line, it's twenty minutes of crochet.
- Do a babysitting swap with a friend once a week to get an hour or more of free time.

If you can't carve out an hour per day, figure out what you **can** set aside for regular crochet time, commit to it and put it on the calendar. Even if it's only an hour per week, or heck just an hour per month, it's something ... and if it's regularly scheduled then it can benefit you. I fully believe, based on my own experience of working with creativity books, that just starting the process and working through it will create positive change in your life. It doesn't matter how long it takes you to get through the book or even if you never finish it. Try one way, adjust it to your needs, adapt it over time if that feels right, try something different. Commit to doing the work regularly but be flexible with yourself about what "regular" may look like at any given time.

Each chapter in this book is designed to help you work on specific things. The skills are designed to build upon one another, setting the stage for safe explorations in the early chapters and then moving towards more difficult inner work in later chapters. For that reason, I'd recommend working through the chapters in order. However, each chapter is able to stand on its own, so if there is a topic that you truly feel you really need to work with at any given time then go ahead and move to that chapter as needed. For example, if you're really feeling like relationships are the toughest thing going on in your life right now then you may want to move through that chapter first. My hope is that once you've worked the book completely through one time you'll return again and again to the chapters that you need throughout different periods of your life. We all face ongoing challenges as things shift in our lives and crochet can always help!

Each chapter is set up in a specific format. First I introduce the topic and share what my own experience is in working with that particular issues. For example, in the chapter on "letting go", I'll share some of the common things that people have trouble letting go of, along with my own experience in "letting go" and how I've worked through some of those difficulties including ways I've used crochet to help me. Then I'll provide a variety of crochet-related exercises that you can utilize to deal with that same topic. Each exercise includes brief information about the exercise and its purpose, more in-depth information on the purpose, the specific steps, tips to help you out and a "taking it further" idea to go beyond the basic exercise. Some exercises also include helpful lists or other information. After the exercises, at the end of each chapter, I've provided what I call "yarn for thought" questions, which you can ponder and work on in your crochet journal (a tool I'll be explaining in the next chapter) so that you can go further with your inner work than you can go with just the crochet work alone. Each chapter also includes inspiration, quotes and ideas related to the topic to help you get the most out of working through various issues and coming to a deeper part of yourself through craft.

I'll add a quick note here that for some people it may be beneficial to work on this book with a partner or a group since it will hold you accountable for keeping to the exercises during times when you may not be as motivated to do it on your own. This could take the form of starting a local craft group specifically to meet formally and work on the exercises together or it could mean just finding an online friend who is willing to do the exercises at the same time and agree to a weekly check-in to make sure that you're on track. Play around with this option if you think that it's something that will work well for you or if you find that working the program alone doesn't seem to take off after your first few efforts to give it a go.

Above all, please trust yourself to use the materials in this book in the way that is most right for you. We know a lot more about ourselves than we often give ourselves credit for, and part of owning our own creativity is owning that self-knowledge. And finally, be easy on yourself. You will slip up on your commitment. You will skip days, maybe even weeks. You may start the program and find it's not right for you right now and come back to it months later. It's okay. Although it's really important to make artistic commitments to ourselves, it's also equally important to be easy on ourselves. We already spend too much of our lives beating ourselves up for not doing "enough" and I don't want anyone to use this book as another weapon for that kind of self-punishment. So try it my way but then do it your way. Consider the book a gift from me to you and also a gift from you to yourself.

Gathering The Tools You Need for this Creative Journey

Before you start a crochet project you need to gather your materials. Typically, you'll need a pattern, yarn and your crochet hook. If you don't have those things, you can still find a way to crochet (freeform, with plastic bags, using finger crochet, for example) but that is a lot more difficult than if you just start with the right materials at the outset. Similarly, you can do this creative journey right now without any preparation but you'll find it a lot more valuable if you take the time to gather some creative materials. I have three tools that I recommend that you work with throughout the duration of your time using this book, which I'll explain in more detail now. Those tools are a crochet journal, the technique of mindfulness and a commitment to your own creative process.

Tool #1: Crochet Journal

The first tool that I find to be invaluable as you work through the exercises in this book is the crochet journal. Don't worry if you're not normally a journaler or don't consider yourself a great writer or whatever other excuses your mind might already be conjuring up to resist the use of this important tool. The crochet journal is going to be a way for you to get in touch with everything that happens for you during this creative process and it can be useful for everyone, regardless of what writing level you see yourself as having. Just try to set aside any skepticism that you may have and work with the crochet journal throughout the process of working with this book. Sure, you may find in the end that it doesn't work for you and that's fine but I'd urge you to really give it a chance and refuse to give in to the temptation to skip this part of the process because I have found that people who choose to work with creativity journals are endlessly surprised by the leaps and bounds that they make thanks to the time spent on those pages.

So, what is a crochet journal?

Your crochet journal is a place where you can take notes about your projects but it's so much more than that. It's a place where you can write about your feelings about your crochet work, feelings that may change from day to day. It's a place where you can vent about how frustrated you are that certain things aren't working with your hook and yarn and where you can express pride about what is working. It's a place where you can brainstorm about different things you'd like to try in the craft and a place where you can give yourself credit for letting go of projects that don't serve you anymore.

Each chapter of this book is going to help you work on different things, from building your self-esteem to improving your relationships. As you work on those things, you are going to experience a wide range of feelings and thoughts. Your crochet journal is a place to write those out. It's a place to figure out what you're going through so that you can process it all and get to the next place. If you are working through this book using the method I suggested in the previous chapter then I would encourage you to use twenty minutes of your daily crochet hour to work on your crochet journal. In each chapter I've included "yarn for thought", a set of inspirational thoughts and questions that can serve as journal prompts for you.

I recommend keeping a crochet journal throughout the entire process of working with this book ... and hopefully beyond! It's okay if you're not someone who enjoys doing a lot of writing. There are alternatives to the traditional journal, which I'll discuss shortly, and keep in mind that the journal is always about the process of uncovering more about yourself and not about the product of the journal itself so it doesn't have to be beautifully written or super creative or stunningly smart. It's just something to do for yourself.

Basically, a crochet journal is a regular journal that you keep to track, explore, understand and expand upon your experience of crafting. I'm going to offer a variety of different suggestions here for what might go into your crochet journal but in the end it's something that you're doing for yourself so you can do with it whatever feels right for you. I'd encourage you to try a few of the different suggestions here, including ones that you aren't immediately drawn to, just to see if they offer you something beneficial. That said, there are no rules for the craft journal. The journal is your place to reflect upon your craft experience, create what you really want that experience to be for you and develop your crafting further through deeper thought about it.

While you're working through the exercises in *Hook to Heal* it can be helpful to use your crochet journal to track that experience. Each chapter includes exercises and "yarn for thought" that offer you opportunities to think about your craft experience in a new way. Many of these are best done through writing out your thoughts and the journal is perfect for that reason. It's also really interesting (and often useful) to have your answers to these exercises in one place where you can go back and look at what you've written before and remind yourself of the ways in which crochet has helped you and can continue to help you in the future.

In addition to the exercises and thought experiments in *Hook to Heal*, some of the things that you might want to include in your crochet journal are:

- **Your daily thoughts and feelings about crochet**. What are you working on and how do you feel about it? What have you learned about crochet lately or what would you like to learn? What did you read about crochet and what are you thinking about that?
- **Grapple with the challenges that arrive in your crafting**. What doesn't feel good? What do you wish was going better? Maybe you haven't crocheted in awhile and want to explore why.
- **Celebrate your crochet joys**. The craft journal is a good place to work with affirmations and truly celebrate your own contributions to the world through crafting. Track your achievements. Include photos of your finished items. Celebrate yourself!
- **Information for your projects**. You can include the patterns, the yarn details, the hook you're using, etc. and in this way use the craft journal to track what you're working on so that if you set it aside and come back to it later you'll know what it was that you needed for that project.
- **Creative ideas that you'd like to explore in the future**. Use your crochet journal to daydream about the craft projects that you're not yet doing but might want to. Dream of yarnbombing a big building someday? Want to handmake crochet gifts for everyone's birthdays next year? Interested in setting and meeting a big goal such as crocheting 100 scarves for charity? Put it in writing, explore it, play with it ... maybe one day you'll do it.
- **Collect stories about crochet**. It can be fun to trace your craft lineage, for example, asking the people in your family if they know about family members who crocheted or if they have any crochet items in the home that have meaning to them. Write these stories down and explore your own connections to the past through crochet.

I personally think that there's a lot of value in having a handwritten crochet journal to reflect in and be able to look back upon. I'd suggest at least trying it out for a few weeks and seeing if it works for you. But not everyone enjoys a written journal so you may need to explore other options until you find what fits for you. Some of the alternatives to a written journal that will still allow you to muse upon your crochet include:

- **Intentional meditation**. Take 20 minutes each day to sit in a quiet space and meditate upon crochet. What does it mean to you right now? Where do you want to go with it? What do you love about it?
- **Visual journal**. You can do a collage-style art journal that expresses your experience of crochet in images. I like to make collage pages that are mostly images but then include one or two words that I either write myself or cut out of a magazine - words that feel like they summarize my experience. You can do something similar with photography (including the use of apps like Instagram) to track what you are working on.
- **Blogging or social media posts**. Some people find it easier to write if they are going to be posting to a public place. You could plan to do a post every morning on Facebook that explores where you are with your crochet work. You could blog weekly sharing your projects and your feelings about them.
- **YouTube or other video recording**. Whether or not you publish it to the web, you may find that recording yourself on audio or video is an easier way to keep your craft journal. You can show the visuals of your work, talk about what you're feeling, etc.
- **Discussions with a craft buddy**. Make a weekly coffee date with a crafty friend specifically to talk about your experiences with crochet. You may want to both select specific *Hook to Heal* exercises to work through and discuss so that you have a focused topic. Alternatively, you may want to just meet and answer the question, "where are you at with your crafting this week?"

Get creative! The point is to have a way to go beyond just picking up a yarn and hook and instead really explore what crochet can be all about for you on many different levels.

Tool #2: Mindfulness

I believe fully in the importance of mindfulness as a tool for self-improvement, self-care and self-awareness. I have written extensively about this in *Crochet Saved My Life*, where I especially shared my experience of using mindfulness to deal with depression and anxiety. In this section I'll share some of that again with additional information about using mindfulness while practicing the exercises in this book. At the end of this section I will include your first set of exercises, a set of mindfulness exercises that you can work with now but that you can also use at anytime throughout the process of working with the materials in the rest of the book. Consider mindfulness exercises to be a foundation of this creativity program, something that you'll use on a regular basis (ideally daily) to keep bringing yourself back again and again to the work that you are doing here.

So what is mindfulness? It is a state of being, one that people generally have to practice to reach, in which you are aware of the present moment and are able to be fully immersed into it without judging it, labeling it or moving out of it. You aren't worried about the past or the future. You are aware of the sensations that occur but you aren't putting names on them to identify them; you simply let them be and let them pass. There are many different paths to practicing mindfulness. Crochet is one of them, and it's one that I have used myself. Mindfulness has been shown to alleviate symptoms of depression, and it became an important part of my own depression healing both in the past and for ongoing self-care. It's powerful to learn to just sit still with what is and to be grounded in the center of chaos; I found that hook in hand enabled me to do that where just sitting "on the cushion" did not. It helped me through a really dark time. That said; you definitely don't need to be experiencing depression or even difficulty to benefit from incorporating mindfulness into your daily life and your creativity practice.

In a moment, I'll share a bit more about crocheting for mindfulness along with a set of mindfulness crochet exercises. But first I want to give you Tool #3, the final tool you'll need as you make your way through this *Hook to Heal* journey.

Tool #3: Your Creative Commitment

Your final tool that I'd like to gift to you at the beginning of this journey so that you can carry it with you for use as needed throughout the process is your own creative commitment to yourself. Of course, I can't give you your commitment, but I'd like to make space here for you to really think about this program as a gift that you are giving to yourself, a gift that works best if you commit to it. So often we put others before ourselves, or we put obligations before desires. You will learn through your work with this book how to stop doing that, how to put yourself first, how to honor your own creativity and how to give great value to the development of your inner artist. This begins with a commitment to your own creativity. I would ask you here to make that commitment, out loud or in writing.

Here is one example of how you might phrase your commitment, which you should certainly adapt to feel true for you:

> *I commit to the work of discovering, expanding and celebrating my own creativity. I commit to making my creative work a priority, setting aside regular time and space to pursue it. I commit to being gentle with myself, allowing many faltering moments and little mistakes, and continuing anyway because I recognize that the creative work is a process, not a final product. I believe in my value as an artist. By keeping this commitment, I help to heal myself and the world around me.*

Determine what you want to commit to, in a way that is positive and self-supporting. It's time to make that commitment, aloud or in writing. In fact, it would be a great first entry for your crochet journal!

Mindfulness Crochet

Going back to Tool #2, let's talk just a little bit more about mindfulness and then explore some exercises that allow you to use your crochet to achieve this important state. Mindfulness is hard to define, and I already described it a bit, but I want to give you a more concise description of the practice as I see it. So what is mindfulness? Put simply, ***mindfulness is the act of focusing non-judgmentally on what is happening in the present moment both internally and externally***.

What does that mean? Let's think for a moment about our normal thinking processes throughout the day. If you're anything like me (and I think most people are in this way) then you have about a million thoughts going through your head each day. You wake up with thoughts in your head and you go to sleep with thoughts in your head and no matter what you're physically or emotionally engaged in during the hours in between, part of your mind is always somewhere else.

As I write this, it's ten in the morning, and I've only been awake for a few hours. I've gotten out of bed, made and enjoyed my morning coffee, cooked and ate some oatmeal with cinnamon apples in it, taken my medications, put on some music and did a little dance-for-exercise around my living room, checked my email and responded to the two most important issues I saw there and then opened up this document and began doing some of the work on it. Each of those actions required some kind of thinking but there were also a bunch of other side thoughts going on in my head. Just a few of them were:

"I really need to get to work on the next part of *Hook to Heal*. For some reason I don't want to work on it. Why don't I want to work on it? I love writing and I love writing about crochet and I think this is a really important book and yet there's some kind of block right now." That thought process led into thoughts about writer's block and what it is and why we experience it and the value of creative work but also the difficulty of a creative life in twenty-first century America. While I was drinking my coffee and thinking about those things, I received a few text messages that made me think about grad school and my classmates and what everyone is doing this summer, about the people I feel like I should get in touch with and the prep work I might want to do before classes begin again in the fall, about the complexities of our group dynamics and the difficulties of adult friendships. I remembered that I'm going line dancing tomorrow and had random thoughts about that. I realized that my inhaler is almost out and so I need to get a new one since I have asthma and don't want to be caught without one. And those are just a few of the thoughts I had this morning, on a regular, average non-stressed not-so-busy kind of day. My mind swirls around and dances with itself constantly, often chattering away without my even realizing it.

The point of all this is that mindfulness helps quiet that chatter. It's the process of coming down directly to the present moment and setting aside all of those random thoughts that are intruding on the potential for some inner stillness. Mindfulness is about seeing what is happening right now in this moment. And yes, there are still plenty of thoughts there, but when you practice mindfulness, you become fully aware of each thought as it arises and you observe it from outside of the emotionality of it and then let it go. It's freeing. So instead of this constant nagging in my head about writer's block and the difficulties of that, I can look directly at the thought arising that I'm having difficulty with writing and address it without attachment by realizing that it's just a momentary thought and I don't have to give it any weight. It's a way of just giving yourself a break.

Those breaks, taken regularly through mindfulness practice, add up to a lot of relief over the course of time. Studies and anecdotal evidence show that mindfulness benefits include:

- Less rumination, which means a calmer mind and can reduce depression and anxiety
- Increased ability to enjoy daily small pleasures and truly savor life
- Improved ability to handle difficult events and experiences
- Assists in reducing impact of chronic pain conditions
- Reduces problems with insomnia
- Strengthens the immune system
- Enhances working memory as well as cognitive flexibility
- Makes you more appreciative and more satisfied with life and relationships
- Stress-relief, which is associated with countless mental and physical health benefits
- Generally improved quality of life
- Increases self-compassion, allowing you to access your inner artist!

There are many, many different ways to practice mindfulness. I encourage you to explore different styles and options and incorporate them into your daily life. But for now, I'll share with you some crochet-specific exercises for mindfulness practice. If you've read *Crochet Saved My Life* then you'll recognize some of the exercises from that book but I've also added new ones to give you a number of different options that you can use throughout your creative journey.

Mindfulness Crochet Exercise #1: Basic Practice

This is a beginner's exercise to get you started with mindfulness crochet. Read through the exercise first then find a quiet space in your home to practice the exercise.

Select a crochet hook and yarn that are both easy to work with. Sit still with your work in your lap. All that you are going to be doing is making a long crochet chain. You will slowly work each loop of the chain, counting each loop as you make it. Focus all of your attention on making one loop at a time and not allowing any other thoughts to creep in. Every time that you notice a thought, frog the chain and start over.

So, for example, you will start your chain … One loop, two loops … (I'm so annoyed that my check hasn't gotten direct deposited yet, I really need to go to the bank … oops, I'm thinking, better start over.) … Frog, re-start the chain … One loop, two loops, three loops … (I really like this yarn but it seems like such a waste to be using it for a mindfulness exercise. Damn. I'm thinking again.) Frog and start over.

Try to continue this exercise until you have successfully focused on the loops at hand and let all other thoughts pass to the length of a ten-loop chain. When you are first learning mindfulness, you may only be able to achieve a chain length of five or six. That's okay. Cut yourself some slack. Mindfulness isn't easy.

This is the most basic mindfulness crochet exercise and one that you can come back to again and again.

NOTE: I selected the "ten loop chain" as a goal because this is a very common count for breathing meditation across many practices that I've studied. For example, in the Zen of Creativity, Zen Master and creativity expert John Daido Loori describes the practice of counting to ten, breathing in on "one", out on "two", re-starting whenever the mind wanders and going up to a count of ten. The ten count is a powerful number used across disciplines. That said, you can obviously modify this exercise to have a goal number higher or lower than ten.

Mindfulness Crochet Exercise #2: Notice Every Aspect of the Stitch

One of the simplest exercises to explain (although it can be surprisingly difficult in practice) is to try to be mindful of every single part of every single stitch that you create in your work. Instead of just working a single crochet, try to pay attention to every micro-motion involved in working it … from the slight twist of your wrist to the way that you are holding your fingers to the almost imperceptible friction between the yarn and the hook. How many little actions can you notice in just a single crochet stitch? With each stitch, try to notice one more action. Notice your breath as you work. Notice the slight split of the yarn fibers. Notice the contrast between your hook color and yarn color. Be truly mindful of the tiniest parts of your work and you can't help but become completely immersed in the entire process of your craft.

Mindfulness Crochet Exercise #3: Mantra Crochet

There is a slight difference between mindfulness and meditation and this particular exercise is a bit more about meditation but it offers the same benefits of relaxation and immersion in your project that the mindfulness exercises offer. You will need to do two things to prepare for this exercise. The first is to choose a project that doesn't require you to count your stitches. The second is to select a short mantra that you will say as you work.

Ideas for projects that do not require you to count your stitches include:

- Any scarf or blanket that uses a **repeating stitch** (such as a simple single crochet) and won't have any increases or decreases. You can start the project before doing your mindfulness exercise so that the chain and first few rows are done.
- A crochet project **worked in the round** without any joining or increases. Again, you'll want to use really simple stitches that you don't have to think about to create. I like the half double crochet, personally.
- **A large granny square**. If you're familiar with the way it's worked then it will come naturally to you without having to focus on the stitch work. This is my personal favorite repeating stitch pattern. The number of large granny square blankets that I have in my home at this point is a bit absurd and growing daily.
- Any crochet pattern or stitch repeat that is so **familiar to you** that doing it is like second nature. What have you crocheted a million times already? That's the pattern to choose!
- A **freeform crochet** art project that doesn't have any specific pattern so that you can do whatever you like with it.

- A project you're **going to frog** anyway. The process is more important than the product when it comes to mindfulness exercises.

The idea here is that you should not have to focus on your stitches because you're going to be focusing instead on repeating a mantra as you work. So, now you have to choose a mantra. *Note: if you don't feel comfortable with the word mantra, think of this as a saying, affirmation or prayer.* You want to choose something really short and simple. Some ideas include:

- **"Om".** This single syllable widely used in meditation can be repeated over and over for a calming effect.
- **"I am."** Repeating this phrase over and over can be astoundingly powerful. It may make you think about what you are or how you came to be or it may just be soothing and relaxing. You can also add a descriptive word to this phrase if there is something specific that you want to focus on in your life, such as "I am strong" or "I am loved".
- **"Mindfulness".** This single multi-syllabic word can be remembered and repeated easily to help you focus on exactly what you're supposed to be doing with this exercise. An alternative is "I am aware" or "I am present".
- **"Crochet."** This is what you're doing so it will ground you in the present moment of the experience to repeat it again and again.

Now that you've done the groundwork, the exercise is easy. Place yourself in a comfortable position with your crochet project. Make sure that it is quiet and relaxing in your environment. Now, do your automatic stitching and with each stitch repeat one word of your mantra. Repeat it over and over again until you are feeling completely calm. Any time that your mind starts to wander, come back to your mantra. Remember why you've chosen this mantra and then focus on repeating the sounds over and over.

Mindfulness Crochet Exercise #4: 60 Second Observation

This is a great exercise because you can practice it any time that you are crocheting, whenever it comes to mind to do so. Simply pause anywhere in your work and stay still for sixty seconds. During that time, consciously observe your project. Just look at it and take in the saturation of the yarn's color, the details of the stitch work, the overall project and how it breaks down into its small components. Notice what you can see through the holes of the stitches and what it feels like to switch your gaze from the work to the point beyond the work through those holes. Just sixty seconds of mindfulness practiced regularly as you crochet can be very healing.

NOTE: As your practice improves, you may incorporate longer periods of observation. You may do meditative observation for fifteen minutes at the beginning of any crochet session, for example. Whether or not you practice longer periods of mindful crochet observation, it's helpful to keep this 60-second tool in your toolbox for regular use because the simplicity and brevity of it allows you to utilize it more often than longer practices.

Mindfulness Crochet Exercise #5: Increased Breathing Triangle

In this exercise, you will crochet a triangle and as you do so your breathing will get deeper and deeper.

First you'll start your triangle. You can use any simple crochet triangle pattern of your choosing. Here is one example of making a basic crochet triangle:

- Chain 2, sc in second chain from hook, turn.
- Chain 1, turn, increase, chain 1, turn. *NOTE: increase means that you crochet two stitches in the single stitch that is there.*
- Now, for each subsequent row, you will increase in the first and last stitch and will just sc in all of the other stitches. *NOTE: increase means that you will crochet two stitches in each of the first and last stitches of the row and one stitch in every other stitch across each row.*

The breathing part is what brings you to meditation. For each odd numbered row, you will inhale throughout the row. For each even numbered row, you will exhale. So you'll inhale as you start the triangle, then you will exhale on row two, inhale on row three, exhale on row four, etc. You want to start the breath on each turn and continue it all the way through to the end of the row. You will always be exhaling for a beat longer than you inhaled on the previous row. Eventually, you will reach a row where you can no longer exhale or inhale to the end of the row. That's when the mindfulness exercise is complete. *At this stage, you could frog the work. Alternatively, you could finish off and over time you'll have a large set of triangle motifs that will remind you of your meditation progress. Turn them into a blanket or wall art display!*

Mindfulness Crochet Exercise #6: Never-Ending Circle

In this exercise, you will crochet a never-ending circle that keeps getting bigger and bigger. Here is my favorite simple crochet circle pattern:

- **Round 1**: Chain 3 (counts as first dc here and throughout). Double crochet 11 times into base of Chain 3. Sl st to close the circle. (Total 12 dc).
- **Round 2**: Chain 3, dc into base of ch 3. Dc twice into each sc. Sl st to close the circle. (Total 24 dc).
- **Round 3**: Chain 3, dc twice into next stitch. *Dc, 2 dc all the way around. Sl st to close. (Total 36 dc).
- **Round 4**: Chain 3, dc in next st, 2 dc in next stitch. *Dc, dc, 2dc around. (Total 48 dc).

For subsequent rounds, you will keep increasing the number of single dc stitches before each 2dc. So round five will be dc in three stitches, 2 dc all the way around then round six will be dc in four stitches, 2 dc all the way around, etc. The rhythm of the continuing increases, as well as the healing features of working a circle, create a meditative experience.

I like to count as I go, sometimes combining the counting with breathwork. For example, on round six, I'll count 1, 2, 3, 4, 5, 6 (with stitches 5 and 6 worked in the same spot) and I'll breathe in for a count of six then out for the next count of six all the way around. The breaths get longer with each round. I like to work at least twelve rounds, usually twenty and sometimes as many as thirty. You can make this circle as big as you want. You can change colors or not; working it as a stashbuster is a good project. When it's done, you can either use it as a blanket or take it all apart and start over again.

Mindfulness Crochet Exercise #7: Choose a Mindfulness Cue

A mindfulness cue is something that you keep in mind as a thing that will always bring you back to your mindfulness practice and the current moment that you are in. For example, some people get cued whenever they feel an itch and scratch themselves. They train themselves that any itch is a cue to come back into the present moment and to focus on the breath, their feelings, the sounds in the room, etc. Eventually, this becomes automatic and they find themselves regularly brought back to mindfulness.

You can choose a cue that relates to your crochet. Maybe it will be every time that you use a crossed double crochet in your work. Or maybe it will be whenever it's time to increase rows. Or perhaps it will be each time that you work with a red yarn. Or maybe it will just be the habit of coming back to mindfulness each time that you start a new project. Pick something that you do frequently but not excessively so that it becomes a ritual but not a hassle. My personal mindfulness cue is weaving in ends; every time that I start to weave in my ends I'm brought back to mindfulness and I pause and focus for a moment on enjoying that specific experience. (Note: I don't particularly like sewing and I dislike weaving in ends. I chose this cue specifically as a way to not only come back to the present moment but also to flip my attitude about this part of crochet.)

Mindfulness Crochet Exercise #8: Micromoments of Crochet

This is an exercise that you can do anytime, anywhere, in your own mind, even without a crochet hook. Simply pause wherever you are, close your eyes, and take a few moments to quiet everything down inside of yourself. Now, picture that you are crocheting. Picture the movement of your hand. Picture the detail of the stitch. Picture each motion, each sense that is affected. Even though you are not physically crocheting, you are bringing yourself back to a place of centered stillness through the mental act of crochet. Incorporate micro-moments of meditative crochet into your entire day for an overall increase in your sense of calm.

Yarn for Thought: More Musings on Meditation and Mindfulness

- What does mindfulness really mean to you? Journal about this.
- Write a story about "the type of person" who meditates. How does this vision cloud your own ability to tap into this powerful resource?
- Where can you go to learn more about meditation and mindfulness?
- Start noticing your breath. Where do you breathe from? Can you move your breath to different areas of your body? Does changing your breath change how you think or feel?
- What creative ways can you think of to be more mindful in your crochet? Brainstorm a big list!

Letting Go, Releasing, Relaxing

Okay, now that you've got the tools in your tool belt, we're ready to really begin our creative work. With your crochet journal at the ready, your mindfulness crochet practices in mind and your commitment to your process in place, you're ready to start looking at what crochet can do for you in terms of healing and personal growth. We're going to start by creating personal safety in this work.

The thing about creativity work is that it's not always emotionally easy even though it is really valuable and ultimately beneficial. We're going to do some tough inner work in this process. However, you can't do that work unless you've created a safe space for yourself. We're not here to beat ourselves up. In fact, self-doubt and self-flagellation are things that have probably been blocking most of us artistically for far too long already. Instead, we're here to gently midwife our own inner artist into the world and to do that we need to make that world a safe, cozy space. That's why we're going to start this process by focusing on letting go, releasing and relaxing.

Letting go of expectations. Letting go of obligations. Letting go of self-criticism. Let go of the end product, release control, be willing to make mistakes. The exercises in this chapter are all about using crochet to release ourselves and relax.

Before we get into the exercises for this chapter, I want to let you know that every single thing I discuss in this book is something that has been a personal challenge for me in one way or another and that I've used crochet to help me get through it. Although not every exercise is going to benefit every person, it's important to me that none of it is fluff either. It's stuff I've tried, stuff I've used in my own life and even when it didn't solve my problems I could see some benefit as I worked through it all. Life is hard, but the thing is that most of the challenges that we face are challenges that everyone else has faced at one time or another as well. When we are open about our difficulties and share ideas about how to get through the tough times, we help make life less challenging for everyone.

At first glance, you wouldn't think that it would be all that hard to let go, release and relax. After all, we're constantly offered opportunities for endless entertainment and ideas for stress-busting, decompressing and chilling out. We all know about the value of rest, the benefits of vacations (and staycations!), the need for downtime. We all know that we should be kind to ourselves if we want to be happy. Every magazine and self-help website tells us these things. Every spa deal and vacation destination offers the promise of that peace. But if you think about it, we wouldn't need to be bombarded with those ideas if letting go and just relaxing weren't such a constant challenge for almost all of us. Perhaps it shouldn't be so hard to just relax and be easy on ourselves but in this society, in this era, it often feels impossible.

At least, that's been my experience. Learning to let go of my own high expectations for myself, my own self-judgment and self-criticism and my own sense of internal obligation has actually been one of the most difficult aspects of my own creative process. It is something I am constantly working on, continually having to stay vigilant about, often having to return to in order to work through it in a different way. Being hard on myself is second nature to me and it doesn't go away easily even though I'm aware of the damage that it does me.

And damage it has done. Depression literally almost killed me when I was in my twenties. There were many, many reasons for that depression and it's a long and complicated story but the important part here is that the depression was significantly exacerbated by how hard I was on myself all of the time. At the time, I didn't even realize how mean I was to myself with all of the "shoulds" and "ought tos" and "not good enoughs" that I was using to beat myself down.

Let me give you the most basic example of how something simple in everyday life can become weighted down with difficulty when you are hard on yourself. I'm thinking back to a time of deep depression when it was difficult to just get out of bed. I'd wake up in the morning, groggy and fatigued from an insomniac tossing-and-turning night, and before my feet had even touched the floor my mind would be attacking itself. "I should get up now." "I should get started on work." "I should be doing work that's more creative than whatever I'm supposed to be working on today. If only I'd finished the boring work yesterday when I had time then I could spend today being creative. I'll never be creative again." "I should call my friends. I haven't talked to any of them in so long. I'm being a terrible friend. I'm not even sure why anyone likes me." "I shouldn't be so hard on myself. Beating myself up isn't going to help. I should relax. I should go to a yoga class. I should learn to meditate." "What's wrong with me?" Should, should, should, bad, bad, bad ... And with all of these thoughts swirling in my mind, just the very act of getting out of bed became too overwhelming. So I'd stay in bed and be mad at myself for staying in bed and then be mad at myself for being mad at myself ... in this endless cycle that just perpetuated and exacerbated the depression.

That's just one example of how being hard on myself worsened my depression. I'm hoping that it's an example that you can relate to – not because I would wish that on anyone but because in my experience this kind of thing is something that we each do to ourselves far too often. We place a bunch of expectations on ourselves – reasonable or unreasonable – and then when we fail to meet those expectations to our highest standards, we feel bad about ourselves. It's terrible. It makes life feel far harder than it should. And it's something that we often do to ourselves in our creative work.

It's definitely a problem that I face in my own creative process. I've chosen to intertwine my work life and my creative life, and there are many wonderful things about doing work I creatively love but the flip side of that is that it becomes even more difficult to navigate those tricky waters of letting go when the creativity is tied up in making a living. There is a lot more at risk, of course, but there's also a lot more socially-sanctioned self-pressure in our work lives. I want to be creative and also to be successful and I have a lot of ideas about what that looks like. The problem is that the expectations I have for success can often block the creative process.

I'm the first to admit that I'm ridiculously hard on myself, although I'm getting better at it with a lot of personal growth work. I'm not 100% sure where this comes from, although I have some suspicions. For example, I think that a lot of it comes from being the eldest child in a family of three with siblings that were significantly younger than me. I've explored birth order theory quite a bit and my family dynamics are pretty straightforward in terms of matching the basics of what it means to be an eldest, middle or youngest child. As an eldest, I tend to be a perfectionist. I was a mother figure to my siblings, the one that they looked up to and mirrored, the one that knew how to do things "better" just by virtue of having learned to do them first. That gets ingrained into you somehow and creates this need to always be the best, the first, the leader, the one who excels. The pressure for that gets internalized and even when nobody else expects me to be on top of my game, I expect it of myself.

This drive is what has led me to succeed in working independently as an author and solopreneur. Many of my friends have told me that they couldn't do my job. Some personalities need the oversight and direction of others in the workplace to keep them motivated, driven and on task. I've not only never needed that; I've never thrived in that kind of setting. I thrive by setting my own deadlines, expectations, desires, goals and then meeting or exceeding those. The drawback to that is that it can create a dangerous cycle; I feel like in order to do well, I need to have high self-demands and I see that meeting those demands makes me feel that I'm doing well so then I set higher demands for myself. And the truth is that I still think that's an important part of being successfully self-employed in creative work. But it's a difficult way to live, and I've had to learn (slowly, surely, often in a one-step-forward-two-back kind of process) that there are ways to manage expectations and be easier on myself even while still setting and achieving goals.

Let's take a look at how this plays out in one area of my creative life – my blog, Crochet Concupiscence. I started this blog in January 2011 as a purely fun, creative thing. I love crochet, I love writing, and I wanted a new and inspiring project that would allow me to explore both of those things in depth. Even from day one, though, I took this side project very seriously. I set a blogging schedule and committed to doing posts every single day. (In fact, I did multiple posts daily in that first year.) I was (and am) dedicated to research, thoughtfulness and honest self-expression in my posts on that blog. I'm happy with this risk. But wanting to do this work well can be a double-edged sword and I run the risk of cutting myself on that creativity.

Some of the ways I've been known to beat myself up with "shoulds" even when it comes to this blog that I love include:

- **Irritation or disappointment** with myself on the rare occasions that I've missed a posting day. I "should" be posting daily, I tell myself. No one else tells me to do this. Likely no one really notices or cares. There's no reason in the world that I must post daily except that it's the goal I set for myself. And yet I get angry at myself when I miss a day.
- **Feelings of embarrassment** when a post doesn't feel up to par. Typos are a particularly common problem for me and although I've come to realize that they don't bother me personally, I still sometimes get embarrassed when other people point them out. I "should" always have a professional writing appearance for my blog.
- **Sense of inadequacy** when it comes to web design and tech things. I get overwhelmed with feelings of frustration when I can't get certain tech things to work right on the blog, when I've had server problems that I didn't understand or when I've had doubts about the blog's design. I "should" have a perfect blog that always looks great and works wonderfully.

So there have been challenges for me in the letting go process when it comes to my blog. I've had to learn that those "shoulds" are things I'm telling myself, and that being mad at myself for not being perfect will not actually make the blog better. There's a difference between striving to create a better product and being mad at myself for not already having it absolutely perfect ... and I've had to work with letting go of expectations and self-criticism in order to understand that difference. I've had to acknowledge that there are areas of the blog that not only aren't strengths for me but aren't actually of interest to me, like the background tech stuff, and I've learned to hire people to help me with some of that and simply to let other things go.

Most importantly, I've learned to shine the spotlight on my creative successes and the things that I am proud of when it comes to Crochet Concupiscence and to make those the focus of my energy. It's easier to improve upon the things that I already like because I'm happy with what I'm doing than it is to work on things that are causing me stress. In other words, if my thought process is "I should never have a typo on my blog" then I can get so mired down in proofreading and editing that the posts stop being fun and I dread doing them and it becomes a joyless blog that nobody can have fun with. In contrast, if my thought process is "I love creating community by celebrating the work of amazing crochet artists" then I get excited about doing the posts, I give them more attention, there are naturally fewer typos and the overall vibe of the blog is one that's positive, spirited and joyful for everyone. **Let's focus on what we're doing well, and on what we enjoy, not what we wish we were doing better, especially when it comes to our crafting and creativity!!**

I'll share one more aspect of my own letting go story before we move forward and that's how I've learned to let go specifically in my crochet work. It is horrifying to me when I think back on all the "shoulds" and expectations and stresses I've had about my crochet work. I crochet for fun. I crochet for myself. I crochet for no other reason than to relax, heal and enjoy my time. And yet, in the past I've managed to make a painful mess of that experience by having "shoulds". Some of the crochet "shoulds" I've lorded over myself have included:

- I should crochet more often.
- I should use more colors when I crochet.
- I should not have knots in my work.
- I should weave in my ends the "right" way instead of the easy way that I actually prefer.

- I should crochet more for charity instead of just for myself.
- I should go back and frog a piece when I realize I've made a mistake instead of just fudging it and moving forward like I usually do.
- I should learn to block my work properly.
- I should photograph my work more expertly so it looks better on the blog.

What the heck?! Why am I using all of those shoulds to make my creative life less fun? Why would I do this to myself? Because the truth is that what underlies all of these "should" messages is the message I tell myself that I'm not good enough just the way that I am. And it's not true. What I make in any given moment is exactly enough for that moment. If I only crocheted once a month in a single color, never weaved in my ends and never fixed my mistakes, it would still be perfect because it's clearly exactly what I needed to do at that time. Crafting shouldn't be stressful; it should relieve stress.

When we put these pressures on ourselves, we actually cause pain in the world around us. When I essentially say to myself, "you're not doing this craft you love good enough" then it's a message I send out into the world that there's a right way to express creative urges and no other way is acceptable. Even if I never say that out loud to anyone else, it's part of the energy that I'm emitting around me, and it infects other people. Everyone around me starts to feel like there's a "good enough" and a "not good enough". This feeling hinders their own creative process because they can't match up to what they think they should be doing. We all suffer as a result.

If we want to improve our own quality of life through crafting, we have to learn to let go. We have to stop seeking perfection. We have to stop saying that where we are at is not enough. We can find ways to strive to make our best work without beating ourselves up for its perceived flaws. We do this by letting go of controlling the end product and focusing on the creative process. And there are many, many ways to do this through crochet.

Common Challenges in Letting Go

Before we get into those exercises for letting go, let's look at some of the common challenges that arise in working in this area. Some that I have encountered include:

- **The fear that letting go of high standards will result in shoddy work**. It's a totally understandable fear that feels very real. It's not. You can find a balance between striving to improve yourself and setting the bar at the impossible height of "perfection".
- **The idea that you need to know what you're doing before you begin**. Creativity is a learning process. It should be messy and fun and filled with "mistakes". You don't know how to do something until you do it. Closely aligned with this is the mistaken belief that there is a "right" way to do something.
- **The incorrect belief that you are in control**. Our brains like to plan and organize and predict because it makes us feel like we are in control of what we are doing and what happens to us. Often, we are not, especially in opening ourselves up to creative work. If you can surrender to the idea that you are not in control, you will have opened up the letting go process.
- **Confusing inspiration and aspiration**. I often look at the work that other amazing crocheters are doing and get so inspired by it. Sometimes, though, I start to cross over into aspiration, into wanting to do what they do. This can be dangerous because we can never be the people we see as role models and that gets very defeating. It's crucial that we stay tuned in to exactly who we are, exploring our unique strengths and motivations and moving forward on our own paths. Aspiring to be someone else makes it hard to let go and relax into who we actually are right in this moment and that aspiration hinders the work.
- **The devil you know problem ...** It can be scary to let go because it means that you're moving forward into an unknown. You may not be comfortable where you are but if the discomfort of not-knowing is greater than the discomfort of the current place then you won't want to take the risk to let go. I dare you – let go anyway!

The Exercises for Letting Go, Releasing, Relaxing

Okay, now that we understand all about the need to let go in our work, we can get into the crochet exercises that facilitate making this happen. Since this is our first foray into the exercises, let me give you a breakdown of how they work. I'll summarize the exercise, then go into more detail about the purpose of the exercise and ways to get into depth with using the exercise as a tool for creative self-exploration and growth. Then I'll provide the steps to the exercise along with some helpful tips. You can often adapt these steps to utilize the exercise in many different ways. I'll wrap up the instructional section with a suggestion for "taking it even further". Remember to use your crochet journal to track your experience, especially as difficult thoughts and feelings arise in the process of doing the exercises; you'll find some ideas about this in the "in depth" section of each exercise. At the end of the chapter you will find the "yarn for thought" questions that you can also journal on to expand your understanding of the work in this chapter.

Letting Go Exercise #1: The "Wrong" Materials

The exercise: Crochet a project using an entirely different yarn and hook from what the pattern requires.

The purpose: Making an item that is impractically tiny or large will allow you to focus on the process of crafting rather than the product. You're letting go of the end product and investigating what the process of the work can offer to you.

In depth: Explore the emotions that come up as you create something you might see as useless or pointless. This exercise can teach you a lot about why you crochet and what you get out of it, information you can use to improve your future crafting experiences.

Exercise steps:

1. **Choose a pattern**. You can choose any pattern at all, of course, but if it's your first time doing this exercise then you might want to pick a fairly straightforward pattern that's easy to follow. I like to pick patterns that will be humorous when done this "wrong way" – hats that look silly when they are too large or too small, for example.
2. **Choose your crochet hook**. You want to select a hook that is very different in size from the hook suggested in the pattern. This is easy if the hook is small or large; just choose the opposite. If you select a pattern with a mid-sized hook (G or H, for example) then you'll have the choice to go smaller or larger (D or N, let's say).
3. **Choose your yarn**. There are two important considerations here. First, you want to choose something that differs from the suggestion in the pattern. You might change the fiber, the weight or both. So for example, if you're working a basic crochet scarf pattern with a worsted weight acrylic yarn, you might instead choose to use

a fine weight silk yarn or a bulky weight T-shirt yarn. Before you finalize your decision, though, make sure that you can work this yarn with the hook that you've chosen. Sometimes it's fun to work a weight that differs from the norm for a hook; for example, I've done a lot of work using an N hook with a lace weight yarn for an open design. Sometimes, though, it's just impossible to pair a hook with a certain yarn; if you're using a tiny thread crochet hook then it may be impossible to use thick T-shirt yarn with it.

4. **Work through the pattern**. Follow the instructions exactly like they are but with your new materials. Practice mindfulness with this exercise, paying attention to all of the senses and all of the feelings that arise as you work this seemingly pointless project.
5. **Enjoy the finished item!** Laugh at it. Share it. Celebrate it. You made something totally pointless and that means that you let go of function, even if just for a moment.
6. **Decide what to do with your finished object.** If you really want to immerse yourself in the "letting go" then the end product doesn't matter at all. You can just give it away or frog it at this point. But you might also find that the finished item is lovely in its own way and actually has a use that you didn't imagine when you began. A smaller-than-normal scarf might be a good gift for a little girl in your life; a too-big bag can become a laundry hamper. Although you shouldn't think about these purposes as you work the project, it's interesting to see how something can become useful or artistic once it's finished. There's magic at work in letting go and also magic in finding inspiration in something finished.

Tips:

- Ignore rules about gauge; they don't apply here.
- Consider choosing the hook and yarn you most like to work with. If you don't like fiddly work, for example, then you might not want to choose a very small steel crochet hook and thread to work this exercise – at least not the first time through. You're supposed to enjoy this, after all!
- It's likely that a thought will come up along the lines of, "what's the point of this?!" Think of it as a practice like in meditation; notice the thought but don't cave in to it. There's value in working through that as you learn to let go of the end product.

- Once you've done the exercise once through, try it again using different materials. (For example, if you worked it using a large hook and T-shirt yarn, do it again in thread crochet with a small hook.)

Taking it further: Run through this exercise six times using different patterns and making different changes with each pass through. At the end, you'll have half a dozen items to put together into a mixed media art display. Get creative! You might put several tiny crochet scarves onto the outside of an oversized crochet bag (appliqué-style). Or perhaps a too-large scarf can serve as a wall hanging and the other items can be attached to that. Play around, explore, get dirty, make something new.

Letting Go Exercise #2: Be a Beginner

The exercise: Learn a new crochet technique.

The purpose: It's important in creative work to always come back to being a beginner. There can be comfort in doing work that we've gotten good at and there's definitely a time and place for that (that's why I have so many large granny square blankets at my house!) but it can be a hindrance to creative growth as well. When we forget what it's like to struggle with a technique, things get routine and the creativity can stagnate. Going back to a beginner's mindset and learning anew can refresh all of the work that we do.

In depth: Explore the emotions that arise as you become a beginner again. Is there fear of doing it incorrectly? Is there frustration at lacking skills? What negative things are you saying to yourself in this process and how can you turn those around into positive things?

Exercise steps:

1. **Select your technique**. What have you always wanted to try in crochet but haven't learned yet? (*Below you'll find a list of possible options.*)
2. **Find the right instructions**. How do you learn best? Crochet books, written online patterns, photo-based tutorials, online video instruction, in-person or online classes ... there are many different ways to learn crochet techniques. Play around with what works best for you. Set yourself up for success.

3. **Gather the materials**. Most crochet techniques won't require anything new; the hooks and yarn already in your stash will suffice. However, some techniques require different materials. For example, Tunisian crochet uses a different type of hook and broomstick lace will require a large knitting needle, dowel or other comparable cylindrical item. Make sure you have the materials you need to get started.
4. **Practice the technique**. Make some swatches. Learn the process.
5. **Crochet a pattern using your new technique**. It's not enough to just learn the steps. You want to take it further and make sure that you can use them to make something. Choose a pattern that uses the technique that you're learning and work it until you've got the hang of it.

CROCHET TECHNIQUES TO TRY

Here is a list of some popular crochet techniques that you might want to learn if you don't know them yet. Of course, there are many different crochet techniques out there and this is only a partial list to get you started. One of my favorite things about crochet is that you can make many things with only a few simple stitches but there is also an endless array of other techniques to learn if you so desire! Here are more than two dozen suggestions:

- **Colorwork Techniques** including Tapestry Crochet, Fair Isle Crochet, Overlay Crochet and Reversible Crochet.
- **Lace Crochet Techniques** including Broomstick Lace, Hairpin Lace, Filet Crochet, Solomon's Knot and Bruges Lace.
- **Alternative Material Crochet** including working with wire, beads, glass, recycled fabric and plastic bags. You can also do mixed media crafting.
- **Alternative Tool Crochet** including Tunisian Crochet, Finger Crochet, Cro-hooking and cro-tatting.
- **Advanced Crochet Basics** including working in different loops, join-as-you-go techniques, chainless foundation, crochet felting.
- **And more!** There is always more to learn in crochet. Try amigurumi, hyperbolic crochet, Bavarian Crochet, entrelac crochet or freeform work.

One of my favorite crochet books that would be great for this exercise is *Crochet Master Class* by Rita Weiss and the late, great Jean Leinhauser. It shares information about eighteen different crochet techniques, each one written by a master in that technique, so you get a lot of information and inspiration about things that you might want to try.

Tips:

- Remember that you may not end up enjoying the technique. You don't have to love it or master it. It's all about trying it and seeing what happens to your creative process as you work through something new.
- Practice non-judgment. A lot of this "letting go" process is about letting go of the inner critic. That critic will tell you that you're not doing this right, not getting the hang of the technique fast enough, not recreating the pattern the right way, that you can't do this ... Work gently with your inner critic, telling it that it's not helping you anyway and you're sending it on its way out of your mind!
- Set emotional goals for yourself. Write them down and keep them where you can see them as you work. For example, I have a tendency to give up quickly if I'm not getting the hang of something so one of my emotional goals when trying something new is to devote at least one straight hour to it before giving it up. That gives me enough time to run through a range of different emotions and get past my blocks to learn something new.

Taking it further: How about making a crochet quilt where each square is done using a different new crochet technique? One way to do this is to learn a new technique each month, finishing the month with a 12" square in that technique. At the end of the year, you'll have one dozen 12" squares to join together to make a large crochet quilt showcasing all of the skills that you've learned. It's a very empowering process to keep learning new crochet techniques all year long, weaving together your beginner self with your experienced self into one whole creative creature.

Letting Go Exercise #3: Join a Mystery Crochet-a-Long

The exercise: Participate in a crochet-a-long (CAL) where you will not know what you are making as you go through the steps.

The purpose: This is the ultimate way to learn to let go of the end product while still feeling some reassurance that you're making something you'll probably enjoy in the end.

In depth: Explore the frustrations that arise as you work through the different steps. One common frustration is being unsure if you're doing the work correctly since you can't see in advance how it's supposed to turn out. Other possible frustrations include wanting to move faster or slower than the CAL, wanting more information for choosing colors, and being afraid that the whole thing is pointless since you don't know if you'll even want the end product that you're making. Whatever you're feeling, work through it and process it!

Exercise steps: You can often find mystery CALs online, hosted through various blogs or online crochet groups. The great thing about the crochet-a-long is that the process unfolds over a period of days or weeks. I strongly recommend finding a current project online that you can follow. But, if you have a friend that is willing to help you, then you can create your own mystery CAL using the following steps:

1. **Ask a friend** to select a crochet pattern for you, but not to tell you what it is. The ideal pattern is relatively long and may contain multiple parts (such as several body parts in an amigurumi pattern or sleeves, body and collar in a shirt pattern).
2. **Have your friend divide the pattern into parts.** One easy way to do this is to copy the pattern over to a Word document and then break it into sections so that each part is on a different page. Each page should be labeled (Part I, Part II, etc.)
3. **Ask your friend to delete any information that identifies the project.** So if the sweater instructions say, "body" and "arms", that can be deleted. You don't need to know what part you're making to follow the instructions.
4. **Crochet your pattern in parts**. Work through each part, one at a time, giving yourself breaks between each part as though you're following along with a group's schedule online. If you can't trust yourself not to jump ahead, ask your friend to email each part in turn on an agreed-upon schedule.

Tips:

- Let your friend know in advance if you have any specific requirements or limitations. If you're a beginning crocheter, for example, you might request that a project is marked for beginners. If you really want to work on a specific technique, such as Tunisian crochet, you can ask your friend to find a relevant pattern.
- Notice your frustrations and really delve into them. You can learn so much about your creative process through this exercise!
- Don't give up halfway through. This is one project that you don't want to abandon.
- Work the CAL with other people. Find a crochet group locally or online to work through the CAL. This will be built-in to CALs that are done online but you'll need to set it up yourself if you're working through the process outlined here.

Taking it further: Once you've completed the CAL, repeat it. This time you will obviously know what you're making. You'll likely make different choices at the start of the project and have different emotions as you work. Pay close attention to the differences this second time around as it can give you a lot of information about yourself, your working style, your inspirations and your limitations.

Letting Go Exercise #4: Rip It, Rip It, Rip It

The exercise: Crochet something to the end then frog it. (Frogging it is the term that crocheters use when they take apart something that they've been working on. Rumor has it the term comes from the fact that you "rip it" back, and your "rip it, rip it" sounds like the sound a frog makes.)

The purpose: What better way to let go of the end product than to completely eliminate it?

In depth: This exercise can bring up a lot of emotions around letting go. What happens when you make something and then it disappears? What do you feel about birthing a creative item that's never going to see full life? What comes up inside of you as you rip back your work? There are some powerful life/death cycles that can be invoked through this process.

Exercise steps:

1. **Choose a pattern** for an item that you think you would like to have. The point is that you're going to have some attachment to this item in the end but you're going to destroy it anyway.
2. **Crochet the pattern with love**. You don't want to cut yourself off from the potential feelings of loss. You want to enjoy the entire crochet process so work it with yarn you like. Pretend it's something you are creating as a special item for yourself or a loved one even though you're not going to keep it in the end.
3. **Photograph the finished item**. This is a way to retain the memory of the project without its physical self.
4. Prepare a calm, safe space in your home and **frog the work**. Unravel everything that you've created until your work is completely gone.
5. Sit still and really **reflect** on this process and what it means for you to undo what you've created.

Tips:

- This exercise can bring up a lot of emotionality around life/death and letting go. Be prepared for that and have a support system in place.
- Work with a yarn that is easy to frog. Mohair and some novelty yarns tend to catch on themselves and are difficult to frog. Cotton and smooth acrylic yarns usually frog easily.
- Find a special use for the yarn that you have left at the end of the project. This will help you honor the process of creating without feeling like you've wasted precious yarn. You may use it to make another special item or you may re-wind it and donate it to a cause that you care about. However, don't simply re-make the item that you frogged, as that breaks the letting go cycle.

Taking it further: Make a shrine to your artistic self using images of the items that you create through this exercise. Create special items, photograph them, then frog them. The shrine is a way to recognize and honor artistic potential, mourn the loss of the artistic projects we've let go of in the past and move forward through celebrating the process of art instead of the product.

Letting Go Exercise #5: Toss Your WIPs

The exercise: Gather all of the works-in-progress (WIPs) in your home and get rid of them.

The purpose: Getting rid of unfinished projects through this exercise can free up your artistic energy; where one creative door closes another will open. It's all about letting go of the past to be tuned into the creativity of right now.

In depth: Sometimes we hang on to creative projects for far too long. They linger over us, not just taking up physical space in our homes but also occupying mental energy in our minds. They make us feel like we have something to get done that isn't done yet, and that can be a creative drain on us in so many subtle ways. Explore why you've held on to the things that you've held on to. Why do you still have these WIPs? Was there a reason that you didn't finish them? What emotions come up when you think about letting them go?

Exercise steps:

1. **Gather the WIPs**. Go through your house and collect every crochet item that you've started and haven't completed. Every single one.
2. **Lay them out** and look at them all as a bunch. For some people, it can take up a whole room but it is important to see all of that unfinished work that has been weighing heavily on the back of your mind.
3. **Pull out any WIPs** that you truly, honestly, really are consistently working on and will actually finish. But be honest with yourself here.
4. **See if there are any items** in the remaining WIPs that can be used or donated exactly like they are. For example, an unfinished crochet afghan might be the right size already as a baby blanket. Give it immediately to a baby charity or home with a baby. Get those WIPs out of your space but use them if you can.
5. **Donate or frog the remaining WIPs.** You can donate half-finished crochet items to many thrift stores; people will purchase them and either finish them or use the yarn.

Alternatively, you can simply frog the item and repurpose the yarn yourself.

Tips:

- Avoid hanging on to WIPs. It's easy to convince yourself that you really will finish something but if you haven't done it, yet, then you probably aren't going to.
- Prepare a little ritual for saying goodbye to the WIPs you're donating or frogging. You might simply hold the WIP in your hands for a moment, reflect on why you started it and give it thanks for serving the purpose that it did at the time that you needed it. You can do this for all of them at once or do each one individually, whatever feels best to you.
- Turn WIPs into art if you can't let them go. For example, you might have started to crochet a baby blanket for a child that was special to you but then it never got finished and the child is all grown. Ideally, you'll donate or frog the WIP and move forward, but if you simply can't emotionally bring yourself to do that then it's best to make use of the item as is. You can frame a WIP and make it a piece of crochet wall art, getting it out of "unfinished" status and giving it a place in your current home.
- Start and finish a new project to replace those special WIPs. For example, make a new scarf for the grown-up child whose baby blanket you never finished. Get rid of the WIP and the guilt associated with not finishing it and yet come full circle with the project by making something that's relevant to the here-and-now.
- Return to this exercise at least once per year so that you aren't allowing unfinished items to linger in your mental space.

Taking it further: One way to get rid of all of your WIPs without actually getting rid of them is to turn them into a mixed media project. Lay out all of the pieces of unfinished work. Organize them into a rectangular wall hanging. Stitch them together or glue them down onto a canvas. Frame the piece. It's like a quilt of your unfinished items. It takes what was in the past and finishes it in a way that suits your current artistic process. Then you can let all of those pieces go and just move on.

Letting Go Exercise #6: Intentional Mistake

The exercise: In this exercise, you will intentionally put one glaring mistake into an item that you are making and leave it there.

The purpose: Many people feel that their work must be "perfect" and are dissatisfied with any little mistake that they see. The practice of allowing mistakes in the work will release you from this perpetual feeling that things could always be done better and let you appreciate the beauty of things that you make just the way that they are.

In depth: Consider how you feel about mistakes in your work. If they bother you, examine why they bother you. What beliefs do you hold about what a mistake says about you? How do you feel when you see mistakes in someone else's work? Do you hold others to the same high standards that you hold yourself to? Think about the voice in your head that belittles your mistakes; who does that voice belong to? What would be the worst thing that might happen if you allowed mistakes into your work?

Exercise steps:

1. **Select a project** for this exercise. It could be something you're already working on or a new project but either way it should be something that you're excited about working on and either keeping for yourself or giving to someone else. Don't make it a throwaway project since that misses the point of the exercise.
2. **Choose an error to make**. You will find some examples below this exercise. Make a note in the pattern where you're going to place the error.
3. **Crochet the pattern**. When you get to the note you've made, intentionally make the mistake. Pay attention to how this makes you feel.
4. **Finish the project**. Keep it in a place where you can see it. Notice if the mistake seems obvious to you and whether or not it bothers you.
5. **Show the work to someone else**. See if they say anything about the mistake. Notice what you're thinking as they look at your work.

TYPES OF ERRORS IN CROCHET

Some examples of the types of mistakes you could put into your work for this exercise include:

- Improperly **joining yarn**. For example, you could put a knot in the yarn if you don't usually do this.
- Improperly **weaving in ends**. Leave a little bit loose so that it pokes through the work.
- A single **incorrect stitch** or even a row of incorrect stitches (a dc where it should be a tr, for example).
- Adding an **extra stitch** or doing one stitch too few in a row/ round.
- Starting with the **wrong number of chains** in your foundation chain and having to cheat it with an increase or decrease.
- **Increasing or decreasing** the wrong amount or in the wrong row.
- **Changing colors** in the middle of a row instead of at the start of a row.

Tips:

- Make a mistake that is large enough to be noticeable in your project but not so big that it will ruin the functionality of the piece. For example, you don't want to change a row of single crochet to a row of double treble crochet in a garment because it will affect fit, but you could change a row of single crochet to a row of half double crochet with less impact on function.
- Noticing is the key thing here. Notice the mistake. Notice how it makes you feel to make a mistake. Notice how you feel when others see your mistake.
- Prepare an affirmation for accepting your mistake. "My work is valuable and wonderful even when it has errors" is something you could remind yourself as you work on this exercise. *NOTE: We will be working with affirmations shortly so if you need more information about that it's on the way!*

Taking it further: If mistakes in your work are something that bother you then it might be worthwhile to do some research into different cultural beliefs that view errors in work differently. For example, there is the Japanese concept of *wabi sabi*, wherein the imperfection of an item is not only acceptable but is actually what makes the item most valuable.

Likewise, there's a wives' tale that Amish women always put one mistake in every quilt they make because they believe that aiming for perfection is a mockery to God. That tale turns out to likely be a myth but it's a concept worth exploring as an alternative viewpoint if you're a perfectionist.

Yarn for Thought: Musings on Letting Go, Releasing and Relaxing

In addition to the crochet exercises offered in each chapter, I'm also offering you this "yarn for thought" section. These are thoughts, ideas, inspirations and questions that I've come up with related to the topic at hand (in this case, the topic of letting go, releasing and relaxing). Take the time to think about some or all of these topics. Meditate upon them, write about them in your crochet journal, discuss them with other creative people in your life (online or offline) and see if you can broaden the benefits of this work by exploring them in depth.

- What "shoulds" are you holding over yourself? What would happen if you let go of those shoulds?
- Whose voice is in your head telling you that you need to be perfect? If you can identify that voice, write a letter (not to send, just for yourself) to that person thanking them for their advice but releasing them from ever giving it to you again.
- Practice sending your inner critic on vacation. This was a technique that I learned from a classmate in a therapeutic dyad exercise that we did. She said that she had learned that you can't ever get rid of that self-critic forever but you can gently suggest that it go on vacation for a bit. It gives you a bit of a break and you're more likely to notice when that negative self-talk returns so that you can banish it more quickly each time. It can even be fun to create a list of places you'd like to go so that you have options in mind for where to send your inner critic.
- Make a list of all of the things that help you to de-stress and decompress. Keep it where you can easily see it so that you can rely on those strategies whenever you feel locked into a stressful situation.
- How can you turn your negative self talk into positive self-encouragement? (In the next chapter, we will work with affirmations.)
- What is the true reason that you craft? Making items to please your creative self is very different from making items to make a living, for example. Examine all of your reasons and motivations for crafting and look at how perfectionism and making-for-function are related to each reason.
- What have you had difficulty letting go of in your life? What feels painful to let go? What feels unfinished? How is this impacting your creative self? How does it affect how you see and treat yourself?
- What are your rituals for letting go?

Self-Care and Self-Esteem Building

Continuing in the interest of making a safe space for our inner artist, we're going to spend this chapter focusing on self-care and the building of our own self-esteem. Releasing negative self-talk and unreasonable expectations of the self is the foundation; building self-esteem helps us to really strengthen our readiness to own our artistic selves and work from them.

Why does self-esteem matter? Because creative work is difficult work that takes us to risky places, places that inevitably fill us with doubt about our own work and ideas. Without a strong base of positive belief in ourselves, we easily falter in the face of creative challenges. We look the demon of doubt in the eye and not only do we go running, we run right back to our darkened rooms and flagellate ourselves with thoughts of "I can't do this", "what was I thinking trying to be an artist?", "I'm not really creative", etc. etc. ad nauseum until we are terrified of ever coming out of the room and into artistic work ever again.

Additionally, the world can sometimes be a mean place. As I write this, I'm thinking about something I saw in crochet news recently that really upset me. A few weeks ago, a woman who had crocheted her own wedding gown made it into the headlines, with many craft channels and even mainstream news sites picking up the story about the 1000 hours that she spent creating her own beautiful dress. Shortly after, a second story came out, emphasizing the fact that a main response to the first story was online bullying from peers who commented negatively on the woman's weight. The woman, who beamed beautifully from the photos with clear joy over her own creative work and her special wedding day, was attacked online over her physical appearance. It horrified me that people will do this, ignoring her creative genius and responding with such cruelty.

Now, I'm not a Debbie Downer. I don't believe that the world is always cruel and that people are terrible and all of that. I genuinely believe that most people are decent people, doing the best that they can. I've seen, especially within the craft community, tremendous generosity and support between people from different walks of life. I believe that people who are cruel are dealing with their own inner demons and should be treated with compassion. That said, I also recognize that there are cases like the one above, some more extreme and some less so, of how cruel others can be when we put our creative selves out there. And because we run the risk of facing that cruelty, we must be especially strong in our own self-esteem so that we can rest within it and let challenging incidents pass without cowering from our own creative process.

You may find that as you open up to your own creativity and trust it more, the people closest to you actually try to shut you down. Most likely, they aren't doing this intentionally, but the impact on you can still be terrible. Why would this happen? Looking at it from a psychological family systems perspective, each "system" (meaning each family, each friend group, etc.) exists in homeostasis, which is essentially just the way that the system has been functioning over time, for better or worse. That system seeks to avoid change and to remain in homeostasis, so when someone in the system creates change, the system tends to try to block that change.

I'll give you a classic example from many of my psychology textbooks. Let's say that you have a family of two parents and two teenage children. Parent A is an alcoholic and the family has found many ways of coping with that. Parent B overcompensates by making sure that the kids are always out of the house at activities and have everything they could possibly want materially. Teen A excels at all things in school and athletics. Teen B checks out and spends time with friends. This is their coping system, and they've managed for a long time, even though they aren't happy. Then something happens in the life of Parent A to cause that person to want to quit drinking. Parent A goes to meetings, gets therapy, quits the alcohol and begins to change for the better in many ways. It sounds great. However, this requires the entire family to change. With Parent A wanting to step up more, Parent B doesn't have to go overboard taking care of the kids, and that leaves Parent B feeling useless. Additionally, with less time focused on dealing with Parent A's problem, Parent B now has time to acknowledge some of the resentment that's been festering and begins to get really angry. Teen A doesn't have to be perfect anymore and the grades start slipping. Neither parent notices at first because they are busy focusing on Teen B, worrying about all of that time out with friends and fighting over curfews. Nobody in this family wants Parent A to start drinking again, but something inside of their psychology is trying to maintain the homeostasis. If they can't work through it to create a new homeostasis, then they'll find a way to recreate the old one. Parent A might start drinking again or might become a workaholic and have the same patterns with this new addiction. Or someone else in the family might become "the problem" (in family systems the term is the "identified patient"). In either case, the problem was within the system itself and the system fights the change.

What does all of this have to do with your creativity and the process of building self-esteem? When you make a commitment to your creativity, you are taking steps towards change, and that change has the potential to alter your system. The change may be obvious; you decide to take an hour per day to work on the exercises in this book and all of a sudden your kids are sick, your husband needs to be out of the house working more and your best friend has a crisis that needs your attention. It's this weird magical thing. Every excuse that comes up feels really legitimate, but really it's just the system trying to adjust itself. And if you don't have strong self-esteem that allows you to continue to carve out your creative space in the face of all of that, you risk returning to homeostasis and allowing your artistic urges to go fallow.

And let me tell you, you don't need to have a big, needy family to be in a system that tries to thwart your creativity. I know this from experience. I live alone. Although I'm close with my family, none of them live here in San Francisco and I've worked hard to have healthy differentiation from them that allows me to recognize my own needs and make these needs a priority. My partner is fairly independent, as are my good friends. I work for myself on my own schedule so I'm not tied up with the demands of co-workers. And in spite of this seemingly idyllic situation for fostering my own creative change, I still constantly have to fight staying in homeostasis. I'll begin to work on an exciting new project (this book, for example) and suddenly everything in my life seems to conspire to make me lose interest. I get sick. My beaux gets unexpected vacation time and wants to go somewhere. A gig I've had forever suddenly disappears and I start worrying about finances so I "need" to spend more time looking for new writing work. Friends who I occasionally petsit for suddenly need me every weekend for a month. When you are aware of it happening, it's almost humorous. You can start your creative activity and then every time something comes up to challenge it you can look up to the universe, shake your head and say, "sorry Universe, I know your tricks, and I'm not giving up this project".

But usually, it's not so cut and dry. The way the system tries to right itself is subtle. The feeling that you need to be doing something else besides the creative work feels so real. The Universe says, "oh, that little cold isn't going to stop you? Okay, I'll put you in the hospital for awhile, you can't work there!" And so often, our initial creative ideas feel so unsure and little anyway that it is really unfortunately easy to let them go instead of insisting on fostering them in the face of this difficulty. If you don't have really strong self-esteem, a commitment to your own self-care during the creative process and a huge belief in the value of your own acts of creativity then you're doomed.

So that's why we are going to work on building self-esteem before we get any further into other creative changes. The cornerstone of this section will be working with affirmations. You don't have to believe in them to be able to get some use out of them. I'd encourage you to at least give them a try even if you find them a little bit silly (like I do!) And this section will also have additional exercises after the affirmations work that are all designed to assist with self-care and building self-esteem.

So let me tell you that I hate affirmations. I also believe that they work.

There is a cafe here in the San Francisco Bay Area called Cafe Gratitude. Every item on their menu is an affirmation, so you don't order a peach salad but instead order an "I Am Pure" and instead of asking for Pad Thai you tell your waiter, "I am Terrific".

I have only been to this cafe once. In talking about it later to people I have had a tendency to dismiss, minimize and admittedly even make fun of it. And yet, I regularly think about it and I consider going back to it and it has left an impression on me because dining there was such a unique experience. I do not remember the food; I remember the affirmations. Or more accurately, I remember the experience of saying and hearing the affirmations.

What I remember is that it felt really awkward ordering the food this way. I was actually very conscious (and self-conscious) in ordering my food, really feeling like I wanted the message to match my mood and intention just as much as I wanted to get a meal I'd enjoy. It was strange to think of food in this way, as something powerful not simply because the nourishment could heal but also because the thought going into the food was meaningful. It felt even more awkward when the waiter delivered my food and confirmed my affirmation: "You are pure. You are terrific." We rarely say straightforward nice things to ourselves and even more rarely do so aloud where others can hear them and affirm them. It is awkward. I ordered an "I am pure" and the waiter affirmed, "you are pure" and it was really strange.

And yet, I think about that cafe often. And I have worked with affirmations, both spoken and written, at various times throughout my life. I usually feel silly doing it. I grumble and wonder if it's pointless and think that I shouldn't do them and feel really skeptical about them. They are too new-hippie, too new-agey, too self-helpy ... too uncomfortable. But why?

Why is it so awkward to just say something nice about yourself, to yourself, for a moment, once a day?

What I've discovered is that working with affirmations can be powerful and so even though I always feel silly doing them I just go ahead and say to myself, "okay, you'll feel silly, that's all right" and I let it go. I tell the inner skeptic to suspend cynicism and just do the work. I let myself believe that even if it's silly, it's certainly not hurting me and it just might help me so it's okay if I feel a little awkward while I do them. It's worth a try, right?

I want to add one more story here that relates to this, about the experience that most stands out to me of all of the moving experiences that I've had during my graduate studies in Integral Counseling Psychology. We had a guest speaker in a cultural awareness class, a woman who had formerly been a Catholic nun and then had studied several other religions and finally found her way to the Muslim faith. She was there to speak about her spiritual journey, and about what it is like about living life as an older, white, female Muslim in California. But what stood out for me was when she talked about doing the prayers five times each day, saying among other things "Assalamu Alaykum" which (to my understanding) is essentially "peace be with you". She said that it doesn't matter what God she believes in or prays to or even if she really believes or not; her entire world changes because she stops five times per day to pray for peace. This stuck with me, long after everything else about the class had begun to fade, because it's a simple, daily act that I can wholeheartedly believe in despite my own patchwork of spiritual experiences and questions. I believe in the idea that if I were to stop five times per day and consider peace for myself and others, my internal and external worlds would alter. Meditation, affirmations, they all relate to this type of practice ...

Crochet and Affirmations

I want to talk about two different ways we can use affirmations in our crochet work. The first is to work with affirmations that are designed to support the positive activity of crafting and honor the work that we're doing when we sit down with hook and yarn. The second is to look at ways that we can use affirmations while crocheting, working with messages that may improve other areas of our lives as well or even help to heal other people.

First, let's look at using affirmations to help us honor our own choice to craft. I think it's always sad when we say negative things to ourselves. And we do it all the time. We look in the mirror and see the extra pounds, the flawed skin, the things we think are wrong with us and we say them to ourselves, sometimes so quickly and quietly and subtly that we don't realize we're doing it. It's always sad. I'd encourage you to look closely at all of the negative messages you send yourself each day and work to stop doing it because it's mean to yourself and the world is mean enough without you compounding the difficulty for your own heart.

But I really think it's especially sad that we beat ourselves up about our crafting. Crochet is something that we do as a hobby (or perhaps a job), something that we do because we enjoy it and it helps us and it heals us and it allows us to express ourselves and it's a way to share our creativity with the world and it's relaxing and it's soothing and it's pretty and it's fun. Crochet is something that we do because we **want** to do it. We do not have to do it. We choose it. And when there is something in our lives that we have 100% chosen as a means to add new dimensions of joy to our days it is tremendously sad to then take that thing and use it as yet another way to abuse ourselves. And yet we do.

In the first three exercises below, we are going to examine our negative self-talk about crafting and then engage in a series of activities to change that thinking. In the second set of exercises, we will explore ways to use crochet alongside affirmations to improve general self-talk. And then there will be some additional exercises at the end for further self-care non-specific to affirmations.

Affirmations Part A: Uncovering your negative self-talk as it relates specifically to crochet and crafting.

NOTE: Exercises 1-3 are all part of Part A and should be worked together, in order, to complete this process.

Affirmations Exercise #1: Uncover Your Negative Crafty Self-Talk

The exercise: In this exercise, you will write down all of the negative things that you say to yourself about crochet and crafting.

The purpose: The first thing that this is going to do is to make you greatly aware of all of the negative energy that you're putting into your world with your statements to yourself about crafting.

<u>In depth:</u> You may experience a lot of sadness when you first become aware of how negatively you've been treating yourself. As a key part of this process, you need to focus on self-care. Make sure that you look at how you can make changes today to benefit yourself, rather than grieving the way you've treated yourself in the past. The exercises from the previous chapter on "letting go" can assist with this so feel free to return to them as needed.

<u>Exercise steps:</u>

1. **Clear a calm, soothing space** for yourself. Give yourself at least ten uninterrupted minutes of brainstorming time.
2. **Make a list of all of the negative things** that you say to yourself about crochet and crafting. Brainstorm, free associate and really get honest with yourself about all of the cruel things that come into your mind about your experience of crochet. (A list of possible examples is below.)
3. **Keep this list** as it will be used in several of the following exercises.

COMMON NEGATIVE SELF-TALK ABOUT CROCHET

Here are some of the most common things I've heard people (including myself) say to beat themselves up about crochet:

- I should crochet more
- I have too many WIPs, UFOs, yarn skeins
- I can't do this (a hard pattern, a niche of crochet)
- I'm not good at this (weaving in ends, blocking, joining)
- I haven't made anything good in awhile (or ever)
- I should be doing something else when I'm crocheting
- I should be crocheting for charity instead of for myself
- I should be crocheting more gifts for Christmas
- I should be crocheting with better yarn
- I'm just a beginner
- I should spend less money on crochet
- I should be involved in more crochet groups
- I'll never be as skilled as that other person

As you can see, the things that we tell ourselves as negative crochet messages have a lot of similarities although there are differences as well. I tend to err on the side of beating myself up for not crocheting more often, not making more complicated projects or trying new techniques more often and feeling like I don't work well with color. Others may beat themselves up for crocheting when they feel like they should be working or reading or spending time with family, or they beat themselves up for spending too much money on yarn that's not yet used. Make your list, be honest, look at where you beat yourself up.

Tips:

- Keep a notebook with you to write down thoughts as they come to mind.
- Pay close attention to thoughts that begin with "should", "must", "always" and "never". These words usually indicate that some negative self-talk is going on.
- Present your work to someone else (in person or online) and notice what negative self-talk comes up around this.
- Imagine that you are presenting your entire body of work to a group of professional crochet designers. What do you fear that they would say? (Often these are the same things that you say to yourself.)
- Ask close trusted friends if they have heard you say anything negative about your crochet work. Add these messages to the list.

Taking it further: One of the trickiest things that happens at this stage is that there are things that we take for granted as truths so we fail to add them to the list. For example, if I have very little money and one of my negative statements is "I shouldn't spend so much money on yarn" then I can easily convince myself that this is a truism and not just negative self-talk. Beware of those things that present themselves as true; sometimes they are the worst culprits. Go through your mental archive of things that you honestly believe are true about your work but could be viewed as negative by an outside observer and add those to your list.

Affirmations Exercise #2: Excavating the Negative Sources

The exercise: We will look at each item on the list and determine the source of that negative self-talk.

The purpose: Usually the inner critic that beats us down is really the voice of someone else that we have introjected into ourselves. By identifying the real source, we can move it back out of ourselves and strengthen our own inner resolve and self-esteem. The goal is to reduce the negative self-talk and increasingly celebrate your experience of crochet.

In depth: Sometimes getting to the root of why we say negative things to ourselves can really release us so that we stop saying them. It can at least be a first step. So let's excavate. Look closely at each item on your list and ask yourself where that message comes from. Sometimes it's actually a message that other people are sending you. Sometimes it's your own message, holding yourself up to an impossible standard.

Exercise steps:

1. **Take one item** from your list and write it down at the top of a blank page.
2. **Quickly brainstorm** all of the possible sources of that inner message (see example below).
3. Identify the most likely **source** of the negative self-talk.
4. **Write a letter** or have an imaginary conversation with the person who is really talking to you. Play Devil's Advocate and act in your part of the conversation as if the negative self-talk is complete baloney.
5. Ask yourself **how much you agree** with the other person's side of the argument. Examine why. Identify ways to break that down further. At this stage, you may have to go back to step three and repeat.
6. **Work through the entire process** until you have come to believe your own argument about the invalidity of the negative statement. Make a list of all of the reasons supporting your argument and use this to battle that negative self-talk whenever it arises.

Example:

- Negative self-statement: "I have a huge unused yarn stash, which is a terrible waste of money."

- Brainstorm sources: Husband always grumbling about money, kids complaining about the yarn stuffing their closets, Depression-era parents who never spent money on luxuries
- Most likely source: After thinking it over carefully and honestly, you determine that you are most stressed out about your husband's grumbling.
- Have an imaginary conversation with your husband addressing the importance of your crafting and why you think it's valuable and not a waste of money after all.
- See if you agree with some of what he's saying in your imaginary conversation? Do you really believe that the yarn is a waste of money or is that his message that you've internalized and are feeling unnecessarily guilty about? Maybe you go back to step three and discover that some of your parents' old messages about money are in there, too.
- Work through until you've come to believe your own argument that money spent on yarn is not wasted. Make a list of all of the reasons why you are right. Support yourself.

Tips:

- Look for the obvious sources first (parents, spouses, teachers) and then for less obvious sources (a childhood friend who said something mean, a critic who rejected a creative work of yours in the past).
- Make sure that you act as your own best ally when you're playing the part where you oppose the negative statement. It may be a case of "fake it 'til you make it" but that's okay. This is setting the stage for learning to battle negative self-talk by flipping it to the positive.
- Recognize that sometimes you might not know the source of the negative statements. Try hard to figure it out but if you can't then an alternative is to make a list of reasons the negative belief feels true and a list of counterarguments refuting it.

Taking it further: Be aware that this kind of work can be really deep and emotional. The inner critic that each of us carries around with us is a strong force that doesn't want to be dismantled easily. A lot of wild emotions can come about from working directly to reduce its negative impact. It may be necessary to work with a professional therapist or talk with a trusted friend or mentor about the things that are emerging as you deal with your inner critic.

Affirmations Exercise #3: Flip It Around

The exercise: Take every negative statement on your list and write it down as a positive affirmation.

The purpose: The only way to break the pattern of negative self-talk is to replace it with something else.

In depth: This will seem simple at first since you're just writing down the opposite of your negative self-talk from the previous exercises. However, it can feel really difficult as you begin to work with the affirmations; they won't feel true and you'll feel silly. Work with them anyway. Ask yourself what the worst thing is that could happen if you say the affirmations; realize that at the very least they're harmless and at best they may help re-build your self-esteem and just do them.

Exercise steps:

1. **Take out your list** of negative self-statements from Exercise One in this chapter.
2. **Write each one down**, one at a time, leaving space beneath it.
3. In the spaces, **write down the opposite** (positive) statement. For example, if one of your negative self-talk messages is "I should crochet more" then write beneath it, "The amount of time I spend crocheting is exactly the right amount". (There are more examples below).
4. **Rewrite your entire list** of just the positive affirmations. You now have a list of positive things that you can say to yourself every single day or anytime that you're feeling down about your crafting.

EXAMPLES: POSITIVE TWISTS ON COMMON NEGATIVE SELF-TALK

- "I have too many WIPs, UFOs, yarn skeins" can become "I am lucky to have such an abundance of materials to work with when the time is right."

- "I can't do this (a hard pattern, a niche of crochet)" can be turned into "This is a new skill for me to keep working at and getting better at day by day."
- "I'm not good at this (weaving in ends, blocking, joining)" … the simplest way to change this one is just to add "yet" at the end, reminding yourself that you're not good at something yet but will be soon. You could also change this one to, "I'm okay at this" or "I'm happy with where I'm at with this technique".
- "I haven't made anything good in awhile" becomes "What a great body of work I have from the number of years I've been crocheting."
- "I should be doing something else when I'm crocheting" gets turned over into "immersing myself in crochet is a great practice in mindfulness; I don't wish to be focused on anything else at that time".
- "I should be crocheting for charity instead of for myself" can turn into "Crocheting for myself is an important act of self-care so I can have energy to give to others."
- "I should be crocheting more gifts for Christmas" is released and the focus is on, "I made x, y and z for Christmas this year – how wonderful!"
- "I should be crocheting with better yarn" has an alternative viewpoint of, "look at the amazing things I've been able to make with such simple yarn."
- "I am just a beginner" can become "I'm lucky to have so much to look forward to in crochet" or "I'm so proud that I've started this new craft".
- "I should spend less money on crochet" is now looked at as "I invest my money in crochet because it is an important part of my life and I am worth it!"

Tips:

- Whenever you catch yourself engaged in negative crafty self-talk, turn it around in your head immediately. Focus on the new positive thought for a brief amount of time and then let the entire thought process go.
- You don't have to believe the new affirmation for it to work.
- Not sure how to turn a negative statement around? Ask yourself what you would say to a friend who said the same thing. If a friend

said, "I didn't crochet enough for the holidays", would you say, "yeah, you're a terrible crafter and no one is going to like you?" No, you would say something like, "you always do beautiful work and what you did give is going to be so appreciated." Say to yourself what you would say to your friend.

Taking it further: The best way to break the pattern of negative self-talk is to emphasize the positive self-talk. Each of these new statements is an affirmation that you can work with daily to improve your self-esteem. One great way to take this exercise further is to spend a little bit of time (each morning, each evening or at the start or end of each craft session) working with the affirmations. You can either write them down or say them out loud. Choose one affirmation for the day and write it or repeat it ten times. This daily practice can offer surprising benefits.

Affirmations Part B: Using Crochet to Support Other Affirmations

NOTE: Exercises 4-7 are designed to help you uncover other important areas of affirmation in your life and to use crochet to support them. Begin with Exercise Four to figure out your affirmations that will be used in the other three exercises. Beyond that, the exercises do not have to be worked in order.

Affirmations Exercise #4: Uncovering Your Affirmations

The exercise: Make a list of other important affirmations for your life. These are things that aren't related to crochet but that you want to incorporate into your sense of positive self-esteem. For example, if you always beat yourself up about your physical appearance, you'll want to work with affirmations about loving yourself just the way that you are.

The purpose: Use the craft of crochet as a time to focus on your affirmations and improve your overall level of self-esteem.

In depth: In the first three exercises, we looked at ways to improve how we feel specifically about our crafting. The second aspect of affirmations and crochet is to use the crochet itself as a time to speak, think or focus on your affirmations. You can select affirmations for any area of your life and then utilize the power of repetitive crochet to work on those affirmations.

Exercise steps:

1. **Identify** areas of negative self-talk in your life.
2. Use your negativity list to make an **opposite list** of positive affirmations (as described in Exercise Three in this chapter).
3. Write down your new list of affirmations that you want to work with. These will be used for the exercises below.

EXAMPLES OF COMMON AFFIRMATIONS

- Creativity fills my entire being.
- Embracing peace is my daily right.
- Every choice is the right choice.
- Every day it all gets better.
- Following my dreams matters.
- I already have everything I need.
- I am beautiful.
- I am courageous.
- I am enough.
- I am stronger than (my illness, my circumstances, my fears).
- I am talented.
- I am unique.
- I am worthy.
- I create my own life.
- I deserve the best.
- I love and approve of myself.
- I overflow with joyful energy.
- I see magic around every corner.
- I radiate perfection.
- I trust myself completely.
- Forgiveness is already here.
- Good comes from everything I do.
- Love infuses everything I do.
- My body is healthy, my mind is sharp.
- My nature is Divine.
- People who are no longer here are watching over me.
- Positive energy fills my entire being.

Tips:

- Notice the negative things that you say to yourself most often about your weight, your parenting skills, your education, etc. These things destroy self-esteem and working to change the patterns of thinking can significantly improve your life.
- Get to the core themes of your list of negative self-statements. For example, you might have ten different statements on your list but when you examine them, you discover that they all relate to the theme "I am not worthy". This gives you a simple affirmation to start with: "I am worthy".
- Try to make the statement feel as true as possible even if you don't believe it, yet. For example, if the above statement of "I am worthy" doesn't feel like something you would ever say to yourself then consider changing it to "I am valuable", "I am special", "I am perfect the way I am" or some other similar statement that addresses the core negative theme but feels honest to you.

Taking it further: Again, be aware that working with these difficult things can bring up extreme emotions. If you are ever in a position where you feel that you can't handle the emerging information on your own then it is best to pause the work and get the support of a therapist or other professional before moving forward with this kind of in-depth exploration. Stretching yourself is fabulous; harming yourself is not!

Affirmations Exercise #5: Simple Repeat Affirmation

The exercise: Work on a simple repeating crochet project while repeating a simple affirmation.

The purpose: The repetition of both stitching and speaking the affirmation will help ingrain into you that you really believe the positive thing that you are saying about yourself.

In depth: Repeating the same simple affirmation over and over again has powerful effects. We stop even hearing the words that we are saying but somehow they get into our hearts, beating in time with them, reverberating deep inside of ourselves and helping to eradicate those old negative messages that have been playing like broken records in our mind for all of these years. The repetitive stitching action helps facilitate this rhythmic motion inside of our psyches.

Exercise steps:

1. **Select a simple crochet pattern** that has an easy repeat so you can focus on the affirmation, not the product. For example, make a scarf made of double crochet stitches with no increases or decreases, or a large granny square blanket, which is my personal favorite repetitive crochet project.
2. **Choose your affirmation** from the list that you created in Exercise Four above. Either memorize it or have it written down clearly in front of you.
3. **Repeat your affirmation** over and over as you stitch, with one word equal to one stitch. Let the repetition of the stitching and the words just wash over you.

Tips:

- You may want to set a specific amount of time, with a timer, for how long you will do this meditative affirmation work. Alternatively, you may decide to do it until a certain portion of the work has been completed (such as when the last skein has run out).
- Start by working with a really short, simple affirmation. The exercise works with longer affirmations as well but when you're getting started it's easiest to choose an affirmation of 3-5 words. "I am creative", "I am valuable", "How I am is perfect" and "What I do matters" are all good examples.
- Tuck an affirmation into each project bag. Write out some of your favorite affirmations on individual index cards. Put them in the bag with whatever WIPs you have going so that you don't have to scrounge around for them when you pick up your crochet work. Other places you can keep these notes for yourself include: inside your crochet hook organizer, in your yarn basket, on the table next to your favorite craft area and in your crochet journal.

Taking it further: Now, I'm the first to admit that when you work with affirmations, it won't always feel comfortable. The statements won't always even feel true. Watch what comes up for you as you say your affirmation. Notice it. Figure out more about it. So if you're stitching your large granny square and saying aloud, "I am a good mother. I am a good mother," you may hear your brain saying, "no you aren't". Try to stitch through it but if it keeps coming up, inquire as to what that's all about.

What do you mean you aren't? Your brain may say, "you never make your kids home-cooked meals". Acknowledge that this may be something you want to try to do better and then go back to your stitching and continue saying, "I am a good mother. I am a good mother." See what else comes up. Work with it. Then drop the negative thought, focus on the stitch, repeat the affirmation again.

I know - it can feel silly. It can feel awkward. For reasons we can't even quite explain, doing this can even feel embarrassing despite the fact that you may be alone in your house with no one to ever know what you're doing. It's okay. Do it anyway. It works. Or maybe you'll find that it doesn't work for you but give it a good solid chance and see what happens.

Affirmations Exercise #6: End-of-row Affirmations

The exercise: At the end of each row or round of a crochet project you will pause and repeat an affirmation.

The purpose: This is a great way to work with more complex affirmations and to keep bringing yourself back to them again and again.

In depth: This exercise allows you to work on more complicated crochet projects, where you might have to follow the instructions carefully, and yet still work on your affirmations at the same time. Each end-of-row is a reminder to come back to your positive self-talk. It combines a mindfulness cue with affirmations work. This is a good habit for the rest of your life where you might find that something stressful is going on and you can habitually bring yourself back to positive self-talk and self-care.

Exercise steps:

1. **Choose your crochet project.** Make sure that you have the pattern ready to go.
2. **Select your affirmation.** Write it down so that you have it in front of you.
3. **Begin your project.**
4. At the end of the first row, **take a pause**. Focus on your affirmation. Say it aloud or repeat it silently in your mind, doing so intentionally and with full attention.

5. **Repeat your affirmations** at the end of each row throughout to the end of the project.

Tips:

- Use the same affirmation throughout the entire project. The repetition helps emphasize the truth of the affirmation for you.
- Make it a point to say the affirmation out loud if possible. It helps to re-train your brain into actually believing it more so than just saying it in your mind.
- Refuse to abandon this idea halfway through. It can be easy to do that, especially if it's a long project. Resist.
- When you've completed the project, take a photograph of it and make yourself a little journal page showing the photograph and the affirmation.

Taking it further: You can extend this exercise by adding extra understanding for yourself with each row. One of my favorite affirmations is "My creativity heals myself and others." In working with this affirmation I might just repeat it at the end of each row. Alternatively, I might repeat it and then at the end of each row add a reason as to why I believe this.

For example, at the end of row one I might say, "My creativity heals myself and others. It allows me to get in touch with my true self and feel more confident in my interactions." Then at the end of row two I might say, "My creativity heals myself and others. When I create something for someone else the gift serves to connect us." At the end of row three I might say, "My creativity heals myself and others. I create and serve as a model to inspire others who want to create." And so on.

This allows me to not only work with the affirmation but to take the affirmation itself deeper and deeper while also producing work on a perhaps complicated crochet pattern.

Affirmations Exercise #7: Setting Intentions

The exercise: Set a positive intention for the item that you are crafting.

The purpose: In intentional crafting you choose for the project to have a significant meaning. This adds value to the work itself and can make you feel purposeful and more positive about doing the crafting.

In depth: An example of intentional crafting is the prayer shawl, which we'll look at in another part of this book, where the crafter says a prayer for the recipient while crafting. It infuses the work itself with love, intention and positivity and it gives the crafter solid positive feelings while doing the work. The same concept is used in working with affirmations for the self.

Exercise steps:

1. **Select an affirmation** to work with. This will be the basis of the positive crafting. For example, I might want to work with, "I feel creative."
2. **Do a brief visualization** before beginning the project. Close your eyes and meditate upon the project. Think about what it will feel like to work on it with creativity in mind. See in your mind's eye the finished product and tell yourself how creative it is.
3. **Do the work** on the project, holding that visualization in mind at all times. Keep bringing yourself back to the project and thinking about how working on it is an act of creativity.
4. When the project is finished, **celebrate the affirmation**. Repeat the affirmation, holding the project in hand, noticing that your intention has been completed. In this example, you might say aloud, "this crochet item is an act of my creativity".

Example:

Just to give you a better idea for this one, I'll share a second example. Let's say that you're going to crochet a blanket for your child. You want to work with the affirmation "my crochet gives loves to the people important to me". This is an affirmation that values your crochet work, ties in with the project and infuses a terrific positive emotion into the blanket. Begin with a visualization of the finished blanket and how that shows your love to your child. Use visualization, meditation and affirmations throughout the project to keep incorporating that loving intention into every stitch. At the end of the project, notice what you accomplished, celebrate that your crafting was able to bring love to your child and congratulate yourself.

Tips:

- Make sure that your intention is in line with your affirmations. For example, if your affirmation is "There is value in crocheting for myself" then you don't want to do a project in which you crochet for someone else. Seek congruence.
- Use repetition to keep yourself focused on the intention of the project. You can use either of the above two exercises (continued repeating or end-of-row affirmations) to help with this.
- Don't skip the part about celebrating the project at the end. Notice that you set an intention, met the intention and worked on an affirmation at the same time. Honor this.

Taking it further: Use your crochet journal to explore your intentions for your project and track all that comes up for you as you work on the project. Sometimes you may find that you regret a project halfway through or that your intentions seem to be shifting and that's worth exploring even if you do stick with the project to the end.

Part C: Moving In To Self Care

The rest of the exercises in this chapter are all about going beyond affirmations and using crochet as a form of self-care. When you commit yourself to recognizing your own needs and wants and making sure to provide them for yourself, you improve your life in myriad ways. It can be so easy to let self-care slip for so many different reasons, and yet it's critical to a healthy way of life.

In fact, although I've talked a lot about how helpful mindfulness practice can be in our lives, it has been found that self-compassion might be as important as mindfulness in many ways. Clinical psychologist Elisha Goldstein writes about this in his book *Uncovering Happiness*, explaining that he found mindfulness works as a natural treatment for depression but is only the foundation and requires the "scaffolding" of self-compassion practice "to make it come alive".

With that in mind, all of the exercises in the rest of this chapter are designed to help you treasure yourself, protect your own creativity, practice that important trait of self-compassion and honor your artist within.

Self-Care Exercise #8: Crochet for Diet Cravings and Addictions

One of the keys to a healthy lifestyle (and good self-care) is to quit the addictions that are doing harm in your life. This is not a prescription by me about what you should and should not be doing or consuming. If you drink every day or smoke constantly and it doesn't bother you and you don't feel like it's a problem then that's your choice. But if you are concerned about some of your habits and cravings and want to quit then this exercise can help.

The exercise: Use crochet as an intentional replacement tool for food, alcohol, cigarettes and other addictions.

The purpose: You can slowly reduce the amount you give in to various addictions and cravings by delaying your consumption of them through replacing them with crochet. With a gradual increase in the ratio of crochet:craving, you might even be able to kick some addictions.

In depth: In the summer of 2014, I conducted a crochet health survey of more than 10,000 people who answered questions about how crafting had helped them. One question was a multiple choice question about which health issue crochet had helped them with (such as depression or chronic pain). There was also an option to write in a different answer from those given in the multiple choice section. By far, the most common write-in was from people saying that they had used crochet to help them quit smoking. Others said that it helped them quit food addiction, drinking and abuse of drugs. A review of the literature on quitting smoking (and sometimes other addictions) shows that they generally suggest keeping your hands busy with something else - and crochet is perfect for that. You can't hold a cigarette, a spoon or a drink while actively crocheting!

More than that, research has shown that replacing a negative addictive activity with a positive activity significantly increases the likelihood of quitting the addiction. Finally, research has shown that addiction is often related to overactivity in the brain and that activities that increase the relaxing alpha waves in the brain can help reduce addiction. You guessed it: the soothing, repetitive motion of crochet helps increase those helpful alpha waves in the brain!

Exercise steps:

- **Identify** what you are trying to quit. We will use smoking cigarettes as an example here. More examples of common addictions can be found below.
- **Keep a daily log** of how often you engage in the addiction. You might count the number of cigarettes smoked in a day, the number of times that you light up or the number of minutes spent smoking. Track every day for one week to get a good average of your daily use.
- **Set a goal** to reduce that amount. A ten percent reduction is a great starting point, but do whatever feels right to you. So, for example, if you smoke ten cigarettes per day, your goal will be to smoke only nine per day for one week.
- **Continuing tracking your daily use**, with an intention of using crochet to replace what you're subtracting. So in this example, when you get a craving to smoke a cigarette, you can crochet instead. If you crochet once and smoke nine cigarettes, you've reduced your use. Do that every day for one week.
- **Reduce again**. For the second week, crochet in place of two cigarettes, smoking only eight per day. Continue decreasing weekly.
- **Celebrate your success**! Reward yourself for achieving your goals. Purchase a new set of crochet hooks, craft something wonderful for yourself, whatever might feel like a reward to you that will celebrate your success while boosting your crafting!

COMMON ADDICTIONS

Some of the things that you might try to quit with the aid of crochet, in addition to quitting cigarettes, include:

- Alcohol
- Drugs (OTC or street drugs)
- Sugar
- Caffeine
- Overconsumption of calories (food addiction)
- Excessive use of TV, internet, social media
- Gambling
- Shopping; be aware that there's a risk of channeling your addiction into shopping for craft supplies

Tips:

- Work on quitting only one thing at a time and do so slowly. You want to set achievable goals and work on them over time so that the new healthy habit of crochet sticks.
- Crochet in place of your addictive activity first thing in the morning. This gets you off to a great start for the day and helps to jump-start your commitment to reducing your cravings.
- Work on projects that you really enjoy and are excited about finishing. This way, you look forward to doing the crafting each day and can easily use that as a focus to replace your addictive behavior.
- Use the money you save from reducing your craving to indulge in luxury yarns. The more you love to touch them, the better! Get something in your hands that feels better than a cigarette!
- Make a list of the reasons not to do your addictive behavior while crocheting. For example, you could technically smoke a cigarette while crocheting (taking stitch breaks to puff) but some reasons not to (beyond the health reasons) include the risk of setting fire to your work and the fact that smoky crocheted items don't work well as gifts or for sale. Keep this list near your work to remind yourself daily of why you don't crochet and engage in the addictive behavior at the same time. One key reason not to crochet while doing any addictive behavior at all is because your mind will associate the two with each other and make it that much harder to quit.
- If crochet isn't taking your mind off of the craving enough, take it up a level. Learn to crochet while walking. Take your crochet on public transit (where you can't engage in your addiction) and craft there to replace your craving. Crochet regularly with a group of friends that supports you quitting your addiction. Go to a meeting and crochet there. Figure out what it will take to replace at least ten percent of your addiction consumption with crochet instead and do that thing!

Taking it Further: Work with a combination of meditative crochet and affirmations (as practiced in previous chapters) to continue reducing your dependence on the substance. Use visualizations to picture your life without the addictive substance. Use affirmations for a daily re-commitment to reducing your addictive behavior. Recognize that you may not be able to quit on your own and that you may need the help of therapy, group support, etc. to quit your addictive behavior but that crochet can be one tool in your toolbox to help you reduce and cease the addiction and stay sober.

Self-Care Exercise #9: Crochet as Part of Your Sleep Routine

The exercise: Make crochet a regular part of your nighttime ritual for good sleep.

The purpose: Lack of good sleep causes / exacerbates a significant number of mood, mental health and physical health issues. Use crochet to help you improve your sleep hygiene.

In depth: Sleep hygiene is a term coined in recent years to describe the healthy habits we must engage in to get enough good quality sleep. It is a term that we need because a significant number of us aren't getting enough sleep and/ or good enough sleep. Developing proper relaxing rituals at night can significantly improve sleep. Crochet, a calming and relaxing activity, can be one key part of your regular nighttime sleep routine.

Exercise steps:

1. **Choose a simple, relaxing, long-term crochet project** that you will work on a little bit each night before bed. Large blankets like granny rectangles, ripple blankets and repeating v-stitch blankets are a great choice.
2. Complete your normal **before-bed activities**, such as brushing your teeth, before you start your project.
3. **Turn off all distractions**, such as television. You might find that light music is good. Make sure that your home is a cool, but not cold, temperature. Light a candle. Turn other lights down, leaving enough on to work on your crochet but as few on as possible to create a low-light area for rest.
4. Settle into a **comfortable position** in a cozy place that is not your bed (unless you are bed-bound by illness of course). Good sleep hygiene says that your bed should be only for sleeping, not crafting or other activities. A chair in the bedroom is a great choice.
5. **Work on your crochet project** until you get sleepy enough that you think that you will be able to fall asleep. Eventually,

your body should adjust to a specific cycle and you'll find that you're always working on your crochet for the same time (half an hour or an hour, perhaps) before you go to bed. *Note that this is a great time to work on meditative crochet and crochet with affirmations.*
6. **Calmly and quietly set your work aside**. You don't want to disrupt your body too much before you go to bed so put the work in a project bag near your craft space so that you can resume it again the following night.

Tips:

- Do what works for you in terms of your setting. The standard rules of not crafting in bed and keeping the TV off are good tips and worth at least trying as you establish a new sleep routine but you may find that they aren't right for you and adjust accordingly. I personally always fall asleep to TV; it's what works for me regardless of what the sleep hygiene "rules" are.
- Try a light-up crochet hook to see if it works well for you. This allows you to see your stitches in the dark, which means that you can create a fairly dark space as you get ready for bed each night.
- Some people (like myself!) have very little trouble falling asleep but struggle with insomnia that wakes them up in the middle of the night or they have early morning wakefulness. In some cases, staying in bed and crocheting for a very short period of time can help you relax enough to go back to sleep. If you find that you are still awake after twenty minutes, get up, make yourself a cup of soothing tea and crochet in your craft area before going back to bed.
- Make sure that you engage in other good sleep hygiene habits throughout the day to promote healthy sleep. Some of these include eating right (limiting caffeine, for example), getting enough natural light and exercise and taking your medications properly.

Taking it further: One great way to go further with this exercise is to crochet yourself items that you can use to improve your sleep hygiene. One terrific project is to crochet a sleep mask that you can put on when you lie down to block out the rest of the light. Some other helpful sleep items to crochet include:

- Cozy pillows that you love
- A stuffed animal to take to bed with you
- Cozies for your phones and laptops to keep them out of sight at night
- Cozies for candle holders in your craft space
- Crochet basket or bag to keep your project in at night
- Scented sachets to keep by the bed; lavender is great for sleep

Self-Care Exercise #10: Decluttering Your Makes

The exercise: Declutter all of the crochet items you've already made that don't make you feel good about yourself.

The purpose: You want to use your craft to celebrate who you are, what's best about you and what you can accomplish. Get rid of any item that you've made that doesn't do this!

In depth: When we keep items in our home that no longer serve us, they not only take up physical space but also occupy us mentally in a negative way. We often hang on to things that we have made just because we've made them, even though they no longer serve us. By only keeping the items that make us feel truly happy and proud of ourselves, we improve our daily quality of life and encourage more crafting in the future.

Exercise steps:

1. **Gather all of your crochet items** that you have made and lay them out together in one space. Yes, every single one of them. If you have far too many to lay out all at once then separate them by category, laying out all of the blankets at once or all of the clothing at once.
2. **Pull out any items** that you see that you immediately feel a tug of love for. I might have two dozen crochet scarves laid out on my floor but when I cast my eye across them, I know instantly which ones I wear all of the time because I love them. These are useful and feel good. Keep these in a "love this!" pile.
3. **Pull out any items** that you absolutely know don't make you feel good. It doesn't matter what the reason is. Don't justify it to yourself. If you look at that pile and see something that makes you feel "ick", pull it out and put it in the "must go away pile".

4. **Now it's time to deal** with the handmade items that lie somewhere in the middle of "love it" and "ick". These are the ones that we tend to hoard in our homes, making reasons to keep them and allowing them to detract from the joy and wonder of our creative space. You'll find lots of tips out there on decluttering. A common one that you see is to ask yourself "do I love this?", "do I use this?", "do I need this?" and other such questions. This can be helpful for some people but a lot of us get mired in the details and find it ultimately unhelpful. I recently read a decluttering book (*The Life-Changing Magic of Tidying Up* by Marie Kondo) that had a much simpler suggestion and one that I've found to be supremely useful. The basic idea is that you hold each item in your hand and feel the energy that it gives you. If what you feel is positive energy, keep it. If it is negative energy, ditch it. In order to do this, you must be sitting in a calm, quiet space in your home with ample time to go through your pile. Sit still. Pick up item one. Hold it in your hands. Close your eyes and feel it. Trust your gut. Stick it in the "love it" or "must go away" pile and move on to the next item. Do this with each item you've laid out. Don't hesitate. Just do it. Your body knows what you should keep!

5. **Immediately** get rid of everything in the Must Go Away pile. If you keep it around, you'll find a reason to keep things. You can get rid of items in any number of ways: frog them to re-use the yarn, upcycle them into other craft items, donate them to charity, gift them to others, go yarnbomb with them. Whatever you decide, do it immediately.

6. **Showcase and celebrate** the items in your Love It pile. These are the things you've created that make you feel good so keep them where you can see them. Hang scarves and shawls out in the open where you can not only easily access them to use them but can also enjoy seeing them. Create a stack of blankets or display a set of them on a ladder. Sprinkle handmade cushions lovingly around your space. Hang potholders in a kitchen display. Treat your home like an art gallery designed to showcase you the artist!

7. **Do this process regularly** - either seasonally or annually - to keep from accumulating items that make you feel less than wonderful about yourself.

Tips:

- It is especially critical that you get rid of any wearables that don't make you feel good when you wear them. I had a crochet dress that was beautiful - on the hanger - but on me it looked dumpy because the proportions just weren't right. Every time I wore it, I'd get these complex mixed feelings, because I didn't feel pretty in the piece but felt that the piece itself was pretty. Get rid of things like this. Fix them, frog them, gift them but get the negative feeling out of your space!
- Remember that you can always make more things. In fact, the more you get rid of at home, the more space you have to create things that you truly love.
- If you have trouble getting rid of the items, a great way to approach it is to thank the item for what it has done for you. This ritual can help in letting go (and is one I learned from the aforementioned decluttering book). When you're holding the item in your hand and determine it has less-than-positive energy, keep it in your hands and silently (or aloud) thank the item for what it taught you, gave to you or served you for in the past. If nothing else, I can always thank a crochet item I've made for helping me to pass the time productively, creatively and with some level of peace of mind. The ritual may feel silly at first but it can be truly helpful in releasing items that no longer serve you.
- Note that this is another version of the "letting go" exercises practiced previously in this book. It takes that to another level by emphasizing the importance of only keeping things that make us feel good. That's an exercise in proper self-care. You are worth having items that you love.

Taking it further: Repeat this process with your handmade items that others have given to you over the years. These can be especially hard to get rid of but shouldn't be in your space if they don't make you feel great. So often those items are laden with guilt, obligations and other negative feelings.

Also repeat this exercise with your yarn stash and any other craft supplies that you have. While there may be financial issues that require you to use whatever you can get your hands on, most people have at least a little bit of flexibility in terms of the supplies that they keep on hand. Choose to keep only those that inspire you and make you feel great about crafting! I keep almost all of the yarn I'm given but every once in awhile there will be a ball that I just get negative feelings about it; I donate those!

Self-Care Exercise #11: Make Something That You Need

The exercise: Figure out what you need and crochet that item for yourself.

The purpose: A critical part of self-care is learning to identify your own needs and figure out how to meet those needs. Crochet can be a part of that.

In depth: You may discover through this process that you aren't at all sure what your needs are. You may also discover that you feel guilty or selfish for having needs, and you may therefore dismiss them as things you don't really "need". It's a common condition of our culture to feel this way; a culture that often drowns out our inner needs through the loud messages of advertising trying to tell us that our needs are different from what they really are. If you are unsure about your needs or feel guilty identifying and taking care of them, you may want to return to the "letting go" chapter and work through some of the exercises there with an emphasis on letting go of the idea that you shouldn't have needs. You may want to also work through some affirmations that help you recognize the voice that tells you not to have needs and assists you in honoring your needs. Needs don't make you needy; meeting your needs makes you a healthy adult.

Exercise steps:

1. **Make a list** of all of the items that you need. Focus on physical items, not emotional needs at this time. For example, you might need to drink more water. (See a list of possible needs below.)
2. **Identify an item** that you can make that would help you to meet that need. It may not be obvious at first but you can get creative with it. For example, if you need to drink more water, you can crochet yourself a water bottle cozy. Buy yourself a brand new water bottle, put it in your cozy and you've taken a step towards meeting that need.
3. **Find or freeform a crochet pattern** that meets this need. Make sure that you create something that is both beautiful and functional. You want to meet your need while also having a continuous reminder of how you engaged in self-care by meeting that need.

4. **Use your item** to meet your needs!

POSSIBLE NEEDS AND CROCHET ITEMS THAT MEET THEM

- Medication. Crochet cozies for your medication bottles or pill dispensers. Alternatively, crochet a placemat that you can store everything on top of.
- Exercise. Crochet an exercise headband, a cozy for the iPhone you use to listen to music while you exercise or even little cozies to go around your hand weights.
- Healthy Diet. Crochet a set of amigurumi food items that represent the healthy foods you want in your fridge and keep them on the counter as a reminder.
- A Good Night's Sleep. Crochet yourself a sleep mask to help meet this need. See the previous exercise on "crochet for good sleep" to get additional ideas.
- Clothing Items. We all wear clothes so in this day and age that's definitely a need. What is a clothing item that you truly need right now? Make it for yourself!

Tips:

- Recognize that one of your needs is simply to be creative. Any act of crochet at all can help you meet this need! Likewise, you may need time alone or downtime and crochet can be the means to meeting that need. Or you may need social time and crafting with friends can meet that need. Consider both the things that you can make with crochet and the act itself as something that can meet needs.
- Engage in your preferred form of meditative or mindful crochet as a way to get in touch with yourself. This can help you regularly understand your own needs better.
- Make a list of things (physical and emotional) that you wish someone else would give to you. Ask yourself if you can meet any of those needs yourself through crochet.

Taking it further: Now that you've learned how you can use crochet to meet your physical needs, take it further by identifying deeper emotional needs and use crochet to meet those needs. For example, one thing that you might need is comfort. What could you crochet to help you feel more comfort in your life? Make that item. Many people argue that we "need" very little and that everything else is a "want". I'd encourage you to take a look at Maslow's Hierarchy of Needs and consider your needs in this way. Yes, at a basic level, what we "need" is food, shelter and safety, but when those needs get met, we have different needs. We need love and belonging, self-esteem, self-actualization and even self-transcendence. Don't limit yourself in terms of discovering and meeting your own needs!

Self-Care Exercise #12: Crochet a Basket for Items You Love

The exercise: Crochet a basket where you can store and display items that are close to your heart.

The purpose: When you collect several items that you love and put them into one display, you essentially create a shrine to your own happiness. This is a place where you can continually re-fuel your own creative spirit. A crochet basket is a great place to store these items.

In depth: The possessions that we have are infused with memories, feelings, and various associations. Whether it's an expensive luxury gift or a rock picked up on a beautiful walk, the things that we keep around our homes are filled with experience. By acknowledging this emotional weight of our possessions, we can change the energy in our homes. Sometimes, as we saw in a previous chapter, this means letting things go. But other times it can mean giving a special place to items to honor the inspiration, beauty and love that they emanate into our lives.

Exercise steps:

1. **Gather a set of items that you love**. Collect all of the items you might possibly want to display in one place.
2. **Curate them by theme**. Imagine that you are creating an art display and select only those items that you want in this display. What is the theme of your personal exhibit? Colors of the Sea, Favorite Family Moments, and Inspiration in Small Things are examples of themes you might choose (more ideas below).
3. **Spread out the items** in your curated collection. Do they all belong? Are you missing anything?
4. If your collection is complete, **determine the size of basket** that you need to hold them all. You may want to make a shallow basket that displays them each side by side or you may want a

deep basket that allows you to layer items so you can only see a few on top. What feels right for you?
5. **Find or freeform a crochet basket pattern** that matches the mood of your collection. If it's a fun and playful collection, perhaps you want to make a really colorful t-shirt yarn crochet basket. If it's a basket filled with items drawn from nature then you might want to make a neutral-toned basket of organic cotton or hemp. Heritage pieces might look best in a doily-decorated vintage basket, etc.
6. **Lovingly place your curated collection** in your new basket. Place the basket on display where you can celebrate and enjoy these items that you love. Visit your mini-shrine often to re-invigorate yourself.

POSSIBLE THEMES FOR CURATED COLLECTIONS

- **Color Themes**. I mentioned colors of the sea already but you could create a collection of rainbows or a collection honoring a single color (especially your favorite color!) For example, many of the favorite things in my kitchen are yellow (a female sculpture a friend gave me, a yellow music box pillow of Sunshine Care Bear from my childhood, yellow flower magnets) and a yellow crochet basket would easily corral these into a beautiful collection.
- **People Who Make You Happy**. Photos of your family and good times with your friends, favorite old greeting cards, items that have been gifted to you that don't really have a place but that make you smile when you see them. These things celebrate the love of the people in your life.
- **Accomplishments and Sources of Pride**. I have a collection of all of the items I've published in print, from the early days of first making 'zines to my most recent self-published book. Your first creative work, your graduation certificate, a business card from a favorite job, maybe even the first wonky item you crocheted ... what makes you feel proud when you see it?
- **Fabric Scraps**. I don't quilt but I love the idea of quilting, where you take a little piece out of each item that you loved but no longer wear and keep it because it's filled with memories. You could collect a single scrap square of fabric - from the scarf you wore on a first date, from your child's clothing - and simply keep the scraps as

they are in a basket of your own making, on display to always enjoy.
- **Favorites of the Decade**. Pick a decade and choose one item that represents each year. Similarly you could create a basket of items from each special event in your life.
- **Nature Basket**. This basket might be filled entirely with items you've collected from nature - rocks, shells, pinecones, branches. Or it might be filled with photos, postcards, mementos and other representations of nature that you love.
- **Creative Tools**. Your basket doesn't have to simply be something you look at; it could also be functional. A basket to corral all of your tools of creativity is a great example of this. A set of baskets is even better - one basket for your crochet hooks, one for your scissors, one for paper, etc. If you have the space, make an entire creative display to celebrate your artistic self.

Tips:

- Choose items that you want to have on display. Old love letters might be a good keepsake but not something you always want on display. In contrast, a favorite shell picked up on a long-ago vacation can be inspiring on display.
- Make multiple mini-shrines that you place in crochet baskets throughout your home. Create a spa-inspired shrine of natural items in a jute basket in your bathroom. Create a play-inspired shrine of favorite toys, books and childhood items that goes on display in the hallway. Gretchen Rubin's book *Happier at Home* has great ideas for making shrines using domestic items throughout your house.
- Create seasonal crochet baskets to inspire you with the things that you love at specific times of the year - baskets for your favorite holidays, for example.

Taking it further: The types of displays we've explored here so far are special but they are not specifically spiritual. The idea of a shrine or altar, however, is a spiritual idea, and if you want to take this exercise further you might consider creating a spiritual shrine that incorporates some of the creativity of your crochet. Shrines are often created as memorials to specific people to help in the processing of grief or the worshipping of a deity whereas altars tend to be spaces that are created for spiritual reflection. What type of shrine or altar would benefit you in your space? How can you adjust the exercise above to create this for yourself utilizing your crochet skills?

Self-Care Exercise #13: Set The Environment

<u>The exercise</u>: Create a craft space that invigorates your senses.

<u>The purpose</u>: The space that you work in holds an energy that can either enhance your creativity or detract from it. Make a space that benefits you.

<u>In depth</u>: You can craft from all of your senses. By paying deeper attention to the entire setting around you, you can facilitate more inspired artwork to emerge from your hands. Set the mood for your space with scents, sounds and sights that truly stimulate you to create more.

<u>Exercise steps</u>:

1. **Carve out an area for your craft space**. If you live in a small spot, like I do, it might just be a single corner of a room, but you can still add all of the elements that you need into this one space. For example, you might put a tray on a shelf near your space that holds the items you need to create the right environment.
2. **Select scents** that you find to be helpful to your creativity. Candles, incense, fresh herbs, natural aromas, perfume ... What scents inspire you? You may find that you need a few different scents for different types of crafting - lavender essential oil for relaxing craft projects and fresh cinnamon potpourri for playful crochet explorations. Keep these scents on hand in your craft space.
3. **Figure out the sounds** that help you be most creative. Some people like to have TV, audio books or podcasts going while they work. Others find that different types of music inspire different creative moods. The natural sounds coming through the window, the white noise of a fan ... the sounds around you may be subtle but they can make a huge difference in the way that you work. Sit quietly in your space, assess the sounds that are already there and figure out if you need to replace any of those sounds (and with what). Create playlists of movies, music

or ambient noise that you can always have on hand as you start a craft session.
4. **Add a bit of visual inspiration** to your space. A beautiful photo that you've fallen in love with, a funky chair that you absolutely adore, a skein of gorgeous yarn that you don't even use but love to touch before beginning a project ... these items add inspiration and make you want to work in your craft space.
5. **Work in some texture.** The act of crocheting is a terrifically tactile act but you can add additional texture in to enhance the experience. I have a super-fuzzy blanket in my craft space that I love to sit on or underneath. For a long time I also had a jar of glass beads that I sometimes ran my hand through as I sat there thinking about what I was making. What textures do you want here?
6. **What else do you need** to make this craft space more comfortable and inspiring? Take away what isn't serving you and add what will.

Tips:

- The color of a space can make a huge difference in the way that you feel in that space. For example, bright red can make some people feel anxious or angry whereas soft blue is more calming and soothing. Notice the impact of the color in your space and use paint or fabric to alter it if need be.
- Take the chance on trying things that you don't think you'll like. Turn the radio station to classical or punk rock one day and see how that impacts your crochet; you might be surprised at what you find. You don't have to like something for it to change you creatively and it can be worth the small risk of changing your space for a day.
- Move your craft space around regularly. The physical shift will create an energetic shift in your work. If you have a studio, you might rearrange the furniture, change up your storage system and paint the walls. If you craft in a chair in the living room, you might move it for awhile to the bedroom or even just across the room facing a different direction.

Taking it further: Different colors, scents and sounds elicit different moods. These can vary from person to person but there are a lot of similarities for many people. Take the time to research and explore color theory, music therapy and the healing nature of different scents to find the best way to create the right setting for your own needs at any given time.

CHOOSING YARN COLORS FOR MOOD

NOTE: This information is an extension of Exercise 13.

There are a lot of details to color theory and each shade within a color can have a widely varying impact (dark blue vs. sky blue for example). Plus each individual responds to colors in her own way. That said, here are some very, very basics of color as they relate generally to mood.

- **Blue is calming**. Color science has found that blue is a very calming color. Being in a blue room can be relaxing and soothing. Blue tones vary a lot, though. An icy blue will be chilling instead of relaxing. And a really dark blue can provoke sadness instead of just calmness. The best blues for a relaxing mood are the bright, dark blues like cerulean and turquoise. Green is both calming and warm so bring in green-blue tones for ultimate relaxation. Because of blue's "coolness" it is good for lowering blood pressure, bringing down fevers and calming angry tempers.
- **Green de-stresses**. One of the most healing aspects of crochet is that it relieves stress. Green yarn might be the best choice for enhancing that aspect of the craft. It is a color that encourages the eye to rest and this rests the rest of the body as well as the mind. Green is the color of new grass and suggests re-birth and liveliness, especially in the yellower tones of green. This makes it a hopeful color in addition to being one that relaxes you. Green is also the color most commonly associated with balance and harmony. Finally, some believe that it boosts the immune system.
- **Yellow is energetic but stressful**. Yellow is a tricky color to work with. On the one hand it makes us think of sunflowers and sunshine and bright, happy days. You may drift to yellow when you're in a really cheery mood because of its light and brightness. And you may want to choose it when you're feeling down to help boost your mood. But too much yellow can be a bad thing. It is considered to be the color that is most stressful on the eyes. It can cause frustration, irritation and anger. So if you're working on a pattern in a yellow yarn and the work is driving you crazy and you just

want to throw it across the wall; try switching to a more calming yarn and see if that helps. Color therapy says that it is also good for digestion problems and skin disorders.

- **Red is agitating but invigorating**. Red is often associated with anger. This doesn't mean that you'll be mad every time that you work with red yarn, of course. But if you're particularly sensitive to color then you should be aware that the over-stimulation of this bright hue can cause your blood pressure to rise and your pulse to raise. If you suffer from anxiety then you may find that working with red yarn heightens your anxiety. On the other hand, this does stimulate the nerves, so if you suffer from a lot of fatigue and need a boost of energy you may find that red projects are uplifting. It brings warmth so if you have an illness that leaves you cold it can be a good choice. Additionally, red is a power color so if you are feeling weak and like you need to regain your personal power then crocheting something for yourself in red can be just the answer.
- **Orange excites without irritating**. People who are seeking the excitement and racing heart of red but find the bright color too overwhelming may find that orange is a better choice. It is less harsh on the eyes and body but still boosts excitement. It can be a good color for some people dealing with depression; that's because it stirs up emotion and may help take away that "numb" feeling. Orange is considered very freeing so if you're overwhelmed with restrictions in your life then pick up some orange yarn! Some people believe that this color helps to stimulate the thyroid.
- **Brown is stable**. Brown is an earthly color so it is all about stability and grounding. It is the color that you're supposed to turn to if you need to heal your relationships or ground your own emotional center. It is a warm color. But be wary of using too much brown – working only with brown suggests a blandness that can be linked with depression.
- **Purple is creative**. Purple is the go-to color for people seeking to get in touch with their creative sides. Deep purple suggests opulence and luxury and stimulates the creative brain with feelings of fantasy and whimsy. Lighter colors, such as lavender, are more restful but still allow you to open up to your inner creative voice. This is a great color choice for doing meditative, artistic crochet!
- **Pink is youthful**. Pink is a joyful color associated with youth. People who have age-related disorders may find that pink brings them back in touch with a younger side of themselves and

reinvigorates them. Pink is also the best color for healing from grief.
- **Grey is the ultimate neutral.** Color theory says that grey is the most neutral of all colors. Because of this, it is useful to neutralize negative emotions and experiences and generally to bring you into balance.
- **Black fights evil.** Black is said to be a color that fights off evil. What does this mean for healing? Well, if you need to end a toxic co-dependent relationship or break yourself free from an addiction then black can be a good choice to surround yourself with. Black is also one of the most meditative colors so if you feel like it is time to go deep into your own psyche then work with this color. However, excessive blackness is obviously associated with depression and should be used carefully.
- **White is totally healing.** White is the balance of all colors together and therefore is considered to be a very powerful healing color. It suggests freshness and so it is great if you feel like you need to "start over" from something. It also suggests spiritual enlightenment and inner peace so if you're feeling at a loss in this world then you might be calmed by working with pure white.

Self-Care Exercise #14: A List of Safe Projects

The exercise: Create a list of safe projects for yourself that you can always return to.

The purpose: Creativity is adventurous and risky. There are times when we also need for it to be a safe space. This list will be that safety net for you.

In depth: Creative artistic work is often infused with self-doubt. This causes many artists to stop creating all together. It is critical that we have areas of our creativity where we can rest, areas that make us not only feel safe but make us feel sure of ourselves and confident in our creativity capabilities, areas we can return to again and again to re-fuel ourselves for riskier artistic endeavors.

Exercise steps:

1. **Make a list** of all of the things that you are good at in crochet. (There is a list of possible options below.)
2. **Make an additional list** of all of the other things that you are good at in life. Next to each item, see if there is a way that your crochet can reflect this. For example, you might be great at letting people know you care about them through small gestures. Crocheting little gifts for random holidays could be an example of how you'd express this skill through crafting.
3. **Re-write the list** into a set of positive reminders about your craft skills. For example, you might have written that you're good at amigurumi. Write down something like, "I have the skills and talent to crochet amigurumi, and I love doing it!"
4. **Post this list** where you can see it (or stick it in the front page of your crochet journal). Return to it again and again to select projects that make you feel safe, creatively confident and able to rest in your craft until you have the energy to try new things!

THINGS YOU MAY BE GOOD AT IN CROCHET

Not sure what you're really good at in crochet? Here are some of the things that you might find are easy and enjoyable for you:

- Crocheting granny squares
- Crocheting neat, even stitches
- Crocheting quickly
- Finishing what you start
- Huge projects (or tiny ones)
- Joining invisibly or in an interesting way
- Making beautiful flowers
- Making blankets
- Mixing crochet with other crafts
- Multi-tasking projects
- Reading crochet patterns or diagrams
- Risk-taking and willingness to learn new things
- Selecting colors that go well together
- Specific techniques, such as thread crochet or broomstick lace
- Working with texture

Tips:

- Often it's easier to think of things that we aren't good at rather than things that we are. When those things come to mind, turn them around to reflect what you ARE good at. For example, I'm terrible at weaving in ends properly, but I can take those ends and allow them to hang loose and adorn them with beads and make them artistic features of my work. So my list might say, "I'm great at turning ends into works of art." This reminds me that when I'm struggling with creative confidence, I should create items that have ends like this to re-inspire me and celebrate what I'm good at. Not good at joining? You might want to work on large top-down crochet projects.
- Regularly add to your list when you notice or realize that you've gotten good at something new in the craft!
- Celebrate what's good about every part of your craft. I've always loved researching crochet ... but when I started claiming aloud that I love knowing obscure facts about the craft I started taking even more joy in the process of researching and sharing what I learned.

Taking it further: Start a set of WIPs that use the techniques and skills that you are good at. Stick each WIP in a project bag with a note to yourself about what talents it celebrates that you have. When you feel down or unsure or creatively stuck, pull out a WIP, see what it celebrates and work on the skill that you already have down pat.

Yarn for Thought: More Musings for Self-Love

Some of the additional things that you might want to think about and journal on related to self-care, self-esteem and self-compassion include:

- What do you really enjoy vs. what you wish you enjoyed? What is really fun for you? Do you think you should join a crochet group but actually really enjoy solo crafting? Do you think that "good crocheters" create really complex, detailed large projects but actually really just like to work on small, simple projects? What's true for you? Erase the "shoulds" and celebrate your real loves in crafting.
- What would be your absolutely perfect crochet day? What projects would it include? Where would it take place? How are some ways that you can incorporate elements of that into your regular crafting experience?
- Meditative walking can be a great way to open yourself up to new understandings of your own creativity. Take one thirty minute walk every day for a week. Keep your phone and electronic gadgets turned off. Go alone, not with a buddy. Listen to the way your heartbeat matches your footfall. Ask yourself what you need more of. Ask yourself what inspires you. Ask yourself how you can crochet differently with this new knowledge.
- What rituals would make it easier and more enjoyable for you to crochet? Lighting a candle before beginning a project, photographing work in the sunshine after you've completed a piece, eating a piece of fruit at the end of each craft session .... these are all examples but you can come up with your own. Make a list of possibilities to try. Keep the five senses in mind as you make your list.
- Explore the highs and lows of your own personal energy throughout the day. How does that impact your choices in crochet? For example, I have really high creative energy in the morning so that is a great time for me to either work on non-crochet projects (like writing) or to work on really innovative and artistic crochet projects. I have really low energy in the afternoon, so that's a great time for me to crochet a meditative, relaxing project like a large granny square blanket. If I haven't slept or eaten properly, I get grumpy and my self-esteem plummets so that's a good time to return to my list of "safe projects" and work on one of those.
- What limits your ability to love yourself?

Embrace a Sense of Adventure

Now that we're feeling safe, it's time to make a leap. (*Remember, as Julia Cameron says, "leap and the net will appear!"*) This chapter is all about learning something new, embracing a sense of adventure and working with setting and achieving goals. The work in this section is a combination of stretching your own limits and encouraging playfulness in your own work. It is designed to allow you to take more creative risks but of course there will be times when that feels a little frightening.

Let me digress for a minute and tell you about a vacation I took last year; it's not about crochet per se but about pushing my own boundaries in terms of adventure. It was December 2014 and my beaux and I were taking our first big vacation together (after the obligatory previous trips to my hometown and his). He has traveled to many of the interesting places in the world throughout his lifetime. I have traveled extensively within the United States but have only been out of the country a few times, so I wanted to go to a place that really excited me but not one that he had already been to. We chose Belize.

Belize is beautiful; it is picturesque in that way that you read about in romantic travel memoirs but rarely get to really experience firsthand. And in terms of travel for an American, it is really fairly straightforward and simple – it is safe, it is an English-speaking country, the money exchange rate is straightforward and they accept US dollars most places. There are certainly pros and cons to this type of travel, and there are certainly socially-minded pros and cons for a country that used to be a small fishing village and now relies almost entirely on tourism for survival. But for me, at the time of the trip, it was perfect, because my anxiety was under control but definitely bubbling close to the surface and the stress of international travel threatened to cause it to boil over. So, pros and cons aside, I was really excited to be spending a warm week on a stunning beach in a gorgeous area of the world that I had never explored but found fairly easy to navigate.

The beaux and I are both pretty laidback and learned that we traveled well together, but there were definitely negotiations that had to take place to allow us each to have the kind of vacation we wanted to have. Truth be told, I would have been totally content writing and reading in the hammock every day, sipping pina coladas and seeing very little. He, on the other hand, wanted to take every tour that existed including the super adventurous ones that require swimming through caves to see skeletal remains. The compromise meant that we did some tours, mostly the slightly-less-adventurous ones, and I was glad because I got to see things that I wanted to see even though my natural inclination was to just rest in the sand forever.

One of the things that we did was snorkeling, which was new to me. Truth be told, it wasn't high on my list of activities. I love being on the water in a boat but I am not a strong swimmer and don't really enjoy swimming at all. I wish I did; it seems like it should be such a peaceful activity, but the reality is that I don't. The beaux, however, is SCUBA certified and the area is beautiful, known for being comparable to The Great Barrier Reef in terms of SCUBA and perhaps even better for snorkelers. So we went on an all-day snorkeling tour.

What I want to share is that I hated it and loved it and wasn't sure about it and got anxious and was proud that I accomplished it and in the end left with really great memories of it although I don't know that it's something I'll ever do again. I didn't like the swimming part, trying to keep my humongous flippers from popping to the surface and flipping me over, trying to keep up with my group when I could barely navigate at all, in a sea absolutely crowded with tourists all doing the same thing. I did like the few moments when everything else slipped away and I remembered that I could breathe and see underwater and the coral created a magical landscape around me while I passed just above majestic sea turtles and eyed eerie eels from a distance. I won't lie; most of the time was uncomfortable and I found myself too much in my head and often thinking, "I would so much rather see this in an aquarium, standing dry outside the tank" and then being annoyed with myself for having such a thought. But those other moments were worth the discomfort. And weeks after we left Belize, I found myself telling people about snorkeling, because it was an experience that left an impression on me, even if I hadn't truly enjoyed the adventure of the activity in the moment. The experience stuck with me, expanded my sense of the world, grew my sense of myself.

I share this story with you here because it illustrates how adventure plays its role in our lives, in small and large ways. In this case, I pushed my boundaries a little bit, not so much that my anxiety would wield out of control but enough to feel uncomfortable. I did something I didn't love but wanted to do anyway. I explored the possibility of exploration. And because of that, I grew. I learned something. I changed, subtly but strikingly. The most important thing is that I did it, I took the chance. I could have stayed sunning on the beach with a book and been perfectly content but then I would have left that beach the exact same person I'd arrived there as, and that's not the way that I want my entire life to go. The less adventure you embrace, the smaller your world shrinks; the more adventure you embrace, the bigger the possibilities are for yourself, even if the possibilities are only within your own imagination and artistic growth.

So what does any of this have to do with crochet? After all, taking a risk with a hook and yarn isn't the same as traveling fourteen hours to a foreign country to go into waters that scare you, is it? No, but yes. Strangely, I get the same sense of trepidation and not-sureness that I did that day when I decide to try something new in crafting, especially if it's something that doesn't have a specific pattern and blueprint to guide me. In the Belizean waters that day, I knew I was more or less safe; I do know how to swim and there were so many people there with me that it's really unlikely anything bad could have happened. Still, my body reacted like it might drown in the waters of doing something I hadn't done before. And although I know that there's certainly nothing life-threatening about trying something new in crochet, my body sometimes still reacts in that same way.

Recently I've been crocheting mandala after mandala for my Mandalas for Marinke project (which you can learn more about in the conclusionary chapter of this book). One of the contributors to the project, Leslie Rayborn, sent in a small set of mandalas that really inspired me because instead of weaving in her ends like we usually do, she left them loose, braiding them and adorning them with buttons. I was so inspired that I decided to try something similar, intentionally leaving long ends so that I could play with braiding and macrame on them.

And let me tell you, I was scared! I knew it was unreasonable to be scared - no one had to ever see these except me - but there was something that happened in my body when I did things "the wrong way" that caused me to feel anxious. Creating and leaving those long ends didn't feel right inside me. And then I wasn't sure if I liked what I was doing with them after. Later, I came to love these creations and I was glad I had taken the creative risk, but during the process I felt all of this trepidation. I thought that I should just be doing the mandalas the way I had done all of the previous ones, "the right way", similar to how I had the thought in the water that I should just be at an aquarium looking at sea turtles through the glass instead of fumbling along gracelessly beside their massive, stunning bodies in the tranquil wonder of Belize. I am glad I swam with sea turtles and I am glad I added macrame to my mandalas and both experiences took a risk that my body didn't recognize as different from each other even though objectively they are obviously not the same.

So, let's practice risk taking and adding adventure to our creative lives. You never know how this might expand your world!

Adventure Exercise #1: Random Lines Pattern

The exercise: Randomly select lines from the instructions of a variety of different crochet patterns and compile them into one new random pattern.

The purpose: This exercise is designed to inspire your curiosity, as you try to guess what the next line will look like and what the finished piece will be. Being curious is a key way to improve your total experience of life and art.

In depth: This crochet exercise combines some of the things we've already worked with in other exercises with a new sense of creating adventure. You'll have to work at letting go of the end project, as it's not likely going to be anything specific (although you may later be able to adapt it into a blanket or at least into wall art). You'll have to explore what it feels like to work on a project without knowing what the end outcome will be (like when you do a mystery CAL, as described earlier in this book). And you'll get the opportunity to see what kind of lines inspire you in different patterns and how you feel when you work each one.

Exercise steps:

1. **Gather together a bunch of different crochet patterns**. You are going to be cutting them up so you will want to use copies if you are doing this physically (which I recommend) but you can also do this with cut-and-paste on a computer. Any patterns will work, although you might want to make sure that every pattern is either worked in rows or worked in the round, not mixing the two at least the first time that you do this exercise.
2. **Randomly select lines from each project** and paste them into a new "pattern" of your own creation. For example, I might have pulled lines from three different patterns that now form the first three lines of my new pattern, which now reads: (1) Chain 80, (2) dc in the 3rd chain from the hook, dc in next chain, *sc once in next two chains, dc once in next two chains, repeat from * until the end of the row, turn. (3) ch 1, hdc in 2nd ch from hook in the 3rd loop, hdc in the 3rd loop in every ch across,

turn. Each instruction comes from a different pattern and isn't intended to go together but now they all do.
3. **Follow this new pattern** from beginning to end to crochet a random item. You will have to make adjustments to compensate for the fact that the pattern lines don't actually go together. For example, a line may say "dc in each sc" but the line before might not have been sc. It's okay; just dc in whatever stitches ARE in that previous line.
4. **Complete the pattern.** See what arises as you work and what you have when you're done. Embrace the adventure.

Tips:

- Start small. Choose just a few different beginner patterns to draw from, patterns that are similar to each other (all blankets worked in rows, for example), and choose just 5-10 lines to create your new pattern. This will give you a sense of how the project will go and provide you with confidence for making a larger project next time.
- Be flexible in your process of following the pattern. The numbers in the rows aren't going to add up, the exact instructions aren't going to match. If you feel frustrated by this, explore your frustration in your crochet journal. Ask yourself if it is a fear of this sense of adventure.
- Use yarn and a hook that you're really comfortable using. It doesn't matter what the original patterns call for, use what you like as you work your new "pattern". Play with whether or not you like color changes. Keeping the same color, or color scheme, as you work the pattern can make the work look cohesive even though at first glance it may not be.

Taking it further: You can take this project further by drawing the lines from disparate projects and even projects that use different techniques in crochet. What happens when you take one line from an entrelac crochet blanket pattern, the next from a crochet pattern for a broomstick lace scarf and the following from a tapestry crochet purse pattern? How does this inspire you as you create and how could you use it to design your own crochet pattern in the future?

Adventure Exercise #2: Found Lines Pattern

NOTE: This is a variation on Exercise One above, so make sure that you read that one first.

The exercise: Choose specific lines from a long crochet pattern and crochet only those lines.

The purpose: As with exercise one, you're adapting a pattern so that the lines of it don't necessarily go together and you'll play with the adventure of finding out what you create. The difference here is that you are working from a single pattern so you will be more selective in what you choose to edit out or leave in. Instead of random selections, you'll be more thoughtful.

In depth: This exercise draws from my love for "found poetry", particularly in playing with it through existing writing. I used to play with this a lot. I would go find a visually compelling book in a bargain bin, usually one with thick, heavy pages that were good for art-making. I'd go through the book and circle or highlight all of the words that appealed to me, crossing out all of the rest. This is "found poetry", using the words that are already there and the process of deletion to create my own new poem. Then I'd use altered art techniques to manipulate the book's pages and I'd have a living work of poetry art. That's essentially what we're going to do here, but we're going to be taking a long crochet pattern, highlighting and eliminating lines to create a smaller poetic version.

Exercise steps:

1. **Choose a long crochet pattern**. I typically choose one for a complex crochet blanket, because even when it is shortened it might still be big enough to serve as a lap blanket or table topper.
2. Skim through the pattern and **highlight** any of the rows or rounds that sound especially great to you.
3. Skim through the pattern and use a **Sharpie** (or your computer tools) to delete any of the rows or rounds that sound especially annoying to you.
4. **Read through the rest** of the lines and use your gut instinct to either highlight or delete them.

5. **Use the highlighted portions** as your new "pattern" and work through the pattern step-by-step.

Tips:

- The original exercise is worked in order, from top to bottom using the highlighted text. However, it can be mixed up for a more interesting approach to the project. Cut out each line of highlighted text. Put them in a bowl and pull them out one at a time to create a new crochet pattern of random lines.
- *See additional tips in Exercise One of this chapter.*

Taking it further: When I create altered art found poetry, I sometimes add lines of my own to the text, writing them in based on inspiration from the piece that I've created through the process of highlighting and deleting what's already there. You can do the same thing with your pattern. When you have the highlighted text ready, read through the pattern and see if there are any things that you feel might be missing from the piece. Add them in with your own hand, incorporating them into your pattern. For example, I love the meditative beauty of working rows of hdc stitches, so I might add a line of just that here and there in my "found pattern".

Adventure Exercise #3: Research a Crochet Artist

The exercise: Research a crochet artist and allow this to inspire play in your craft.

The purpose: Immersing ourselves in the world of someone who inspires us creatively can open up new channels in our own work.

In depth: There are many artists out there who work in the medium of crochet. Learning more about the entire body of work created by one of these artists can spark new creative approaches to your own work that you never even imagined were possible. You have to let yourself take the time to really absorb and explore the work of this other artist, seeing what they do, learning about their life, practicing the techniques that they practice.

Exercise steps:

1. **Broadly research** the topic of crochet art to get a sense of what types of artists might inspire you. (You can find a section of my site, Crochet Concupiscence, devoted to crochet art and artists.)
2. **Choose 3-4 crochet artists** to explore in more depth, browsing through their portfolios of work.
3. **Select the one crochet artist** that most inspires you at this time (*there is a short list below to get you started*). Research this artist in depth. When was the last time that you got passionately obsessed about a topic and had to know everything about it? Let this be that time. Find as much information as you can on the artist - what they are like, what they have made, how they created what they did. You don't have to make anything at all, yet, just learn about this person, see where the sense of adventurous inspiration takes you.
4. **Choose a technique or style or approach** from this artist and practice it in a very small way in your own crochet work. For example, perhaps you've fallen in love with the crochet artist Olek who does elaborate crochet art installations and yarnbombing, covering entire rooms with her work. Maybe you love how she incorporates text into her work through crochet. You don't need to crochet a whole room. Choose one word and learn to crochet it, letting her style inspire your style. See where it takes you. Play with it.
5. **Continue learning** about this artist and choosing projects inspired by this person until you are completely maxed out of all possible inspiration from this source. Then begin the process again with a new artist! The more you research, the more you'll discover what you really love in crochet art and this will help you discover your own voice as well.

SOME CROCHET ARTISTS I ADORE

I absolutely love crochet art and I do a lot of exploration into it. You can see all of the crochet artists I've written about it on Crochet Concupiscence by going to the crochet artist category, which you can reach by clicking on the "crochet art" icon on the homepage or visiting
 http://www.crochetconcupiscence.com/category/crochet-art-crochet-artists/.

If you want to explore crochet art I'd also strongly recommend that you check out the book *The Fine Art of Crochet* by Gwen Blakley Kinsler; it is a one-of-a-kind art book featuring the work of many amazing working crochet artists. That said, here is a short list of some of my very favorite crochet artists that you might want to use as a starting point for your research:

- Olek, who combines crochet with the street art of yarnbombing, interactive performance art, and text in art. *Other great yarnbombing artists include Magda Sayeg and London Kaye.*
- Jo Hamilton, who uses her own unique technique to crochet the most amazing realistic-looking portraits of people. *Other great portrait crochet artists include Pat Ahern and Katika Art.*
- Kate Jenkins, who makes knit and crochet installations of food and other objects that have a witty, humorous twist. *Other terrific artists who crochet food include Clemence Joly and Twinkie Chan.*
- Joana Vasconcelos, a mixed media artist whose large crochet installations have been featured in major museums around the world. *Other large-scale crochet installation artists include Orly Genger and Toshiko Horiuchi-Macadam.*
- Su Ami, a crochet artist who specializes in making teeny-tiny amigurumi crochet animals. *Other micro-crochet artists include Elin Thomas and Lam Linh.*
- Nathan Vincent, a crochet artist who tackles topics related to masculinity, with installations including guns and locker rooms. *Other male crochet artists include Dale Roberts and Ivano Vitali.*
- Nick Cave, who makes wearable crochet art and "sound suits". *Other wearable crochet artists include Aldo Lanzini and Huckleberry Delsignore.*
- Arline Fisch who crochets terrific jewelry and art installations using colored wire, and has been doing so for six decades. *Other terrific crochet artists working with wire include Ruth Asawa and Yoola.*

Tips:

- Don't compare yourself to the artist in question. You are two different people. Although you will allow this person to inspire your work, do not aspire to be this person. You are your own artist;

this is just an exercise in stretching yourself by allowing someone you admire to infuse your work with ideas.
- Not sure what to crochet in the technique of the artist that you like? Sometimes that can be difficult or seem overwhelming. For example, I love the work of Catherine Carr who actually takes glass and somehow melts and uses it to crochet. I have no idea how she does that and don't imagine that I could do it. Instead, I try to imagine what I could make that she might like, something she could wear while working or something that would complement her pieces if they were housed together in the same exhibit space.
- Some crochet artists have small bodies of work, or have crochet as only a small portion of larger collections. It is okay to start small with your research. If you can't find a lot of information about someone's work, see if there's a contact address for them and email them, or ask around through social networks to see if someone knows more. If you get stuck, that's okay, write down what inspired you about the person's work so that you can look for other artists with similar traits.

Taking it further: The most amazing things happen when we allow ourselves to just randomly follow what interests us. Let your research simply be the starting point of a journey of creative exploration. Follow your heart wherever it wants to go, setting time aside regularly to research your passion. For example, you may be in the midst of researching the work of Su Ami who crochets the tiniest amigurumi and you naturally wonder how she crochets that small, so you start researching that when you come across some literature on miniatures and the next thing you know you're visiting a Miniatures Museum, watching documentaries on people who make miniature dollhouse furniture and collecting your own miniatures from around the world. One interest leads into another as long as you don't place limitations on yourself. Embrace the research as a creative adventure!

Adventure Exercise #4: Research a Period of Crochet History in Depth

NOTE: This is a variation on Exercise 3 above.

The exercise: Choose a period of crochet history and research it in depth for inspiration.

The purpose: As with Exercise Three above, this exercise helps immerse you in new creative possibilities as you explore the way it was done before.

In depth: Allow the creativity of the past to inform the future of your own creative work by learning as much as you can about a specific era in crochet. Researching a favorite period in depth will turn you on to areas of the craft that you never knew, and it will give you a whole new appreciation for crochet that might impact your work in a positive way.

Exercise steps:

1. **Choose a decade** in history between 1810 and now; *see a list below for some good options*. Do a quick search to see if there is at least a little bit of available information about crochet during that decade. (If not, you might wish to select a larger time period or a different decade, at least if this is your first time trying this exercise.)
2. **Research** the decade in depth as it relates to the history of crochet. What were people crocheting? Who were the ones making items? Where were people getting crochet patterns? Who was using the crochet that was made? What types of tools were used in the craft at that time?
3. **Crochet a project** inspired by this period in history. It might be a pattern written at that time. Alternatively it might be a contemporary pattern or project that is simply inspired by that era; a modern cloche hat inspired by the fashion of the 1920's, for example.

POPULAR DECADES IN CROCHET HISTORY

Here are some of the decades of crochet history that you might wish to learn more about for inspiration:

- 1860's. Crochet had been around for a few decades, some patterns had been published, industrialization made crochet hooks more readily available and Harper's Bazaar began to come out with published craft ideas.

- 1920's. This was an important decade in fashion history, which makes it worth learning more about as someone who might like to crochet clothing.
- Wartime Crochet (late 1930s, early 1940s). Many women were using crochet in war efforts, making items for the troops, and when the men returned home many women who had been working had a lot of time on their hands for crafting at home.
- 1970's. There is some really interesting crochet art that emerged at this time, especially from the people who were crafting at The Pratt Institute in New York. You can still get your hands on some of the books that were published then. (You'll also find a category on Crochet Concupiscence devoted to 1970s crochet designers.)
- The early 2000's. Crochet saw a great revival at this time in recent history. Yarnbombing was developed, crochet hit the fashion runways, middle schools launched crochet clubs, craftivism emerged strongly and so much more happened that's worth learning about.

Tips:

- The history of crochet is often intertwined with the histories of knitting, lace and other needlearts. Don't limit yourself to articles and books from your chosen era that are just about crochet; look for crochet information in materials about these other crafts as well.
- Watch movies from your chosen decade to discover whether crochet turns up in fashion and home items from this time. Look for knitting and lace, too, since these items were often also made by crocheters around the same time.
- Consider starting a vintage crochet collection. I collect vintage craft and fashion magazines, and I also love old crochet books. Some people that I know collect vintage crochet hooks and scissors. Others collect vintage crochet patterns (or reproductions of such). Imagine that you have an art studio of your very own and you have room to store any collection at all; what would you want? Even if you don't have the space, you can collect a few of the items as special tokens to your craft. (You might even put them in your crochet basket / shrine that you made in the previous chapter on self-care!)

Taking it further: Immerse yourself fully in the decade as you research, learning not just about crochet but everything there is to know about that time period. My father, for example, loves the 1920s, and I swear he could tell you everything there is to know from that era, particularly about the women who were silent film stars and especially about Louise Brooks. He didn't set out to know everything about Lulu; he just followed an interest and that's where it led. Learn about who was famous in your decade, what was going on politically and socially, the music that was heard, the films that were created, the artists that were active ... You can get crochet inspiration from all areas of the decade, not just how crochet was done at that time!

Adventure Exercise #5: Other Areas of Crochet Research

NOTE: This is an expansion of the ideas presented in Exercises Three and Four above.

The exercise: Make a list of different things that you would like to learn about and explore their relation to crochet.

The purpose: Expand your own opportunities for additional research in crochet to broaden your crafty horizons.

In depth: Researching a crochet artist in depth and researching a particular part of crochet history can each be a great way to explore adventures in crafting. However, you can obviously do all different kinds of different research in crochet that will work similarly in your craft life.

Exercise steps:

- **Make a list** of every single thing that you feel inspired to learn more about. Don't limit this to crafting - include languages, cultures, hobbies, anything at all. *See examples below.*
- **Next to each item** on the list, include at least one note about how this might relate to research in crochet. Want to learn to read Braille? That might inspire you to learn if there are blind crocheters; (there are, many of them actually). Interested in Native American mythology? How was crochet used in native cultures? Want to be a fashion designer? What do you know about the history or technicalities of crochet in fashion?

- **Choose** the thing off of your list that most inspires you. Research it in depth (using the tips, tools and ideas practiced above in Exercises Three and Four).
- **Crochet** at least one item related to your area of research. Want to learn tennis? Crochet a tennis racket cozy or a tennis skirt.

THINGS MANY PEOPLE WANT TO LEARN

- An **art**, such as glass blowing, woodworking or painting
- A **skill**, such as cooking, upholstery or car repair
- A **spiritual practice**, such as monastic teachings or walking meditation
- **Beauty tips**, such as creating a cat eye or making a French Braid
- **Cultural, historical or regional information** such as the history of your relatives or the native landscaping of the area where you live
- **Entertainment** activities: juggling, face painting, balloon animals
- **Homesteading:** canning, bread baking, beekeeping
- **Kids' crafts** including science experiments and building with blocks
- **Language**, including sign language
- **Memorization** of your favorite poem or selection from a play
- **Performance art** including instrument recitals, acting and dance
- **Practical things**, like learning to tie a tie or plant a garden
- **Sports** such as tennis, pilates, yoga, bicycling or mountain climbing
- **Technology**, such as mastering Photoshop, YouTube or audio recording

Tips:

- You don't have to know the answer to the question of how an item relates to crochet. Simply pose the question. It is through your research that you can learn more.
- If you can't find any crochet information at all through your research, expand a little. You can do this by expanding crochet to a larger category or by expanding your research area with respect to crochet. For example, let's use the Braille example above. I posed the question, "are there any blind crocheters?" There are and there is actually tons of interesting information about adaptations made by these people, but let's pretend for a moment that there wasn't

such information. I could expand crochet to a larger category and ask what types of crafts are common in the blind community? Alternatively, I could expand the category itself, asking what type of crochet is done by any type of differently-abled people.
- Think outside of the box when looking for items that you can crochet that are related to your topic area. Using the above example of wanting to learn tennis, you don't have to be so obvious as to crochet a tennis racket cozy. Instead, you could crochet an amigurumi doll of your favorite tennis player or crochet an item using a yarn purchased in England, which is where the sport originated. What inspires you?!

<u>Taking it further</u>: Uncover a mystery, question or problem in your area of study and come up with a way to solve that problem in crochet. For example, let's say that you are studying a particular sport where the players are prone to a specific kind of injury. What kind of crochet item or exercise could you invent that would help to solve that problem?

Adventure Exercise #6: Go on a Crochet Retreat

<u>The exercise</u>: Attend a crochet retreat (or go on your own self-designed crochet vacation).

<u>The purpose</u>: Traveling is always an adventure; apply that adventure specifically to your love of crochet.

<u>In depth</u>: A crochet retreat is a vacation designed specifically to give you both time and inspiration for crochet. The destination doesn't really matter, although it's ideal to go somewhere that has yarn you can buy and people you can craft with. Set the reset button on your crafting just by taking it someplace new.

<u>Exercise steps</u>:

1. **Research the available crochet retreats**. Even if you don't go on one of these, they will give you ideas for creating your own crochet vacation. As of the writing of this book, I'm able to locate several different options online. One that I haven't had a chance to do but have always wanted to go on is the Cool Crochet Workshop held each spring and autumn at the Chambres d'Amis in Marrakech, Morocco. This retreat includes

yarn purchases at the local souk, crocheting in the open air with locals and more as well as traditional tourist activities. (Details at http://www.chambresdamis.com/cool-crochet.)
2. **Choose** the crochet retreat that is right for you. This may entail creating your own retreat that is inspired by an existing option. See tips below.
3. **Book it, go on it and enjoy it!**

Tips:

- Be open to planning far in advance so that you can take advantage of the available retreats that are planned. If you're multi-craftual, consider knitting and other fiber retreats as well.
- If you can't get away for a full vacation right now, maybe you can plan a weekend getaway instead. A weekend away in a beautiful place, with a trip to a yarn store and maybe a drop-in craft meetup can be an excellent mini-retreat. If that's still not possible, what is possible? Taking your yarn to a cute cafe in a new neighborhood for an hour of crafting, visiting a new book store and checking out their craft section, taking a day trip to see a yarn store that you've never been to …. make something happen for you that feels like a getaway!
- In her books on happiness, author Gretchen Rubin explains that there are four stages of happiness: anticipate it, savor it as it is happening, express this happiness to others and reflect upon it later. Apply this to your crochet retreat by embracing the planning, remembering to enjoy the activity, share that joy with others while you're on the trip and take photos, make a scrapbook or save a special project you crocheted during the retreat to reflect back upon the experience in time.

Taking it further: Design your own ideal crochet vacation and plan a trip with your craftiest friends. It can take time, energy and money to make this happen but if it sounds exciting to you then it can definitely be worth it! If possible, make this an annual trip, just like a family reunion!

Adventure Exercise #7: Use Unpredictable Colors in Crochet

The exercise: Use unusual colors for common items in your crochet work.

The purpose: You can turn the most common of things into an adventure if you are just willing to look at them a little bit differently.

In depth: Crochet something that is common for you to make but use colors to change the elements into something unpredictable. For example, if you crochet an item that has a heart on it and you are someone who always crochets hearts in pinks and reds then it is time to turn your hearts into blue, black or olive green. If you are making a baby mobile that has a crochet rainbow, skip the ROYGBV colors and crochet the rainbow shape in camo colors instead. Feel weird? That's the point! If you can't take a risk in crochet, where can you take one?!

Exercise steps:

1. **Look at your current projects** and figure out which elements have common colors. Brown teddy bears, red hearts, yellow suns, green leaves, grey elephants and even colorful flowers can all be worked in non-traditional colors for different effects.
2. **Choose a project** from step one that can have elements altered. If you don't have one available then consciously pick a project like this to start.
3. **Crochet** your project using a color that is totally out of line with what would be expected. See how this feels!

Tips:

- Stay open and aware to the process that you go through when you crochet something in the "wrong" color. Does it feel weird? Do you hate it? Are you embarrassed by it, as if you are caught coloring outside of the lines?
- You can also do a variation of this project in which you crochet a wearable item for yourself in a color that you'd "never" wear. A crochet hat, scarf or shawl can be a huge statement piece and you can really challenge yourself by wearing a handmade item in a color that's not comfortable for you. People who wear all black can change their entire impression by putting on a bright orange scarf!
- Learn a little bit more about color theory to get an understanding of what different colors mean. Use this information to select "wrong" colors that give you the right feeling!

Taking it further: Crochet an entire scene using the "wrong" colors as a practice in the art of the craft. If you like amigurumi, make a set of animals all in colors that don't seem quite right for them - blue bunnies, purple elephants and green dogs infuse your space with a sense of fun. If you don't like making amigurumi or sculptural crochet, you can do the same thing with flat appliques.

Adventure Exercise #8: Crochet in an Unexpected Place

The exercise: Crochet in a place where you don't think you'll be comfortable crocheting.

The purpose: Getting outside of your comfort zone in a small way can really help you expand your own artistic possibilities.

In depth: So often we place these rules on ourselves and limit ourselves with "should" and "shouldn't" and sometimes we don't even realize that we are doing it. We think that society has told us we can't do something and when we discover that we actually can it is so liberating. Crochet isn't going to hurt anyone so take the risk on doing it somewhere that you're not "supposed to".

Exercise steps:

1. **Make a list** of places that you don't think you're allowed to crochet. *See possible suggestions below.*
2. **Take your crochet** work to one of these places.
3. **Crochet** and see what happens!

POSSIBLE PLACES FOR CROCHET

The places that we typically don't think we can crochet are places where we are afraid someone will be bothered by our crafting. Here are some examples of places that you can take your crochet even if you think it's not going to be welcome there:

- Airplane (yes, crochet hooks are allowed on planes)
- Church
- Day spa
- Hospital
- Movie theater

- Public bathroom (weird? perhaps, but it will challenge you!)
- Restaurant
- School
- Yoga class
- Wine bar

Tips:

- If you are too afraid to start crocheting in one of these places, start by just taking your yarn and hook out and placing it near you in one of these places. See how that feels.
- Remember that you are not hurting anyone. In fact, you might be helping others by inspiring them and showing them your craft. And you might be helping yourself; for example, I crochet in classes because it helps me to focus and sit still so I'm actually more present than I am without the hooks. Does it bother some teachers? Yes, but usually if I explain the purpose and make sure that I'm not being particularly distracting then they are fine with it.
- Stay calm if someone does challenge you. Keep in mind again that you are doing nothing wrong. You can put the work away when confronted if you want to but you can also choose to speak directly with the person, explain why you're doing what you're doing and ask them what the problem is (in a loving way). Your right to crochet is a simple but powerful way to stand up for yourself.
- This exercise is designed to push your limits but not to cause you unbearable anxiety. If it really causes you a lot of stress, take it in baby steps and work on your anxiety as needed with a therapist or other professional.

Taking it further: Go yarnbombing and place an item that you've crocheted in a place where you think it is not allowed. (Be aware of any legal ramifications in your area. Yarnbombers are usually not prosecuted but you should know what is okay in your region, be aware of any possible fines, avoid trespassing issues, etc. The point is to be daring, not criminal!)

Adventure Exercise #9: Order Surprise Yarn!

The exercise: Purchase yarn through the mail without knowing what you're going to get.

<u>The purpose</u>: Embrace the sense of adventure through yarn by allowing someone else to pick what you are getting.

<u>In depth</u>: First you get the sense of adventure that comes while you wait for the mail. Then you get the sense of possibility when you receive a yarn you didn't expect and get to decide what to make with it! If you like to have control over every element of your project the then this exercise is going to challenge that.

<u>Exercise steps</u>:

1. **Order mystery yarn**. You can order mystery yarn balls, bags and boxes from various sources around the Internet. Search around. Mystery yarn balls are balls that are made from yarn ends (you can even make your own) whereas mystery bags and boxes are filled with different types of regular yarn.
2. **Wait** for it to arrive. Don't let it too far out of your mind; allow the anticipation to build because that's part of the adventure.
3. **Make a special event** out of opening the package when it arrives. Wait until you have time to really enjoy it. Use some of the setting-the-mood craft rituals explored in the previous chapter on self-care. See what your reaction is to the yarn when you finally see it. Touch it and smell it to indulge your full senses.
4. **Use the yarn**! How will you use it? Be creative.

<u>Tips</u>:

- Prefer to purchase yarn locally? Go to your local yarn shop and ask the store owner if she would be willing to put together a small mystery yarn bag for you. Give her your budget and any other requirements you have (such as only cotton yarn) and see what you get!
- Don't have money to buy new yarn right now? Arrange a mystery swap with a crafty friend. Set some parameters (number of skeins you'll trade or dollar value of yarn to trade). Create a really pretty surprise package for your swap partner.
- Sometimes the yarn that arrives won't speak to you right away. That's okay. Keep it out in your craft space where you can see it and

give it time to marinate in your mind until it inspires you and you know what to make with it!

<u>Taking it further</u>: Join a subscription or membership club to get mystery yarn in the mail on a regular basis. There are yarn box clubs available online where you get monthly deliveries (usually with patterns and other goodies); they are the BirchBox or BarkBox of the yarn world. As of the writing of this book, a few top choices are Darn Good Yarn's monthly membership, Yarn Box, Yarn Crush and FicStitches. Another option is to join a Fiber CSA (community supported agriculture) where you pay an upfront fee to support a fiber farm and then you get yarn when the sheep are shorn. This is a great way to support small, independent, ethical farms that produce beautiful fiber for crochet.

Yarn for Thought: More Musings on Developing your Sense of Adventure

- Write a story about going on a crochet retreat. What would your ideal crochet vacation look like? Where would you go? What would you study? Who would you crochet with? What would you make? You might not be able to go on your fantasy craft retreat right now but you can certainly write it out on the page. Write it in the first person as if you're already there!
- What are your passions? What do you wish you knew how to do? How does crochet relate to this? How can you pursue a passion wholeheartedly through the lens of crochet?
- What colors do you always use in your work? What colors do you never use? What are the different associations that you have with these colors - what do they remind you of?
- Take a different route to an everyday destination (school, work, grocery store) and pay close attention to everything along the way. Little experiences of adventure can infuse your everyday life in this way.
- Make a list of all of the games that you liked to play when you were a child. Sometimes we can move our sense of adventure forward by working backwards. My childhood love of Nancy Drew stories might spark an interest in Betty Hechtman's crochet mysteries as an adult, the dances that I made up with my siblings could make me want to take a dance class. Whether it's directly related to crochet or not, it could take me new places.
- Make a bucket list. If you've never done this, it's time. If you've done it before, revisit it. A bucket list helps you remember all of the amazing things that you want to do in your life. Allow this to spark your creativity in new directions.

Facing Fears

The things that you are afraid of are holding you back. You may be aware of some of your fears while others are working against you without your awareness. In this chapter we're going to face our fears head on so that we can diminish their power and stop them from the ways in which they are holding us back. Some of these exercises might actually feel frightening (designing and submitting your first crochet pattern to a magazine, for example). However, most of them are a symbolic form of facing fears, allowing you to play and create your way to a stronger sense of yourself that can face fears with more curiosity and a problem-solving mindset.

At the end of this book, in my conclusion, I share with you the story of how I chose to Dive Fearlessly Into The Ocean with my sister and how it changed my life. You'll discover there that I don't have a fear of the ocean itself and running into that water wasn't particularly scary (although very cold!) Instead, it was a symbolic act, setting the intention for my new year that I would dive into things that were a little cold, a little ridiculous, a little scary. By making the choice to engage in that symbolic act, I made the choice to face fears slowly, one at a time, sometimes without even realizing that was exactly what I was doing, and it allowed my world to grow and expand.

But let me give you a more tangible example of how I chose to face a fear. It was the beginning of 2013, just after I had dived into that ocean, and I was trying to start dating again. A couple of years before I'd ended a relationship with someone I loved immensely, someone I thought could be my whole world forever except that in the end we each had mental health issues (and childhood issues and relationship issues and other issues) that directly conflicted with one another and we made each other worse by staying together until we finally realized that to let each other be individually better we had to let go. In the years that followed, I got individually better, and we were able to remain friends, but my heart had been broken by the experience and I was terrified of starting a new relationship.

The thing about that kind of fear is that it's not just one fear. It's a whole slew of fears tied up in one. It is fears from a time before I can even remember being scared tied up with years and years of different experiences that reinforced those fears. It was fear of:

- Being hurt again

- Not being lovable
- Losing myself
- Falling back into dependence and then into depression
- Vulnerability
- Having my space and time encroached upon
- Allowing my whole world to change
- Not knowing what I wanted
- Knowing what I wanted and not being able to get it!

It was a fear of repeating the past and a fear of not knowing what the future would bring. But I love love. I always have. I remember the crushes I had on boys starting in kindergarten (with Jesse, then in first grade it was David who in a funny twist of fate I would meet again ten years later and who would be my boyfriend throughout high school). I have gone through a million changes about my ideas of love but I love love and I want to be in a relationship (and I can finally admit that!) and the desire to have a partner in life became stronger than the fear of what that could mean so I decided to start dating again.

And I met my current beaux. But it took some faltering tries. We met online in late 2012 on the site How About We, where you don't share a ton about yourself but instead list suggestions of things that you want to do on a date and then meet up to go do them, because at the very least you get to have an experience you want to have even if the date doesn't work out. So I met this boy online and he suggested that we go on a photography date to the Conservatory of Flowers and I thought that was genius and we made a plan and exchanged numbers. And then I freaked out. My anxiety got the best of me and I sent a text message postponing the date. A few weeks later, I reached out again and we planned a date to meet at the San Francisco Museum of Modern Art. And yes, I freaked out and flaked again. Ultimately, after diving into the ocean, I took the risk and sent him a long email telling him the truth about not having dated in a long time and being really anxious but really wanting to meet him and suggested a video chat first. I'm not really sure why I suggested that since I'm not a particular fan of phone calls, even video calls, but I did and we "met" on the computer and we ended up talking for two hours and I liked him and the next day we had a real date.

But not before I had gotten scared again. After that phone call I called my mentor friend who had been wonderfully supportive through this entire journey of my romantic nonsense and I told her the story and explained that we were going to meet the next day but expressed all of these reasons (fear) about why we probably should not meet, how I wasn't ready and it wasn't the right time and I needed my own experiences first and on and on and on. And this friend, bless her heart, decided to be direct with me. She is a great listener and she usually trusts me to find my own way through things but finally she just called me on my BS and said, "it sounds like you want to learn to swim without getting in the water".

Bang. Well isn't that the truth. In fact, that's always been my story. I want to know how to do something well before I've ever tried doing it at all. This reminds me of when I was in fifth grade and took private flute lessons. I'd taken some lessons in school and liked the flute and thought I was good at it because I was better than some of the other kids in my elementary school orchestra. My mom, who was always awesome at encouraging our interests, signed me up for private lessons across town where we'd drive each week and I'd arrive with my flute in hand to practice with this elderly lady who also taught piano. And every week, I'd cry. I'd bawl. I'd sob. Because she wanted me to learn more in flute than I already knew and each time I felt like I wasn't good enough. (There's more to this story, really. Looking back from today's vantage point I can see that this was the very early stages of a battle with depression and anxiety that would last the rest of my life, although I had no way of knowing that then.) I didn't really understand why I was crying. I'd get there and I would usually not have practiced during the week, then I'd try to play whatever song we were supposed to be working on and I'd do fine, but not well, and she'd correct me and I'd freak out and sob. I wanted to be the most amazing flute player in the world, someone whose music instantly brought the audience to tears (or at least to polite accolades) but I didn't want to have to learn how to play the flute.

I wanted to learn to swim without getting in the water. Incidentally, I actually did take swimming lessons when I was a kid. I think it was the summer before first grade and my then-best-friend Colette was taking lessons at the local pool near my house and I wanted to take them with her, so we signed up together. The first lesson was easy, if I recall correctly, because Colette didn't know how to swim at all and I'd been swimming since the age of two when I'd jumped fearlessly into a pool at my dad's athletic club without my floaties on my arms, so I was able to take a lesson with her doing something I already knew how to do, and it felt great. But then they bumped me up to the next level of swim lessons, because apparently they think they're supposed to teach you something new when you go to learn something new, and in that class I was supposed to learn how to dive. I didn't know how to dive. I was terrified of diving. I probably cried a lot, although I don't recall. I quit swimming lessons. I still can't dive. And occasionally, when I see someone diving, I think that I would love to be able to do that - to throw myself with both strength and grace off of the side of the diving board and spin through the air before slicing into the water headfirst. But that is definitely something I want to know how to do before I try to do it.

I want to learn to swim without getting wet. I'm afraid of not doing well. I'm afraid of failing. I'm afraid of getting hurt. I'm afraid of not liking what I thought I'd like. I'm afraid of being wrong or bad or not good enough or just not enough. These fears hide inside of us, disguise themselves, turn themselves into all kinds of different excuses until we fail to even realize that we are acting from fear. Through creativity, we can pull out those fears, in manageable ways, understand them a little better, address them through small actions, and in so doing we can heal ourselves and begin to take bigger risks.

So what are you afraid of? You can do any of the exercises in this book to make small changes in your life but it might help if you first take a little bit of time to journal or meditate upon what things you are afraid of. Usually, the first things that come to mind are true but obvious and you have to dig a little bit deeper to assess the underlying fears. Ask yourself, "what's below that?" So if in the experience of beginning to date again I'd asked myself, "what am I afraid of?" then my first answer would likely have been "getting hurt again" but if I then asked myself, "what's below that?" I would come to see that I was afraid of loving someone who might leave me and below that what I was really afraid of was that I might not be lovable. Dig deep, but dig slowly, and remember to return to the chapter on self-care if you need to.

COMMON FEARS

- Fear of change
- Fear of losing control
- Fear of not being perfect
- Fear of disappointing yourself or others
- Fear of being laughed at, embarrassed, disliked, not loved
- Fear that you don't deserve better
- Fear that you are a fraud, that you don't have a voice of your own
- Fear of not being supported, fear of being alone
- Fear of not being good enough
- Fear of loss

- Fear of scarcity
- Fear of abundance
- Fear of intimacy/ vulnerability
- Fear of failure
- Fear of success; fear of getting what you want and finding it doesn't make you happy after all

Facing Fears Exercise #1: Fear of Change

The exercise: Felt an item that you have crocheted.

The purpose: You will symbolically face the fear of change by intentionally transforming a work that you have created.

In depth: If you've never felted anything you've crocheted before then the process itself might be a little frightening and that will allow you to face that fear. The fear that arises in that instance could be fear of failure; will you accidentally destroy what you've created?! More than that, the process of taking an item you've made and intentionally (and irreversibly!) turning it into something else without necessarily knowing if you'll like the outcome allows you to take a small risk in your life and symbolically face the fear of change.

Exercise steps:

1. **Choose a yarn that is good for felting**. Animal-based fibers including wool and alpaca are good choices. Cotton and other plant-based fibers don't felt well, and you certainly can't felt any acrylic fibers that are designed to be machine washable.
2. **Crochet a simple project** using a hook size larger than called for in the pattern. That's because loose stitches tend to felt best. A good starting project is a basic crochet scarf, worked using a worsted weight yarn and a size J or K hook.
3. **Felt your piece**. There are several different methods of felting, including felting by hand and felting with a washing machine. I like the "by hand" option because then you are really actively involved in the transformation of the piece. In her article titled All About Felted Crochet, published in Interweave Crochet Fall 2007, Amy Swensen writes, "You can felt fabric in the sink using hot water and rubber gloves to protect your hands. It's as simple as placing the object in the sink with the hottest water

and a little soap and agitating it by stirring, rubbing or whipping the piece against the side of the sink. After enough agitating, the yarn will mat and grip together, shrinking the overall size of the piece, sometimes quite dramatically." That's felting.
4. **Block your project**. Take your wet felted item, wring out the water as best as possible, and then stretch it out to the desired shape and size of your project. Allow it to dry.

Tips:

- Read more about felting to learn about all of the different ways that you can felt.
- Different stitches will felt differently. Make the same item using single crochet and treble crochet and see a major difference when felted!
- You don't have to create full items like scarves to play with felting; you can create just squares and swatches and have a lot of fun!
- Felting changes the size, texture and even somewhat the color of your project. Explore all of these changes through repeating this exercise. Every project will shrink when felted but play around with different fiber and hook sizes and felting times to alter the shrinkage. Explore how you can make different colors blend into each other through felting. Regina Jestrow is a visual artist who makes amazing felted crochet bags; check out her work online for inspiration!

Taking it further: Another way that you can transform work is through dyeing it. You can dye yarn itself or you can dye a finished item. A great option is to dye the yarn, crochet it into something that you like and then felt that item. You'll face the fear of change twice. First, you are changing the yarn, trying to make it something else and wondering if you'll like the results. Then when you have yarn you like, you'll work with it and get more attached to it since it's running through your hands. And finally, you'll face the fear of change again when you take what you've created and felt it, not knowing if it's going to ruin what you already took time and effort to create. (Conversely you could felt the item first and then dye the felted item.)

Facing Fears Exercise #2: Building Blocks of Growth

The exercise: Crochet rows that grow taller and taller with each turn.

The purpose: Symbolically face a fear of growth and change by growing your work with your own hands.

In depth: Oftentimes we want to grow and embrace transformation but we are so afraid of change that we block ourselves from that growth. In this exercise, we will crochet long rows of increasingly taller stitches to manifest growth through our crochet work.

Exercise steps:

1. **Crochet a chain** of 200 stitches.
2. Turn, chain one and **single crochet** in each stitch.
3. Turn, chain two and **half double crochet** in each stitch.
4. Turn, chain three and **double crochet** in each stitch.
5. Turn, chain four and **treble crochet** in each stitch.
6. Turn, chain five and **double treble crochet** in each stitch.
7. Turn, chain six and **triple treble crochet** in each stitch.
8. **Continue growing** the height of your stitches!

Tips:

- Each taller stitch is crocheted by adding one extra "yarn over" to the number used in the previous row. You can find a photo tutorial for "taller stitches" on Crochet Concupiscence; tutorials are at http://www.crochetconcupiscence.com/how-to-crochet-crochet-tutorials-roundup/.
- Try to keep growing the height of your stitches for as long as possible. You'll notice that the tallest stitches are much harder to make than the short stitches, and yet you've established a pattern of slowly growing the work so that it is not as difficult as if you'd just started out by trying to crochet triple treble height stitches into the foundation chain. This represents how big growth is difficult but can be done when you take baby steps!
- Some people aren't comfortable working with long foundation chains like this. You can start with a shorter chain if you'd like. Alternatively, you can start with a foundation single crochet chain.

Taking it further: There are several variations on this exercise that you can implement to watch growth happening in your hands:

- Increase the number of stitches in each row. Note that if you do two stitches into every one below, you'll be growing your work exponentially and will create hyperbolic crochet pieces. Instead, you might wish to simply increase in the first and last stitches of every row to show gradual growth.
- Crochet the same stitch in each row but increase your hook size each time. Crochet a long row of single crochet stitches with an E hook, turn and use an F hook, turn and use a G hook, etc.
- Crochet a set of motifs that get bigger each time. Granny squares are great for this. Crochet a three round granny. Then crochet a four round granny. Then make a new one with five rounds. You'll have a set of grannies that you can lay out (or string into bunting) to represent gradual growth and change!

Facing Fears Exercise #3: Fear of Trying New Things

The exercise: Practice skill-building in crochet by learning new techniques.

The purpose: Confront a fear of failing at new things by slowly adding new techniques to your crochet skill set.

In depth: The greatest thing about crochet is that once you learn the basics, you can make just about any item you could ever want. And yet, there are so many techniques in crochet that you could continue learning new things all of the time. The idea here is to build upon your existing skill base in crochet by taking the chance on learning something new. You can always fall back on your old favorite techniques as a safety net for comfort. (Remember that list of safe projects you created in a previous chapter?!)

Exercise steps:

1. **Make a list of crochet techniques** that you already know, which you can keep as a reminder of how great you are at the craft in case you have missteps as you learn new things.
2. **Make a list of at least twenty things** in crochet that you don't know how to do yet. It could be as simple as learning new joining techniques or as complex as discovering an entire new niche of crochet. (Some of the lists you've made in previous chapters can be a good starting point for Steps One and Two here. This exercise is an expansion on letting go by "being a

beginner"; this time you are directly facing all of the fears that arise when trying something new.)
3. **Choose the item** off of the list that sounds the least intimidating and learn it. That might mean that you take a class or simply that you sit down for an hour and teach yourself the technique.
4. **Practice that technique** every day for a week, or a month, or however long it takes until you feel absolutely comfortable that you've essentially mastered this new skill. Notice your fears, notice why you want to quit, notice what's difficult. Being a beginner brings up fears; you have the strength and ability now to deal with those. Use your affirmations again if they help.
5. **Go back to the list** you made in Step One and add this new skill to your list of techniques that you know.
6. **Go back to the list** you made in Step Two, cross off the item you've already learned, add a new item to the bottom of the list (so that it's always growing).
7. **Repeat steps** three - seven again and again!

Tips:

- Regularly seek out new information about crochet and see what inspires you. Add those things to your list. For example, I often look at the portfolios of crochet artists and consider what techniques they are using that I don't already know how to do. Even if it seems completely out of reach, I put it on my list. Who knows - I may be ready to learn it someday.
- What are the boundaries of your comfort zone in crochet? Step just to the line of those boundaries, challenging yourself without making the process unbearable.
- Be willing to work through your frustrations. You have to be a beginner sometimes and it can be difficult to learn a new technique. You may decide you don't like the technique and give up. It's okay if you don't like it in the end but persist through that and learn to do it at least moderately well. Even if you never use the skill, the confidence you build up by learning it will serve you well in both your crafting and your life.
- Don't overlook the simple things. Many of us have developed shortcuts and cheats for basic steps in crochet and could benefit by going back and learning how to do those steps differently. A book I

highly recommend for examining this is Dora Ohrenstein's *The Crocheter's Skill-Building Workshop: Essential Techniques for Becoming a More Versatile, Adventurous Crocheter.*

Taking it further: Take a bigger risk by trying a project that you know is a little bit too hard for you in terms of your skill set. The basic exercise here asks you to choose the technique that seems least challenging but in this variation you should choose one that seems really intimidating. See how far you can get with it. See what emotions it brings up for you. Work on it. If you get overwhelmed, go back to one of the easier-to-learn techniques or even back to the self-care chapter and then return to this variation on the exercise later.

Facing Fears Exercise #4: Fear of Not Being Perfect

The exercise: Make a crochet item that has some kind of flaw and display it to the world.

The purpose: Face the fear that others will know you aren't perfect by showing them that indeed you are not!

In depth: Nobody is perfect. No crafter is perfect. No one person crochets everything exactly right all of the time. That's okay. Who cares? You can show the entire world that you are not perfect and discover that nothing terrible is going to happen when this is revealed.

Exercise steps:

1. **Crochet an item** that has some kind of mistake in it. (See the exercise earlier in this book on making an intentional mistake; this is an expansion of that.)
2. **Share the crochet** item with others. You can display it in your home, take it to your craft group or share it on social media.
3. **See if anyone notices it.** If they don't, what goes through your head? Do you worry that they're judging you behind your back? If they do, how do you react? Tell them what the project is all about! Ask them to celebrate with you that it's okay not to be perfect.

Tips:

- DO NOT apologize for mistakes in your work. (The exception here would be if you are hired to craft something for someone and they are legitimately unhappy with your work. That's a different thing. But in your own crafting that you do for you, especially in the exercises for this book, do not apologize!)
- And don't make excuses. Just say, "I'm not perfect, and I know there was a mistake in this work but here are the things that I love about this piece." Encourage others to accept your imperfections. Not only is this good for you but it sets a great example for everyone else that it's okay to make mistakes.
- If this work is challenging for you, make your mistake intentionally in a technique that you know how to do correctly. So, let's say that you're great at making crochet granny squares. Crochet yourself a granny square that's got only one cluster in a corner instead of two. It's a glaring mistake but it's one that you know in your heart of hearts you could always do perfectly if you wanted to. It teaches you that it's okay to make mistakes without sacrificing any huge blows to your self-esteem.
- Deal with bullies head-on. I've definitely had people point out my mistakes when I've shared things online, and sometimes they have done it in really cruel ways. Work on standing your ground. If someone points out a mistake in a well-intentioned way, respond accordingly, letting them know that you appreciate that they were paying enough attention to your work to notice the error and perhaps even sharing your (new) views on how it's okay to make mistakes in your work. If you've got someone being mean to you, you can choose to ignore them (it's not always healthy to get involved in online arguments) or you can choose to confront them; either way, definitely make sure that you deal with your own emotions around the situation in a supportive environment so that you can maintain your sense of self through the situation.

Taking it further: You can take this further by actually drawing attention to the imperfection in your work. Make the mistake in a completely different color than the rest of the work. Or say flat out in your announcement to the world, "see this big glaring mistake?!" Another way of taking this further is to return to this exercise every time that you notice an accidental mistake in your work. Before correcting it, ask yourself if you can live with it, going through the fears and self-judgments that arise. Just because we've faced these fears once doesn't mean that they don't come back!

Facing Fears Exercise #5: Fear of the Unknown

The exercise: Crochet an item using a wacky color scheme with no plan for how it will turn out.

The purpose: Challenge yourself to just create, emphasizing process over product.

In depth: This is an extension of some of the work that we did in the "letting go" chapter, including the mystery CAL. Some people need to know what they are making in their work and it can be related to a fear of the unknown. Embrace the unknown. Just make something. What's the worst that's going to happen?

Exercise steps:

1. **Choose a crochet project** that is based on colorful motifs. A blanket made of small granny squares or hexagons is a good choice. For this project, do not use a join-as-you-go technique.
2. **Select yarn colors** that you fully believe don't really go well together. A lot of them. Use colors you would never use. Use colors that are opposites of each other according to color theory.
3. **Crochet the project**. If you are using a crochet pattern, that's fine for the shape of the motifs but ignore all color suggestions. Change colors willy nilly! Use multiple colors within each motif.
4. When you have all of the motifs, **mix them together** into a big bag. Now dump the bag out on the floor. The order they fall in is how you'll stitch them together. (You'll have to separate out the ones that are on top of each other and create the correct shape for your blanket, but do this loosely, letting the random order generate the design.)
5. **Stitch them all together** into your finished crochet blanket. You didn't know how those colors would go together in each motif or how they'd lay out next to each other but you did it!

Tips:

- This project is especially good for the people who like to use color generating tools or graph out the layout of their colors before stitching together a project.
- If you don't like the "dumping out" process in step four, you can keep all of the motifs in an opaque bag and pull them out randomly one-by-one, adding each motif according to how it comes out of the bag.
- You might find yourself intentionally choosing the yarn throughout the project to create a color-pleasing palette. That's fine but if you want more "unknown" then stick each color of yarn in a matching opaque bag or container, mix them up randomly and work from left to right using whatever yarn is "next".

Taking it further: Crochet the same blanket twice, once using the original crochet instructions and colors in the pattern and once using the exercise steps outlined above. Compare the two blankets to one another and see if one is really "better" than the other. Examine your own process in each of these blankets; did you like it better when someone else dictated the outcome and you knew what the end result would be or did you like the mystery process?

Facing Fears Exercise #6: Make a Magic Ball of Yarn

The exercise: Use your yarn scraps to create your own magic ball of yarn and use it to crochet something.

The purpose: This is similar to the previous exercise in that you are going to be crafting something with no idea of the color layout.

In depth: As with before, you'll be confronting your fear of the unknown by intentionally creating a yarn ball that will rapidly change color as you work so that there's no way to predict the outcome of the color pattern.

Exercise steps:

1. **Collect all of your yarn scraps.** You don't want tiny yarn ends here but rather slightly longer "leftovers" from projects. Make sure that you have a lot of them and that they've come from a

variety of different projects. You want a good selection of different colors, fibers and weights.
2. **Place all of the yarn scraps** in a brown paper bag (or other opaque bag) and give them a good shake to mix them up thoroughly.
3. Without looking into the bag, **pull out two little balls of yarn**. Stitch them together to begin making your magic ball. (There are several ways of joining yarn together. I don't mind working over knots so I just knot mine but you can also do a Russian Join (also known as an invisible join) to secure one yarn to the next without knots.)
4. **Randomly pull out the next ball** of yarn and add it as the next color in your random yarn ball. Repeat until you've created a magic yarn ball using all of the colors in your leftovers bag.
5. **Crochet an item** for yourself using your entire magic yarn ball. Watch the work unfold in front of you. Embrace the unknown as it develops into something tangible.

Tips:

- Sometimes when you pull out that next bit of yarn to add to your growing magic ball, you'll have an immediate reaction about the way the two adjoining yarns are going to clash. Ignore it. Remember, you do not know how this is going to turn out in the end!
- Choose a crochet project where gauge isn't super important. Since you're working with different fibers and weights of yarn, it's hard to get exact gauge with this project. Blankets, scarves, and shawls are good choices because their exact finished size doesn't generally matter so much; an approximate size will do.
- Don't choose a motif-based design for your crochet item. These can definitely look great when worked with a magic ball of yarn but working on a continuous project, such as a top-down shawl or a scrappy blanket, will allow you to really experience the full impact of "crocheting the unknown".

Taking it further: Want to take this exercise to the next level? Take the item that you've made and try to felt it. There is truly no way of knowing how this is going to turn out, especially since some of your fibers will felt and others that are machine-washable won't felt at all. Felt it by hand so you can watch the changes take place. Remember that it's okay if you mess up the entire thing. You didn't know what would happen, now you do and you can learn from it and make changes the next time. No big deal!

Facing Fears Exercise #7: Jealousy & Fear of Not Being Good Enough

<u>The exercise</u>: Crochet a gift for someone who has crafty skills that you are jealous of.

<u>The purpose</u>: Dealing directly with jealousy allows us to confront our own fears of not being good enough.

<u>In depth</u>: Being jealous of someone else in our craft is common and is usually related to the fear of not being good enough. We think that someone else is doing a great job and by comparison we think that we aren't doing a great job and we don't like the way that makes us feel so it gets transmuted into jealousy. Sometimes it gets transmuted into pettiness and meanness. Working through the jealousy can help us reduce our fear of not being "good enough".

<u>Exercise steps</u>:

1. **Identify someone** in the crafting world that sparks your jealousy. It may be someone you know in your personal life or someone that you see online.
2. **Journal** through all of the reasons that you feel jealous about this person. This is an important step because you need to recognize the roots of your feelings here. In particular, ask yourself how you feel about being "good enough" in comparison. It's okay to be petty here. Let your real feeling flow.
3. **Honor this person's work and talents**. Collect images of their crafty work (or their actual handmade items) and celebrate them in your own space. Use one of their images as your computer desktop background. This may spark more jealousy that you must work through. That's okay. That's the point.
4. **Pay homage to their work** by crocheting a gift for the person that celebrates what they do. If it is a crochet designer, use one of their patterns. If it is a crochet artist, use one of their favorite techniques. If it's someone else, see what their work inspires you to create.

5. **Complete the crochet item**, paying particular attention to the thoughts in your head about how it's not going to be good enough to give to the person. What are you embarrassed about or afraid of?
6. **Give the person the gift**. If this is someone that you don't know personally, you may not actually send them the gift but could send an email sharing a photo of what you have created. Or you might just do a post online letting the world know that you have made this work. Share how this person has inspired you. Share what you love about what they do. Take the risk to say, "I love what you do and look, I can do it, too!"

Tips:

- This exercise is intended to help you overcome the fear of not being good enough (or as good as others). However, you may find it helps you in dealing with other fears as well. Some people have a scarcity mindset, fearing that if someone else gets the talent then there's not enough for them. Others have a fear of rejection. This exercise can help you work through both of those things as well.
- You may find it too difficult to actually gift the item to the intended recipient or even to write them an email. Try to do it because overcoming this fear will really get you to a better place in terms of recognizing your own value is equal to the value of everyone else. That said, if you can't do it at this time, try writing an unsent letter to the person addressing all of your jealousy and celebrating their work. Keep this letter in a special place with the finished item, to be looked at later on in your creative process.

Taking it further: Make a weekly habit out of finding crochet work that inspires you and sending short messages to the people that created that work. You can combat all jealousy by celebrating the work of others. If you're on social media, choose someone new there each week to send a message to or repost their work in celebration of who they are. If you're not active on social media, write letters or emails to strangers and community members alike celebrating what they do. Can't find someone in crochet to celebrate on any given week? Branch out to another craft that inspires you. When you send this loving energy out into the world, it will come back to you, and you will find more appreciation and value for your own crafting, not only from others but also within yourself.

Facing Fears Exercise #8: Fear of Rejection

<u>The exercise</u>: Design a crochet pattern and submit it for publication.

<u>The purpose</u>: Put yourself out there in a way that has a high chance of rejection.

<u>In depth</u>: We have all heard stories about the writers who papered their walls with rejection letters before finally getting a great work accepted for publication. Sometimes you just have to take the chance that you're going to be rejected again and again before someone wants to publish your work. Facing that rejection is a humbling but growth-inspiring part of the creative process. Even if your work gets rejected, you have developed new skills and strengths by designing and putting yourself out there in this new way.

<u>Exercise steps</u>:

1. **Design a crochet pattern**. If you've never done this before, start really simple, with a crochet scarf or crochet washcloth pattern. If you've already done some crochet design, work on taking your skills to the next level with a different technique.
2. **Work on the design** until you are proud of it and want to share it with the world. A design may work up quickly or it make take you months; either is okay as long as you're consistently working on it and making it something you love.
3. **Hire a few pattern testers** to see how the design works for them. Not all crochet designers do this but it is a great step towards professionalism and a good practice for this exercise. Ask your testers for honest and thorough feedback and incorporate what they say into the final tweaks for the design.
4. **Submit the crochet pattern** for publication in crochet magazines. You'll need to find the magazines that you like and request their submission guidelines. They often follow specific themes so you may need to tweak your design to fit the theme or wait until there's an appropriate theme for your submission.
5. **Deal with the response** that comes. Published? Awesome? Publishable but needs major edits? Make them! Not publishable at this time in this way? That's okay. Let's see where you can publish it - for sale on Etsy? on a blog? Take the rejection in

stride and see what you can do to make the piece work for someone somewhere.

Tips:

- Already a crochet designer or absolutely not interested at all in crochet design? Submit a finished crochet piece to an art competition instead. Or write an article about crochet and submit that instead.
- Does submitting work to a magazine seem completely out of your reach? You can start smaller. Submit your crochet design to a blog instead or publish it online (for free or for charge) and see what kind of response you get.
- Notice what comes up for you when your pattern testers give you feedback. They are just doing their jobs but sometimes we take it personally; working through this helps eradicate the related fear.
- Don't give up on submitting your work. Keep playing with designs. Keep exploring what people want to publish. There is no reason that you have to become a well-established professional crochet designer if this isn't a goal for you, but it can really help you face your fear of rejection to work on designs until you get published somewhere.

Taking it further: If you really want to embrace a long-term project that will challenge you and force you to face a fear of rejection, work on a crochet book proposal! Design your own crochet book - of techniques or patterns or whatever you most want to make. Spend time working on the pages and the patterns and the text. When you've got a good solid book in the works, it is time to seek out small craft publishers and pitch your work. You'll find lots of material online about how to make book submissions; the important thing here is that you're putting yourself out there! You can always self-publish your book, too, of course, which will also help you face fear of rejection in case you invest in putting it out to market and don't see sales.

Facing Fears Exercise #9: Addressing Excuses

The exercise: Deal head-on with the most common excuses you make for not crocheting.

<u>The purpose</u>: Obliterate your own excuses that block you from creative productivity.

<u>In depth</u>: We often find a million reasons, some of them even good reasons, not to take time for our craft. Those excuses are almost always related to fear even though we call them by another name. By forcing ourselves to see that the excuse is a lie, we challenge ourselves to face the real fear underneath and get past it.

<u>Exercise steps</u>:

1. **Make a list** of the usual reasons that you don't crochet even when you want to. (See a list of the most common reasons below.)
2. **Choose the excuse** off of the list that you use most frequently. Write it at the top of a blank page.
3. **Brainstorm** a list of ways to address the problem. For example, if your excuse is that you don't have enough money to crochet, brainstorm all of the ways that you can get yarn for free or cheap.
4. **Post this list** where you can see it everyday - either in your craft space or inside of your crochet journal.
5. **Notice** every single time that you say that excuse to yourself. Immediately go to your list and choose an action that counteracts the excuse. If your excuse is not having enough money, an action on your list might be to crochet with plastic bag yarn. As soon as you tell yourself that you can't crochet because you can't afford yarn right now, get out all of those plastic bags you're saving for no reason and make some plastic bag yarn and crochet with it.

COMMON EXCUSES FOR NOT CRAFTING

- I don't have enough time.
- I don't have enough money.
- I'm too tired.
- I don't feel well.
- I don't have the skills for a particular project.
- Someone else needs me right now.
- I don't know what to make.

- I have to finish another type of project first.
- I "should" be doing something else.

Tips:

- Practice saying to yourself over and over, "So what? I'm going to crochet anyway". Use this every time you find yourself making excuses. "Oh, I'd like to crochet right now, but I'm really tired. ... So what, I'm going to crochet anyway." Even if you just do five minutes of crochet in the face of your excuse, you're helping yourself beat that excuse down one stitch at a time.
- Typically when you are actively conquering one excuse, you'll find that another subtly pops up. Pay attention to this happening and refuse to allow it. This shows you that your excuses aren't real, they are just fears trying to block your creative action.
- Combine this exercise with your work using affirmations. Turn your common excuses for not crocheting into affirmations that will help you crochet more.

Taking it further: Work through your entire list of excuses one by one until there are no excuses left. If others pop up in the process, add them to your list and work on them, too. Don't allow your inner artist to be squelched by the voices everywhere saying that "you can't". Actually, you can. It doesn't matter what else is going on, just crochet anyway.

Facing Fears Exercise #10: The Value of Craft

The exercise: Assign price tags to a set of your finished crochet items.

The purpose: This exercise helps you confront issues with finding value in your work and deals with fears around money.

In depth: Many people have fears about money, which can manifest as shame about spending money on your craft as well as guilt about asking for money for your handmade items. The nature of our society doesn't help with this issue. We are used to two competing things in this society - number one is having our worth determined by the number of dollars we make per hour and number two is being able to buy super cheap factory-made items. Handmade items don't fit with these contrasting issues; there's no way that most people would pay a high dollar amount for a handmade crochet item that might have taken the crafter 200 hours to create because in their minds they could go buy a comparable or even "better" item for much cheaper in the store. We aren't likely to immediately solve this huge social issue but we can work with the way it manifests financial fear and shame in our own lives.

Exercise steps:

1. **Collect** a set of the finished crochet items that you have in your home.
2. **Lay out the items** side by side and use Post-It Notes or labels to assign a price value to each one. What is each one worth? Do this by gut instinct. Don't overthink it.
3. **Turn each of the items over** on its opposite side so that you can't see the price tag you've placed on it.
4. **Calculate** the approximate cost of each item including the amount that you spent on yarn and the number of hours that went into the work. I use the San Francisco minimum wage for calculating my labor costs; as of 2015 that's $12.25 per hour so if I made a one-skein item that took one hour and used a skein that cost me $5 then the item's price would be $17.25.
5. **Sit with each item** individually and compare the value you gave the item and the price value you calculated. Are they similar or very disparate? What might this say about the way that you value your craft as it relates to money? It may not be realistic to price all items for sale at a dollar value comparable to the hours that you put into the piece but it can help you appreciate your own value as a crafter to go through this process.

Tips:

- When calculating the price in Step Four, feel free to be approximate rather than exact but when in doubt round up instead of down.
- Use what you learn about yourself from this exercise to add to your list of affirmations that you are hopefully still working with from the earliest chapters in this book!
- This exercise can definitely bring up lots of financial fears and stressors as well as issues with how you value your own work. If this is a particularly difficult area for you, you might want to work with a counselor specializing in money issues before proceeding

with this type of exercise. *If you have financial issues to work through, I recommend the book Prosperity Pie by SARK.*

<u>Taking it further</u>: Ask a loved one or friend to place monetary values on your work without seeing your numbers. Simply ask them to place a price tag on the item indicating what they would pay for it. This allows you to go deeper by confronting your fear of what your work is valued at by others around you. You might turn this into something of a party game to make it less stressful. Create a game similar to what you might see on the television show The Price Is Right by making a stack of tags that say that value of each item (as you see it) and asking your friend(s) to put the tags on the items they think most closely match those prices.

Yarn for Thought: More Musing on Fear

- What are you afraid of? What are you *really* afraid of? Write about this in your journal and then go back over your list and dig a little bit deeper to see what the fear is that lies underneath the surface fear. One great way to explore this is to listen to what your inner critic (or superego) is telling you and see how that relates to fear. For example, if your mind is constantly accusing you of being lazy, you'll probably find underneath that you aren't lazy at all but are actually afraid of something. Procrastination is almost always also a sign of fear.
- They say that the only constant is change. What is your relationship to change? Some people don't even want to change their hair color whereas others are so afraid of stagnating that they are constant transformation. Where do you like on that spectrum?
- Gretchen Rubin, author of books on happiness, says that it's okay to be uncomfortable, that happiness isn't comfort but instead "happiness is feeling good, bad, and right in an atmosphere of growth". What are some times that you have felt uncomfortable or even bad but were ultimately happy because the experience led to growth?
- Do you buy handmade items from other people? Why or why not? How do you personally determine whether or not they are worth spending your money on?
- Explore your negative core beliefs. These are things that we all have inside of ourselves, and that we believe, even though they aren't true. These things often relate to our underlying fears. Common negative core beliefs include, "I'm different from others", "nobody understands me", "I'm not smart enough", "life is not safe", "I can't do it", "I'm needy", and "I'm a failure". I promise you that none of these things are true but that you'll have to do a lot of strong inner work to convince yourself of that.
- Make a list of all of the things that make you unique. So often what people fear is not being the same as others and therefore not being liked. You are not like anyone else because you are uniquely you - celebrate that!

Create Abundance

One of the fears that we didn't discuss in depth in the last chapter but which plagues a lot of people is the fear of scarcity or the opposite fear of abundance. Fear of scarcity comes from this feeling that there is not enough; fear of abundance comes from the belief that if you have too much then you'll have problems associated with corruption and obsession with material goods over spiritual matters. In both cases, the individual is creatively restricted by these fears (and let me just say that most of us do have one or the other or perhaps even both!) By building abundance in our creative work, we are able to generate more of the things that we want, not only for ourselves but to give to the world around us. In this chapter, we are going to be working with creating abundance in a number of ways, particularly in dealing with feelings of limitation and transforming those feelings into feelings of abundance by maximizing our existing resources.

One of the most basic, and very common, ways that this manifests in people's everyday lives is in the "saving" of nice things "for the right occasion". In recent history we typically saw this with "the good china", the most beautiful dishes were only taken out to celebrate huge holidays at home and collected dust the rest of the year. Although this sometimes still happens, what is even more common now is to save our favorite clothing for some other day instead of just wearing it "for no reason". Think about it; do you have a favorite dress or even a favorite t-shirt or pair of jeans that makes you feel so great when you put it on that you never want to wear it just to go to the store but instead save it for some "big event". So often, those events don't come. Or if they do, you have ten different things to wear that you've been "saving". You can celebrate abundance in your everyday life by allowing yourself to use all of the things that are special, that make you feel great. There is certainly a time and place for really fabulous things - the wedding dress or the irreplaceable ancient heirloom - but for the most part our nice things can be used in regular life, adding abundance to the everyday and infusing life with more magic.

Something like this that I use is a set of table linens from my maternal grandmother. She received a beautiful white satin tablecloth set as a wedding present in the late 1940s and never used it. As far as we know, it wasn't used even once. I definitely never saw it in my childhood and my mother doesn't remember it ever being used in her childhood either. After my grandmother passed away, my mother asked if I wanted it. I don't usually take items that other people want to pass along to me, because I like a less-clutter kind of life and don't want to feel responsible for someone else's "special things", but I really don't have much to remember my grandmother by and I thought it would be a sweet thing to add to my life. So my mom sent the package, in its original old box.

The first time that I used it, I just used two of the beautiful napkins, for a barbecue slider dinner that a friend and I had at my home. He and I had recently had a small bump in our relationship - nothing major but something that needed a little talking through. We were relatively new friends who had met in graduate school and started hanging out together outside of school about six months later, really hitting it off although only spending time together occasionally. About fifteen months after we met, we had plans to get together but I was dealing with a small relapse in depression and I was very flaky at the time. I kind of blew him off and he kind of seemed irritated and we were both trying to deal with it like mature adults who nonetheless had our feelings hurt. It was not a big deal and a conversation later we were fine but I wanted to have him over for dinner to let him know that our budding friendship really was important to me. So he came over and I made barbecue chicken sliders and salad and a few other small things and we drank good wine in front of my fireplace and caught up. And I used my grandmother's wedding linen napkins, which at some point during the dinner I mentioned. My friend looked at me, horrified that he had wiped his barbecue-slathered mouth all over these precious napkins that had never been used before. I laughed, because I think it is much more important to infuse those napkins with the wonderful energy of a memory-building, friendship-fortifying night than to leave them sitting in my closet awaiting some special occasion. My grandmother lived until she was almost ninety and never found that special occasion; I choose to make my everyday life a special occasion!

Now don't get me wrong. It's not like I dress in ball gowns every day, careful not to snag my diamonds on my yarn or tap them too hard against the fancy champagne glasses I never fail to drink out of. I'm not suggesting living a ridiculous life or even one that necessarily values the most expensive things that we own. I actually don't even own ball gowns or diamonds or expensive champagne glasses. But I do make it a point to drink out of my favorite coffee mugs, even though I know I might drop and break them since I use them every day. And I do use my handmade crochet dishcloths in the kitchen, the ones that I made with some terrific cotton yarns, even though I know that using them wears them out. I don't want to live a life where I'm waiting for the "someday" occasion.

And yet I definitely fall prey to the "someday" syndrome, thinking I'm saving certain things for some other time. It happens with clothes, like I described above, where I don't wear a particular thing (usually because I don't want to have to wash it to wear it again to the "special" place) and I have to remind myself that I like to wear the clothes that make me feel good. It also happens with yarn. I love to buy expensive hand-dyed hand-spun yarns, especially at fiber festivals where I can sometimes meet the animals that gave their wool to me. And then I don't want to use those yarns because usually I'm just making some random item that is a lot more about process than product and it seems a "waste" to use that yarn on a random granny square that doesn't even have an intended purpose yet. And that's okay in its way. I can keep a few of those skeins on my work table and handle them and enjoy them just the way that they are, but I have to be careful not to let my stash of "too good" yarn overtake my space while only using the yarn that doesn't feel "as good".

Life is abundant. Let's look at the definition of abundance, which my dictionary tells me first is "a very large quantity of something" but then goes on to a definition I like better which is: "the state or condition of having a copious quantity of something; plentifulness". It's not about having excess; it's about having plenty, it's about having a lot of what we want and knowing that there's more around the corner. My dictionary's example is "vines and figs grew in abundance"; I love that image. Nobody *needs* tons of vines and figs but it is beautiful that they grow in abundance! And when we look for it in the right places and treat ourselves to it in the right ways, we have beautiful abundance as well.

Abundance Exercise #1: Fear of Scarcity

The exercise: Use your nicest skein of yarn to crochet something frivolous.

The purpose: Use something that you're afraid to let go of in order to open the door for more to come in.

In depth: Many people are afraid that there isn't "enough" … enough money, enough yarn, enough love, enough support. They operate from a fear of scarcity, which can severely limit your experiences of life. It can be helpful to build up your faith and trust that there will indeed be enough, that your family will always get fed and the universe will provide you with creative tools and that there is always more yarn where that came from!

Exercise steps:

1. **Take out your most precious skein of yarn.** You know the one, the one that you felt a little bit guilty paying so much money for and have had in your stash for three years now because you are waiting for the exact right item to make with this super special skein of yarn.
2. **Crochet something less-than-special** with that skein of yarn. Make a dishcloth or a really basic scarf.
3. **Go to the yarn store** and buy a new special skein of yarn. Take your time to find one that really calls out to you. This is reinforcement for your brain that there is always more out there.

Tips:

- Keep your best skeins of yarn out where you can see them and enjoy them and get inspired to use them!
- Ask yourself how "Step Two" above made you feel. Many people react strongly to this part.
- If you can't go buy a new skein right now (Step Three above), that's okay. Go through your stash of yarn and see which skein calls out to you as the most precious skein now that the favorite one has been all used up. You will likely discover that your view has shifted and a skein you previously thought was "okay" is now "the best". Challenge your perspective.

Taking it further: Donate your crocheted item to a thrift store. You have no way of knowing if it will be treated well and that beautiful skein might very well be "wasted". It's okay. Really. Confront your feelings about this in your crochet journal.

Abundance Exercise #2: Abundance of Projects

The exercise: Crochet every project in one crochet book.

The purpose: Remind your mind that there is an abundance of inspiration available in the world.

In depth: A lot of times people feel like their inspiration is going to run out, like they are eventually going to stop being creative. I know that this happened to me at one point while I was writing *Crochet Saved My Life*. Most of it had flowed right out of me but I hit this block, common in the middle of big writing projects, and I suddenly had this fear that I had run out of words - that I had been allotted a certain number of words in this lifetime and that I'd used them all up, wasted them on emails and blog posts and would never write another word ever again, might never even be able to speak again. Of course, that was ridiculous and the first new words came and then more words came but for a time I felt a scarcity of words and needed to be reminded that there is an abundance of them, an abundance of creative inspiration. By working through every single project in one crochet book, you remind yourself that there is more crochet inspiration out there than you could ever possibly work through and there will always be an abundance of projects to choose from.

Exercise steps:

1. **Select one crochet book** that inspires you.
2. **Flip through the book** and see which projects inspire you most. Notice if there are projects that don't inspire you.
3. **Work through the book** from beginning to end, crocheting every single project that comes up. As you do this, work in your crochet journal - take notes on anything that inspires you and pay attention to your feelings about working through projects that you don't like as much.
4. **Collect all of the finished items** in one place and photograph them together. Celebrate the abundance of items that you can make using just the crochet patterns in one book. Imagine how many more crochet patterns are out there in the world!

Tips:

- Choose a crochet book that really excites you and that has at least 20 projects in it.
- Get your crochet book from the library. This shows you even more that there's an abundance of creative inspiration out there and you don't have to have money to access it.
- Keep your photograph of the finished items where you can easily see it for inspiration.
- I once kept a journal of 30 days of working through one crochet book. See it on Crochet Concupiscence here:

http://www.crochetconcupiscence.com/2012/08/diary-of-a-month-spent-crocheting-sharon-silverman-scarves/

Taking it further: Crochet every single pattern designed by one particular crochet designer. You can get all of that designer's books or you can access their patterns online through a site like Ravelry. Note that this will also help you work through any jealousy you have related to the skills of another crochet designer (something we looked at in a previous chapter and can always come back to!) As you work through each pattern, see how it inspires you; perhaps you'll want to change it up and add your own twists on the design! This also builds on the adventurous explorations we did in a previous chapter.

Abundance Exercise #3: Have the Right Tools

The exercise: Get rid of craft tools that you don't need and replace them with ones that you do.

The purpose: Refuse to hang on to broken or inferior items out of a fear that "something is better than nothing".

In depth: It is tempting to keep items that are just a little bit broken or not of the greatest quality or are past their prime, using the excuse that we can still use the items in some way at some time. Crafters are notorious for this, keeping the tiniest fragments of yarn and fabric to use someday. And there is nothing wrong with that kind of creative thriftiness. In fact, in a throwaway world, it's a great thing to do for the environment and the pocketbook. That said, it's important to challenge that in yourself from time to time. You absolutely deserve to have the best quality stuff possible, to not have to work from broken leftovers, and to allow yourself to feel that there is an abundance of rich creative materials out there to work from.

Exercise steps:

1. **Gather all of your crochet tools** including crochet hooks, buttons, sewing needles, storage containers, etc. If you have many, many of them, do one category of things first (such as just hooks) then move on to the next category.
2. Take any items that are **broken** and put them in the trash or recycling bin.

3. Take out any **doubles** and donate them. It is unlikely that you need ten different aluminum crochet hooks that are all size N; donate nine of them.
4. **Sort the rest** of the items that you have into the following categories: love it and use it, love it but never use it, don't love it but do use it, don't love it and don't use it.
5. Take the "**love it and use it**" pile and put it away for keeps.
6. Take the "**don't love it and don't use it**" pile and immediately donate it.
7. Next we will tackle the "**love it but never use it**" pile. This is a great pile for celebrating abundance because you already have great items that you don't need! The ideal option here is to gift these items to someone else; you have so much wonderful stuff that you can share! If there are items that you can't part with, create a beautiful collection for display made up of some or all of the items. (*You may also want to return to the letting go chapter to work with this section but in terms of celebrating abundance, the display works perfectly.*)
8. Now it's time to deal with the "**don't love it but do use it**" pile. This is the stuff that you are likely hanging on to even though it is not of ideal style or quality because you do use it (or will eventually) and it seems like a waste to just get rid of it. That word - *waste* - is a warning word that signifies you're hanging on to something you don't actually need. Letting go of that item to make space for what you truly love is how you create abundance. The goal for these items is to get rid of each one and replace it with an item that you'll use but do love. For example, my aluminum D hooks kept getting bent and I finally replaced that particular size hook with a more durable brand that was more expensive but not as likely to bend. The bent hook worked and I "needed" a D hook but hanging on to that one wasn't as satisfying as making room for the better quality hook.
9. **Look through your supplies** and see if there is anything missing that you really want. For example, you might want a set of a particular type of crochet hooks. Make a wish list of everything that you want to buy and treat yourself to each item on the list as the resources become available. They will become available. Life is abundant if you allow it to be.

Tips:

- If you are not comfortable with throwing away items then put everything in a box for donation. Immediately donate those items; do not hang on to them.
- There may be items that are an exception to the "doubles" rule in step three. For example, I use my G and H size crochet hooks constantly and often have more than one project going at a time so I'm fine with keeping extras of those on hand. I almost never use my Q hook so it would be silly to have more than one.
- You may not have the resources to replace the items immediately. That's okay. Add each of these items to your wish list and when you're able to buy them, get rid of the old item that it is replacing. Hold yourself accountable to this.

Taking it further: When you purchase new craft items, make it a point to invest in higher quality items that you are really going to love and that are likely to last over time. These may come from surprising places. For example, some people find that very old vintage tailor's scissors are far more durable (and beautiful) than the cheap scissors bought in the store today so they shop vintage instead of new. Consider quality over quantity in order to have the abundance you need for crafting without accumulating a bunch of excess items that are subpar.

Abundance Exercise #4: Enjoy Your Yarn

The exercise: Replace uninspiring yarn with blissfully wonderful yarn.

The purpose: Don't keep icky yarn just because it's "better than no yarn at all".

In depth: The work here is to have faith that the world will supply you with the things that you want. It can be frightening to get rid of yarn you don't love and see your stash dwindle down to nothing, especially if you don't have the money to replace it all. The resources will come when you make space for them.

Exercise steps:

1. **Cull through your yarn stash** and pull out every single skein of yarn that does not inspire you. Yes, every one. Too small, too

splitty, not the right color, not a fiber you like working with ... pull it all out.
2. **Get rid of it!** Donate it. Gift it. Recycle it. Get it out of your space.
3. **Go through the yarn stash one more time**. Hold each ball of yarn that is left in your hands. Ask yourself what you are inspired to make with it. If no answer comes, it's not inspiring enough. Get rid of it, too!
4. **Replace the yarn** with yarn that does inspire you. You may need to get creative - shopping clearance sales, doing yarn swaps with crafty friends, saving up for awhile to get the skein that you want, repurposing yarn from old projects. In the meantime, just work from what's left in your stash. Have faith!

Tips:

- Make this your mantra: life is too short to work with crappy yarn.
- Remember that inspiring yarn doesn't have to be expensive yarn. Sometimes even the least expensive yarn on the shelf is really inspiring in the right color!
- Work with affirmations. With each stitch, remind yourself, "there is enough yarn, there is always enough yarn".
- If you simply can't get yourself to get rid of the yarn, then put a shelf life on it. Literally label each skein with a use-by date. It might be one week or one year but when that time is up, the yarn must either be used or donated. If you do this then be sure to go through your stash seasonally to get rid of the "expired" yarn.

Taking it further: Only allow new yarn into your home if it inspires you. Don't give in to the temptation to buy up all of the skeins of yarn at the dollar store simply because they are on sale. (That is, unless that yarn inspires you, then buy it up!) Don't accept gifts of yarn from people if you don't look at the yarn and instantly think, "oh, I love that!" (You don't have to be rude; you can accept the yarn and re-gift it to someone.)

Abundance Exercise #5: "Not Enough Time"

The exercise: Create time for your craft.

The purpose: So often we use the excuse that we don't have enough time to enjoy our craft. It's not true. Make the time.

<u>In depth</u>: We all have busy lives. There are people who need us, tasks that must be done, jobs we have to be at, etc. etc. Hopefully if you've gotten this far in the book then it means that you're making the time for your craft. If you still feel like you don't have enough time for crochet then it is the perfect time to tackle that issue. You deserve to have an abundance of craft time!

<u>Exercise steps</u>:

1. **Take a moment to daydream** about what the ideal situation would be in terms of the time available to you for crafting. Is your dream to be able to crochet through a whole movie without interruptions? Or to have time each day for your craft?
2. **Get out your calendar**. If you don't use a calendar, it's time to start one, at least for a little while.
3. **Block out your ideal amount of time** on your calendar for an entire month. This might mean that you need to reschedule other things or even cancel some of your commitments. That's okay. Give yourself permission to do that! Make it work on the calendar and you'll be able to make it work (or close to it) in real life.
4. **Stick to what the calendar says**. Check your calendar every day. Consider this a commitment that you "must" keep, just like you "must" go to the doctor and you "must" show up at work. Stick to it for one full month.
5. At the end of one month, **make an assessment**. Was that enough time? Do you need more? Less? Figure out what worked and what didn't, tweak it and then set your new craft schedule for the following month.

<u>Tips</u>:

- Remember that you can crochet in many different places since it is a terrifically portable craft, and allow that to factor in to your scheduling. For example, I always block out a half hour extra before any doctor's appointment and use the time that I'm there early as crafting time. Always pick your kids up at school at 2? Get there at 1:45 each day and get in fifteen minutes of crafting time five days a week!

- Watch yourself wriggle out of the calendar you've set. This is a way that you are creating limitations for yourself so that you don't feel the abundance of time that can exist if you allow it. You would probably never tell a job, "well actually I just can't fit work in today" or say to your young children, "sorry, I won't pick you up at school today because there's just not enough time". Make your crafting an equal priority.

Taking it Further: Schedule yourself a crochet vacation. I live alone so if I want to I have the luxury of booking a two week staycation when I can indulge in my ideal amount of craft time (which is basically all day, with the TV on and lots of nap breaks). You might not have that luxury, but book what you can. Schedule a weekend alone somewhere or take a "sick day" from work and treat yourself to abundant craft time.

SOCIAL VARIATION ON EXERCISE FIVE

Some people do feel that they have craft time but don't feel like they have enough time with specific people in their lives, be it quality time with the kids or time to catch up with a best friend. We'll explore this in more depth in the chapter on relationships but for now you can use this same exercise to schedule craft time with the person you're wanting to see. Invite them to learn your craft, craft with you or catch up with you while you craft. Put it on the calendar and commit!

Abundance Exercise #6: Crochet In Excess

The exercise: Crochet more of a single item than you could ever need.

The purpose: There is abundance when you can make more for yourself than what you will actually use.

In depth: When you have plenty of something, plenty more than you actually need or maybe even want, there is clear abundance. It is even better when it's something that you've made yourself because you can see that if you ever run out of that particular item, it would be simple to just make more for yourself.

Exercise steps:

1. **Choose a specific type of item** that you enjoy crafting.
2. **Ask yourself how many** of that item would be a reasonable number for the average person to have. For example, I love crocheting big warm blankets, but I live alone in a one bedroom house so even if I had three blankets for the bed, another three for guests on the couch and a bonus three on my loveseat, that's nine blankets. I don't need more than ten blankets in this house. Write that number down.
3. **Crochet yourself 3-4 times the amount** that you just wrote down. So for my exercise, I would make 30-40 crochet blankets. (I hope you aren't thinking that sounds absurd because I really love crocheting blankets and have actually made that many without even trying to!)
4. **Use as many of the items as you can** and display the rest, at least for a short time. Make sure that they are out where you can see them. I have stacks of blankets on my bed, my couch, my loveseat, under my desk, next to my table. I can look around my house and feel absolutely that I will never run out of blankets. I have an abundance of blankets!

Tips:

- Choose a craft item that you enjoy making and that you can afford the time and cost to make a lot of. Blankets might be too much. I confess I also have an abundance of dishtowels and washcloths in my house. Nobody needs as many as I have made for myself!
- Look to your stash as a source of gift giving. You will have so many of this item that you can easily grab one off of the stack and give it away to someone else. Share your abundance! Often when someone visits my home I ask myself (and them) if there is a blanket that should go home with that person. I always make sure that they have a never-used washcloth available to them in the bathroom.
- You run the risk of overcrowding your home in celebration of crafty abundance. If that happens, work back and forth between the chapter on Letting Go and this work to create abundance so that you achieve a great balance of creative energy in the home. Some times it is the season to let go, sometimes to create too much of an item.

Taking it further: Choose to create an abundance of items that may seem difficult or time-consuming to make. The number may not have to be that large. For example, I find it intimidating to think about tackling a huge tapestry crochet quilt. Instead of caving in to that fear, I'll set a goal to make two of them! I'll prove to myself that I have an abundance of time, skill, and creativity that I didn't think I had.

Abundance Exercise #7: "Not Enough Space"

The exercise: Create an abundance of space for crafting even in a small home.

The purpose: Setting aside space for your creativity honors its value.

In depth: I live in San Francisco where many people live in micro apartments that are just about 200 square feet in total, so believe me when I say that I've seen some really tiny living spaces. Luckily, I don't live in such a space. My spot is small but it has a separate bedroom, a large kitchen and high ceilings with good natural light that all make it feel roomier than its square foot size. That said, it still often feels like there's not enough space, so I've learned over time how to create an abundance of space in small ways. You can do the same.

Exercise steps:

1. Make an honest **assessment of your home** and determine where there is space to set up a crafting area. If you have a whole room, awesome, if you only have one shelf, that's okay. I know of at least one crafter who set up a camping tent in her living room and designated that as her craft space.
2. **Make this space entirely your own**. Decorate it. Organize your tools in it. Post one of your favorite affirmations there.
3. **Use this space** regularly. The more you infuse it with creative action, the more energy it's going to generate. You'll be surprised to find that sooner rather than later your crafty area actually expands.

Tips:

- Make do with what you have and celebrate it. If you only have a shelf, make it the prettiest shelf possible. Put only your very favorite skein of yarn and crochet hooks on that shelf. Add a pretty postcard of a famous place. Add a shelf liner that you love.

- Sometimes a craft space has to be convertible. For awhile, I used my kitchen table as my craft space, but I needed to be able to allow people to eat there when they visited. In this case, keep some pretty storage containers where you can quickly and easily pack away your craft supplies as needed. When you get your crafty space back, put those items out where you can see them as quickly as possible. Try to make the space a craft space for as large a percentage of time as you can.
- Journal about what your very favorite creative space would look like. It could be big or small. Set the daydream in motion on the page. Mine, for example, is a summer retreat space with my siblings that includes large rooms, ample crafting time, creativity workshops and many animals. I haven't made it happen, yet, but I'm certain it's going to one day because I've envisioned it so clearly.

Taking it further: Create a craft studio for yourself. This is a dream of so many crafters and it can feel out of reach but it might not be. Do you have a guest room or old nursery that could become your new craft room? What about a large closet? Maybe a shed can become a small craft space in your backyard or you could enclose the porch for that purpose? Your craft studio might not be on your own property. You might rent a studio space or even see about co-working spaces in your area where you can get a desk that is just for you. Another creative option is to swap services for space with a friend ... turn her basement or spare bedroom into a craft studio in exchange for cooking her weekly meals, doing some babysitting or even making some of your handmade crochet items for her!

Abundance Exercise #8: "Not Enough Energy"

The exercise: Set and meet a tiny crochet goal.

The purpose: Generate energy to craft even when it feels impossible.

In depth: I love crochet. I find it relaxing and soothing and wonderful. But I also struggle with low energy a lot of the time (due to depression and anemia and who knows what else) so sometimes I don't feel like I even have the energy to crochet. What I find is that if I force myself to do just the tiniest bit of it, I feel better than if I did none at all.

Exercise steps:

1. **Set a really tiny crochet goal** for the week. I'm talking miniature, like just crocheting for ten minutes.
2. **Meet your goal**. No matter how low your energy is, you can find a way to crochet for ten minutes in a week. Two minutes of crochet each day will surpass your goal!
3. **Celebrate your success** at the end of the week. Pat yourself on the back for meeting your tiny goal. You had more energy than you thought!
4. **Start over** at step one, increasing your goal just a little bit if that feels possible!

Tips:

- Your goal doesn't have to be a time-based goal. You might set a goal to crochet a certain number of stitches or a set number of rows on a project or to complete a really tiny crochet item like a flower or a granny square.
- Know your boundaries. The idea here is to set a goal that feels slightly hard because you have no energy but one that is truly doable. Don't push yourself beyond what your energy really allows. Push right up to that edge, do one more stitch and then allow yourself ample rest.
- Embrace daydreaming about crochet. There are times when I simply can't get myself up, off of the couch, to the yarn to pick out a project and pull through the stitches. It is unfortunately tempting during those times to beat myself up for not working on my craft, but of course that just makes the whole situation worse. So instead, I try to just sit there quietly and daydream about crochet. What would I crochet if I had all of the energy in the world? What was my favorite thing I've made? Daydream in any way that feels inspiring to you. This, too, is creative energy, even if nothing is specifically getting made in your hands at this moment.
- You can actually generate energy. Try crocheting really, really fast. Then crochet really, really slow. You will likely notice that when you crochet fast, you create an energy in your body that wasn't there previously. (This is similar to when you take a walk instead of taking a nap and find that the walk refreshes you.) If this topic

interests you, I recommend checking out the book *Kick-Ass Creativity* by Mary Beth Maziarz.

Taking it further: It's worth it to explore the reasons that you are lacking energy and to see if you can fix those underlying causes. It may be that you have a chronic (or temporary) illness, a nutrition issue, a problem with sleep, etc. While we've addressed some of those issues in this book and looked at ways that crochet can even help with them, consistent low energy may require more attention. You may want to work with doctors, counselors, nutritionists, holistic healers, etc. to find the right solution for you. You want to feel good as much as possible and crafting can be one piece of that.

Abundance Exercise #9: The Stages of Happiness

The exercise: Move intentionally through the four stages of happiness with a crochet project.

The purpose: Create an abundance of joy in your craft work through attending to the four stages of happiness.

In depth: Creativity author Gretchen Rubin says that there are four stages of happiness and that by eking out as much happiness as possible from each stage, you truly maximize your joy. Her four stages, put briefly, are anticipation, savoring the experience, expressing happiness and reflecting on it.

Exercise steps:

1. **Take your time** in choosing a crochet project that excites you. This is about getting happiness in stage one - anticipating the pleasure. Allow your excitement to build as you look at possible options for projects.
2. **Take yourself yarn shopping** (at the store or in your stash closet) and really focus in on the pleasure of anticipating how you're going to make these colors come together to create this amazing project. (We're still in stage one of happiness).
3. **Set the crafting area** up to really embrace the project that is about to come. By embracing rituals like lighting favorite candles or laying all of the yarn out in front of you, you really let the anticipation get as full as possible.

4. Now we move into the second stage of happiness as defined by Rubin: **savoring the moment**. Really take the time to focus on this project as you work through it. Notice what you love about the craft, the yarn, the experience, the downtime of crochet. Mindfulness crochet techniques can help here.
5. During the crafting, and also once the project is complete, you can **extend your happiness** by expressing it to yourself or others. This is a great opportunity to open your crochet journal and write about the wonder of this particular project. You can also blog about it, share it on social media or take the work to your craft group to share.
6. Finally, you can close the circle and squeeze out that list bit of happiness by **reflecting on the project**. Again, your crochet journal is great for this, as is meditation. Reflect upon each stage of the work. How did it make you happy? Take photographs for posterity so that you can look back again and see that happy work at a future time.

Tips:

- Don't be shy about sharing your work with others. This is crucial to the third phase of happiness: expressing it! This isn't bragging in a bad way; it's celebrating your creativity and the joy you have when making.
- Maximize attention on what makes you happy and minimize attention to what doesn't. I, personally, don't enjoy weaving in ends on my work, but instead of grumbling and allowing unhappiness to seep in during that time, I can practice meditative crochet to reflect upon the parts of the crafting that have made me happy so far.
- Affirmations while crocheting can boost happiness levels.

Taking it further: Do something big and silly to celebrate the accomplishments of which you are most proud. You can maximize the happiness in stage three, expressing it to others, by hosting a party for yourself in honor of a work that you've completed. Make and send birth announcements about your new creative baby and invite everyone to an open house to come see what you've made! Too intimidated by that idea? Host a monthly show-and-tell with crafty friends where you can each go around in a circle and share something that you've created and are proud of.

Abundance Exercise #10: Crochet for all Five Senses

The exercise: Crochet with an attention to all five senses.

The purpose: Experience an abundance of sensory stimulation while crafting.

In depth: Our brain filters out so much of what is happening around us all of the time. This is a necessary thing so that we don't get completely overwhelmed and stop functioning all together. But if you have ever taken a super slow photography walk down your block or engaged in other acts of mindfulness activity then you know that there is an abundance of beauty right under our noses. This exercise brings our attention to that abundance in our crochet work.

Exercise steps:

1. **Select a crochet project** to work on that is going to be pure delight for your eyes. Favorite colors or bold graphic designs are a great choice but choose whatever is right for you. You want something that you are going to love looking at as it grows beneath your fingertips.
2. **Select yarn** that is an absolute treasure to touch, the kind of yarn that we call "yummy yarn", the kind of yarn that you want to pet. It's about the color, which might be dictated by your decisions in step one, but it's also about the way that it feels in your fingers.
3. **Create a playlist** of the perfect songs to go with this crafting experience. They may be your favorite songs or they may be songs that are themed to the project. For example, a rainbow-colored crochet project could go well with a playlist of songs about rainbows. Have fun making the music set that you'll listen to while you are crafting.
4. **Figure out what scents** are going to be perfect for this crafting project. You might already have some favorite candles to use. Alternatively, you may want to make a choice that reflects the project itself. For example, a floral patterned crochet project might call for potpourri or fresh cut flowers in your space.
5. **Now it's time to consider taste.** What would this project taste like if it were a food and how can you bring that into your

space? Maybe it's a summer project and you want to chew watermelon gum while you craft. Perhaps it celebrates winter and a bowl of mints on your craft table is the perfect accompaniment.
6. **Crochet your project slowly**, with intention, and with attention to each of the five senses. When you get to the end of each row, ask yourself which of the senses you may not be paying enough attention to and recalibrate to notice it.

Tips:

- You can work on Steps One and Two together to make sure that the project that you select meets both your need for a great visual pattern and a need for a great tactile experience. You might want to select a project that has richness of texture, like a basketweave stitch or ribbed crochet, for example.
- If this exercise starts to feel overwhelming, try it with a really small project. For example, make a single-color crochet square in a favorite yarn, listening to your five favorite songs on repeat, with a favorite candle scent burning and a favorite chewing gum in your mouth.
- Return to the exercise we did early on about setting the stage for self-care. Remember that we explored the five senses then in a general way but are now tuning in to them as they relate to a specific project and to create a sense of abundance. You may want to make alterations now to your craft space based on what you learn in this project.

Taking it further: Practice planning out your projects in advance, writing about them in your crochet journal to determine the best things for all five senses as you craft. This can become a regular part of your project process (and speaks to Gretchen Rubin's first stage of happiness (anticipation) explored in Exercise Nine above). Embrace the opportunity to turn even small crochet projects into indulgent works of art through attention to these decisions.

Abundance Exercise #11: Crochet Yourself a Special Gift

<u>The exercise</u>: Crochet yourself a special item.

<u>The purpose</u>: Use your craft skills to make something that you really want but won't buy for yourself.

<u>In depth</u>: We often choose not to buy items for ourselves because we want to put our money into something else. This can be related to a fear of scarcity or some kind of guilt about spending money on ourselves. But we can use our talents to crochet some of the special items that we wouldn't otherwise purchase for ourselves.

<u>Exercise steps</u>:

1. **Ask yourself**: "what is an item I really want for myself but don't want to pay money to purchase?" *See examples below.*
2. **Find a crochet pattern** for that item that is exactly what you'd love to have. Don't compromise!
3. **Purchase the yarn** for that item. If it starts to feel too expensive, remind yourself that you are worth it. Set aside money over time to make this purchase if you need to, as long as you are committed to completing the project for yourself.
4. **Crochet yourself the item**. Really take time to celebrate that you can create this amazing thing for yourself.
5. **Use the finished crochet item** in a way that really shows it off. If it's a wearable item, wear it out where people will notice and praise it. If it's a home item, have a few people over and show it off.

EXAMPLES OF ITEMS THAT YOU MAY WANT

- A beautiful dress
- A quirky hat
- Body pillow
- Comfy pajama pants
- Cozy socks
- Jewelry box
- Ottoman
- Purse with enough pockets for everything

- Set of decorative jars
- Statement jewelry
- Stuffed animal
- Wall art
- Wire cords and cozies to hide all of your electronic doohickies

<u>Tips</u>:

- Be willing to choose a pattern that might not be in your crochet wheelhouse yet and to learn the skills necessary to make the item. For example, you might really want a beautiful beaded necklace but don't yet know how to do wire crochet; that's okay - be willing to learn!
- Take your time to make the item right, exactly the way that you want it to be. I'm personally a fast crocheter who prefers process to end product but in this exercise it is really important that you focus on making the end item the thing you have really dreamed of. Wearing a perfectly crafted sparkling crochet necklace can feel as abundant as wearing million dollar diamonds to some of us!
- Don't have a lot of people in your life who will praise your crochet work? Visit a yarn store or craft fair wearing your creation; those folks are always good at noticing what we have handmade!

<u>Taking It further</u>: Use crochet to create the most special items in your life. Many people have begun to crochet their wedding dresses for example.

Yarn for Thought: More Musings on Abundance

- What do you want more of? Make a big list of everything you wish you had more of in life. Time, money, quality experiences with your family, healthy days, education ... anything at all. It is important to figure out what you feel is lacking in your life so you can create abundance around the right things.
- What are some of the limitations that you impose upon yourself? In what ways do you deprive yourself? How can you create more abundance around these areas?
- Creative abundance requires faith that God or The Universe will provide you with what you need to create. What is your reaction to this statement?
- If you had all of the money in the world, what would you buy for yourself? Make a list of how you might provide yourself with some of those items in crochet.
- Begin a journal entry with, "living a life of abundance would mean" and fill at least two pages with the thoughts that follow.
- It is possible for every single person on this planet to experience abundance. Do you agree or disagree? Explore.
- In what ways are you competitive in your crochet? (With other bloggers, Etsy sellers, craft fair artisans, etc.) How can you change your mindset from competing to collaborating?

Relationships and Connecting

For most of us what really makes up the richness of life is the relationships that we have with others. And yet, those relationships are also what can bring us down in so many ways. In this chapter we are going to work with exercises that will help us honor, appreciate and improve our relationships so that we get something out of them every day instead of allowing them to take anything away from us.

We as individuals live our lives in relationship to other people. Those relationships, especially (but not only) our relationships with our chosen life partners, are critical to our own personal wellbeing. They are an area many of us struggle in. I have used crafting to heal within relationships, to facilitate communication with my relationship partner and to heal from relationship wounds on my own.

If you ask almost anyone in my life to describe me in just a few select words there is a very good chance that you will hear something along the lines of "strong" or "independent". There is truth to this. I have always taken care of myself. I have always been fiercely loyal to my own personal growth. I have spent more years than not living alone; I have exited relationships even when I was scared to because I was more scared of losing myself; I have gone to great lengths to maintain my independence as a creative solopreneur. That is the me that most people will see. She is very real. She is true and honest. She does exist. But there is a flip side to her as well. She co-exists with the other side of me that is driven to pursue growth through personal relationships.

I fervently believe that the nurturing of our own individual selves is what is most important in this life. But here is my truth ... for all of my adamant (and I think accurate) beliefs that all healing starts with a focus inward on the self, the reality is that it is my relationships that have ultimately shaped me. It is in love (and in a sense of lacking love) that I have flown, soared, crashed, recoiled, burned, fizzled, re-emerged. I am always me, but the me that is mirrored back to me in small and large ways through the eyes of a romantic partner has always been a critical part of who I am.

While there may be a small select group of people who devote their lives to art or meditation or craft within the solitude of a spiritual, monastic, artistic life, most of us create within the confines of our society. It is the relationships closest to us that can most confine us. It is also through the healthy development of understanding and nurturing those relationships and finding our own voices within those connections that we are able to really grow as people and as artists. All of the work we do on ourselves is important; in the end it may even be all that matters. However, this is done within the shared space of our relationships.

I can remember chasing boys (Jesse, Anthony, Marc) around the playground for kisses when I was in first or second grade. I remember being ten and being a part of a group of four girls who spent hours upon hours trying to understand each other, the world, the boys around us. I had my first sort-of-boyfriend (Gilbert) when I was ten and my first real boyfriend (Jeremy) when I was fourteen. And in the intervening eighteen years I've navigated a world of complex female and male relationships that defined me, shaped me, changed me, inspired me and ultimately not only made me who I am but actually reminded me of the truth of who I am that I already knew before all of those relationships began.

How can it be true that I am so committed to my own self-development and self-awareness while simultaneously having spent a lifetime watching myself develop in the eyes of others? It is because we do not live in a bubble. I do not live on a mountaintop alone where I can hold theories about the world that don't work when you have to share the world with others. It is because I am a solid rock of self but the people who enter my life are the waters that have the potential to erode and move me. It is precisely because I am committed to my own personal growth as an individual that I seek out life-altering relationships with others. In the end, what I build with someone else is important, valuable, meaningful ... but ultimately what matters is the way that I grow as an individual as a result of that connection.

This section is about relationships, but bear in mind that the point here is that it is really all about my relationship with myself, your relationship with yourself. Think of it this way: I can crochet in a room full of people; I can and do share my crafting with a larger online community; I crochet items for others and hold them in my heart as I make those gifts ... but in the end, regardless of all of those important connections, I am still a girl sitting alone with herself and her hook. At the end of the day, it is about me creating me. And I hope in this chapter you'll have the opportunity to think about how to utilize your own crafting to better understand your own relationships and not only improve them but also improve your own self-understanding in the process.

Relationships Exercise #1: Swap Craft Love With Your Partner

The exercise: Teach your partner to crochet. Learn your partner's favorite craft or hobby in exchange.

The purpose: Show the person that you love the craft that you love while also sharing in their joy of experiences.

In depth: We feel loved when our partner expresses an interest in the things that we love doing. You can share this with your partner by being open and willing to partake in their favorite activity in exchange for time spent doing yours together. The "teacher" gets to share their joy, skills, knowledge and crafting experience and the "learner" gets to see the partner in a new way and celebrate their passions. This builds connection between the two of you. Loving gestures and time spent together go a long way towards improving relationships.

Exercise steps:

1. **Explain the exercise** to your partner and ask what (s)he would like to teach you. Make the emphasis on your willingness to learn something new from them!
2. **Set aside time** together alone to teach each other your crafts. Put it on the calendar and commit to it!
3. **Begin by learning something** that your partner loves. The tone that you set as the student will help set the tone for sharing your craft later on. Be as engaged and interested as possible, allow yourself to be surprised by what you might like in this craft.
4. **Share with your partner** what you liked about the experience. Pick out three things that you enjoyed. Even if this is a craft or hobby that you'll never do again, you can find details to appreciate.
5. **It's your turn**. Teach your partner to crochet! Emphasize what you like about the craft.
6. **Ask your partner** what they liked about the experience. Thank him or her for trying it out!

Tips:

- Make something that commemorates the experience. Crochet a heart in your lesson, glue it onto a blank card and give it to your partner a week later with a written thank you for sharing activities with you.

- Don't currently have a romantic partner? You can also do this exercise with a family member or friend.
- Being a beginner at something and trying hobbies we might not be passionate about can be tough. Turn your focus to the purpose, which is to celebrate something that your partner enjoys in service of improving your relationship and understanding of one another. The point is not to be great at your partner's craft or have them suddenly want to do yours all of the time; it's to value how each of you spends your time.

Taking it further: Make a regular date night with your partner to teach each other new things! Embrace the opportunity to share interests with one another.

Relationships Exercise #2: Family Craft Hour

The exercise: Institute a regular family craft hour in your home.

The purpose: Create time together to be creative in the same space to expand your connections with one another.

In depth: Rituals build traditions. Creating time together opens up space for many conversations and deepening of your relationships. Many families have a dinnertime ritual (no phones, sharing your day). Some families have a bedtime ritual. Craft hour can become another of these rituals that provide space and time for sharing deeply with one another over the years.

Exercise steps:

1. **Determine when** family craft hour is going to be. It might actually be a briefer period in the evenings each day or a longer period that happens once a week. Set it in stone and make it a non-negotiable with your family.
2. **Create a space** for family craft hour that includes all of the materials that you'll need to enjoy this time. You want to make engaging in the craft activity easy, without having to do a lot of set up each time.
3. **Come together as a family** to agree to a set of rules for craft hour. Write these down together. See some possible rules below.

4. **Start** having family craft hour! Enjoy! Adapt times and rules as needed until you get the rhythm right.

COMMON RULES FOR CRAFT HOUR

- It is a technology-free time. No phones, televisions or other electronics allowed (unless the item is required for a particular craft; such as using the phone for photography).
- Everyone commits to showing up all of the time except in highly unusual circumstances.
- There is to be no judging of the art work. That means no negative comments about anyone else's work and no negative comments about your own either!
- The last ten minutes are clean-up time. Everyone participates.
- This is time just for the family. No friends invited. (Conversely, some families might have a rule that anyone who is visiting joins, too!)

Tips:

- Carefully consider your family's schedule when setting up the family craft hour schedule. You want to make it possible for everyone to attend. Some families do Sunday Dinner, you might do Sunday Craft Time ... but only if your family is actually able to make Sundays available each week.
- Some families will want to work on a single craft together while other families will want to do their own projects in the same space. Either way works and it may change with time depending on the ages of those involved. Be flexible in this way and do what works for your family!
- It's best not to place a lot of expectations on what will happen during family craft hour. Don't force serious conversations. Just like with the family dinner, the magic happens over time, through the commitment to coming together regularly to be creative in the same space.

Taking it further: Put longer family craft outings on the calendar as well. This might include a visit to a hands-on museum or science center, a shopping expedition to a favorite craft store together or a weekend getaway to craft together while camping.

Relationships Exercise #3: Appreciation Blanket

<u>The exercise</u>: Crochet a "mood blanket" based on your love for the recipient.

<u>The purpose</u>: Celebrate what you appreciate about someone every day and then share that with them in the form of a handmade gift.

<u>In depth</u>: This is a variation on the mood blanket, in which you typically crochet a single row or motif of a blanket each day based on the mood of the day (using a color coded system that you create). In this instance, you're going to use the colors to indicate the positive emotions that you are having about the person who will receive this gift.

<u>Exercise steps:</u>

1. **Create your color code** and write it down. For example you may decide that the blanket will have rows of red when you feel love, pink for gratitude, and white for awe. (See more appreciative mood options below.)
2. **Choose a crochet pattern.** This blanket pattern can be done in rows or motifs; you'll be working one row or one motif daily.
3. **Purchase plenty of yarn** for daily crochet based on the color code you've created.
4. **Crochet one row or one motif** for the blanket each day, using the color that best expresses your mood towards the person that day.
5. **Crochet every day** for a full year.
6. **Put it all together** into a blanket!

APPRECIATIVE MOODS TO CELEBRATE

- Love
- Gratitude
- Awe
- Nostalgia
- Commitment
- Passion
- Joy
- Comfort

- Romance

Tips:

- Select a small motif that can easily be done each day. A three round granny square is one example.
- Use join-as-you-go techniques to allow the blanket to come together steadily instead of having to do it all at the end.
- Commit to a set of positive emotions. You may not always feel positively about the person but this helps you focus on what you do appreciate about him or her, even on difficult days. At the end you'll be able to see the emotion that stood out the most for you while you were crafting.
- You don't have to do a year-long blanket. You might instead do a month-long blanket consisting of 30 daily squares. You also don't have to do daily squares; you could do weekly squares instead.

Taking it further: Incorporate a journal into the project. Each day, write down one sentence about why you chose the color that you did that day. Gift this journal along with your blanket to the recipient.

Relationships Exercise #4: Re-Create a Favorite Memory in Crochet

The exercise: Crochet a favorite memory that you have with someone you love.

The purpose: Celebrate something you loved in your relationship through the act of crochet.

In depth: One of the ways that we strengthen our relationships is through savoring our positive memories that we've experienced with the other person. This can be done alone, in our own minds, as we celebrate the greatest of times and let that love wrap itself around us, or it can be done together through sharing a memory aloud. This exercise puts that into physical form with crochet.

Exercise steps:

1. **Brainstorm** a list of memories that you'd like to celebrate.
2. **Choose one** memory from the list.

3. **Brainstorm** a list of images that relate to this memory. For example, let's say that the memory happened at the beach; include a list of beach items.
4. **Crochet** each of the items on your list from Step Three. You might do them as flat appliques or as amigurumi stuffed characters.
5. **Organize** them into a scene that represents the memory.
6. **Identify** anything that is missing from the scene. For example, did you forget to place yourself in it? Crochet any missing elements and add them in.
7. **Preserve the scene.** You might glue it all down, stitch it all together, set it up as a display in your home or simply photograph it.
8. **Share it** with your loved one.

Tips:

- The items that you crochet can be abstract representations instead of exact replicas. For example, when I put myself and others into a scene, I use crochet hearts in different colors to represent each of us rather than trying to actually crochet a self-portrait.
- That said, if you are skilled at (or want to try) tapestry crochet to create portraits and landscapes then by all means crochet your memory in this way!
- If you're sharing the experience with a loved one in advance, ask them what they remember about that day and incorporate what they share into your physical representation.

Taking it further: Create a play telling the story of the memory. Use your crochet items to tell the story of the play. Present the play to those who participated in the event that is memorialized. You can also use animation and video to present the story.

Relationships Exercise #5: Crochet a Gift with Intention

The exercise: Use crochet with affirmations to make an intentional gift for someone.

The purpose: Infuse a gift with love and positive energy as you crochet.

In depth: The act of crocheting with gratitude for someone amplifies your love for them and creates an item that they can treasure forever.

Exercise steps:

1. **Identify someone** who needs more love from you right now.
2. Identify a **meditative crochet item** that would be perfect to make for that person. Prayer shawls are a popular choice but they aren't the only option.
3. **Choose a simple affirmation** that you can stitch into the work. For example, you might meditate upon the thought, "I surround you with love and peace."
4. **Say a blessing** when the piece is completed. This helps solidify your intention and brings the crafting experiences to a positive close.
5. **Gift** the item to the recipient!

Tips:

- We tend to craft for the same people over and over, the ones who appreciate it, but consider making this item for someone who doesn't usually receive your handiwork but truly needs your support right now.
- You might want to let the person know that you are crafting something for them and explain the spirit behind the piece. These intentions can improve the relationship between the two of you in many stages of the work. You can also include a tag or card with your intention written on it.
- See the tips in the previous chapter on affirmations for working with Step Three of this exercise.

Taking it further: Use affirmations to crochet a gift for someone you are having a difficult time with. Do you have an enemy? This work can help you let go of grudges and move forward, which is something that you do a little bit for the other person but really do mostly for your own wellbeing.

Relationships Exercise #6: Make Friends Through Crochet

The exercise: Join or start a crafting group.

The purpose: Widen your circle of friendships through this activity that you love.

In depth: Crafting can be a great way to form friendships. The people who craft together regularly help each other with their stitching, but they also help each other through so much more than that. This group can be your support system through things big and small. Many people who are introverted find that they are more comfortable meeting people through a task-oriented group like a crochet group.

Exercise steps:

1. **Find a local crochet group**. Check local yarn stores, libraries and meetups.
2. **Get their schedule**, find out how to join them and put a date on your calendar for meeting up.
3. **Visit the group** with an open mind and see what happens!

Tips:

- If you can't find a local crochet group, expand to look into knitting groups and general craft groups, which typically also welcome people who crochet. If there is really nothing in your area, be brave and start your own crafting group!
- Intimidated to join a group on your own? See if a crafty friend or family member will take that plunge with you. It can strengthen your friendship with that person while at the same time opening up your circle of friends.
- If at first you don't succeed, try, try again. Give the group a fair chance. You may be surprised over time at how friendships develop with people you initially don't feel like you share a lot in common with. That said, if you really don't fit with the craft group and it's not providing what you need, try another group down the line!

Taking it further:

Once you have a group, there are many activities that you can engage in together to expand your crafty love and creativity. Some examples include:

- Everyone in the group makes a different version of the same thing (crochet-along style) and celebrates the unique features of each person's finished object.
- White elephant or Secret Santa gifting using your craft-making skills. This is great for holidays and other celebrations.
- Each person in the group teaches a skill to someone else in the group. This might be done one-on-one or through workshops that are taught to the whole group.
- Everyone makes one part of a larger item, such as one blanket for a square or one motif for a bunting. You can make a single item and keep it in the shared space where the group meets or make one item for everyone in the group in this way.
- Show-and-tell days! Host weekly, monthly or seasonal days where each person brings in some of their favorite handmade items to share stories about.

Relationships Exercise #7: Create a Crochet Book Club

Note: This is a variation on Exercise 6 above.

The exercise: Start a crochet book club.

The purpose: Widen and deepen your crafty friend circle by incorporating shared reading.

In depth: A crochet book group is a group of people who all agree to read the same craft-related book and then get together to discuss it. The books aren't crochet pattern books but either fiction or non-fiction books that relate to crochet in some way. (See suggested titles below.) During the discussion they also bring their crochet work and craft together as they talk. Some crochet book groups do a CAL where they are all working on the same project during the sessions whereas others opt to work on their own individual pieces. This type of group provides inspiration, information, support and friendship.

Exercise steps:

1. **Determine the basic ground rules** of your crochet group. These may change with time but you'll want to consider how many people you want in the group, how often to meet, where you'll meet,

whether it will be an open or closed group (accepting new members over time), and the level of formality of the discussions.
2. **Invite members to join your group.** Start by asking your local friends and family who crochet. Ask your best friend who doesn't crochet but would like to learn. Send out a social media announcement to your online friends. Put up a flyer at the local yarn store.
3. **Hold a mixer meetup.** Your first meeting should be a gathering to explain the rules of the book club and figure out all of the details, as well as a way to get to know one another. Have a few icebreakers, talk while crocheting, see what additional thoughts people have about the format of the group. Assign the first book!
4. **Enjoy regular meetings!** The meetings can be as formal or informal as your group determines is right. You might want to have an official person who establishes a set of conversation questions about each reading, or you might just all say what you liked or didn't about the book. Adapt as needed.

Tips:

- If you can't locate enough people for a just-crochet group, consider expanding to other fiber arts. There are a lot of good readable books out there about knitting and quilting, too!
- Include a mixture of fiction and non-fiction titles. Include a range of intended age groups. Explore outside of your reading comfort zone.

Taking it further: Begin a crochet book journal (or devote a section of your regular crochet journal to this). Use this space to write reviews, thoughts, experiences about the books that you are reading and the crafty book club experience.

RECOMMENDED READING FOR CROCHET BOOK CLUBS

- **Crochet Saved My Life** by Kathryn Vercillo. This is my own non-fiction book about the health benefits of crochet. It includes my story of crafting through depression, the stories of many other women who crocheted to heal and research into the mental and physical benefits of crafting. It's a great discussion starter!
- **Hooked for Life: Adventures of a Crochet Zealot** by Mary Beth Temple. This is a collection of essays about the crochet life. It has a great sense of humor to it, which is great for breaking the ice with a new crafting group!
- **Love in Every Stitch by Lee Gant**. This is a selection of stories about "knitting and healing" that also includes some crochet stories.
- **Yes! By Deborah Burnside**. This is a young adult novel about two boys who start a crochet business together. Many adults enjoy YA novels because they are easy and heartwarming reads, making this a good non-controversial choice for a book club.
- **The Betty Hechtman crochet mystery series**. You can have a whole book club around these books or you could just include one or two in the rotation of reading.
- **Dying to Crochet by Bendy Carter.** This is a book in the same style as the work of Betty Hechtman.
- **The Crochet Woman: A Novel** by Ruth Manning Sanders. This is a vintage book from the 1930s about an evil queen who uses her crochet work to cast spells. It may be tough to get your hands on enough affordable copies for your group but could be worth a try.
- **Crafty Girls Talk** by Jennifer Forest. Although not strictly a crochet book this collection of essays by women sharing their crafty lives makes for a great group read.
- **One Plastic Bag: Isatou Ceesay and The Recycling Women of the Gambia** by Miranda Paul. This is a children's book, a true story about plastic bag crochet saving a village. It's a short read and can be a charming, whimsical selection for a crochet book club.

Relationships Exercise #8: Crafting Family Tree

The exercise: Research your family tree as it applies to crafts.

The purpose: Feel connected to the generations before and after you by exploring the history of craft in your own family.

In depth: What has happened in the generations before us filters down through our lineage and impacts us in ways both big and small. What we carry forward with us can greatly impact the generations to come. (*If this is a topic that interests you, do some research into "intergenerational trauma"*). One of the things that we can do to heal our relationships with ancestors is to celebrate the little things that we do have in common, despite any major family differences that may exist. Crafting is one of those things. A crafty family tree can be a great legacy to pass on to your children and grandchildren so that they can see the hands-on artistic bloodline that they come from.

Exercise steps:

1. **Draft out your basic family tree** as you know it. If you aren't sure how to do this, you'll find ample resources online to get started. You can keep it very simple.
2. **Does anyone in your family crochet**? Think about who taught you or memories that you might have of family members crocheting. Make a note of those on the family tree.
3. Does anyone in your family do any **other yarncrafting or needlework**? Knitting, sewing, and embroidery are all common things that someone in the family might know how to do. Add those to your family tree.
4. **Now how about any other crafts**? Woodworking, painting, boat building ... you can expand the categories as far as you want to explore what creative things were done in your own family.
5. **Dig deeper** into researching your family's crafty history. Ask other family members what they know about the crafting that was done. Add this information to your crafty family tree.
6. **Make a creative version** of your family tree based on craft lineage. Your first family tree will show the lineage of you with children below you and parents above you. Rearrange the

information to show how crafts were passed down through the generations. Which ones did only boys do? Only girls? Perhaps your aunt was your "crafty mother" who passed crochet down to you? Draw as many connections as you can to create a display for your family tree that resonates with you.

Tips:

- Keep the tree simple in terms of who was who. Most family tree resources ask for birth and death dates and other details but you don't need that information when you're making a crafty family tree. This is a version focused on creativity.
- When exploring memories, try to think of what people did in their free time but also what they did for a living and how they helped the family around the house. In generations past, mothers mended everyone's socks; it may have been a necessity but it was also a crafty skill.
- You can add people to your family tree that are honorary members through crafting. For example, a schoolteacher might have taught you to crochet. If that means a lot to you, give her a branch on your crafting family tree! We have birth families but that's not all that "family" means.

Taking it further: Make a version of the crafty tree that you can pass down to the generations younger than you. This might be a scrapbook that includes photos of various craft work, for example. This can make an amazing gift, especially for someone else in the family who has budding artistic tendencies. Alternatively, consider making a big visual tree in crochet, with a crochet leaf for each member. You can label the leaves using fabric paint.

Yarn for Thought: More Musings on Crafting in Relationships

- What does it mean when you craft for others? How does the receiving of a handmade gift shape your self image? What happens inside of you when you feel that something you made is not appreciated by the person that you made it for?
- Where do you lose yourself in relationships? How do you find yourself in relationships?
- Do you believe in the curse of the boyfriend sweater? (This is a knitter's legend; you can look it up if you're not familiar with it.) Why or why not? What else might explain this phenomenon?
- What is your experience of crafting with others? Have you had any bad experiences? Great ones? What would be your ideal crafting group?
- During what phase of your relationships has crafting lessened or stopped? And when does it tend to grow and soar? How can you harness that energy to craft the way that you want to?
- What does your crafting right now say about your current relationships? For example, if you are in a lull with your creative work, is it because you're too busy having fun in your relationship and are getting artistic sustenance there or is it because there is something in your primary relationship that is draining you? This is an important area to pay attention to because it can alert you to warning signs through your crafting that things are "off" in a relationship.
- Write a letter to your partner thanking them for the ways in which they support your craft. Let them know that you appreciate the time, space, money, and energy that is given to your crafting.
- Do you need to have a serious or difficult conversation with a loved one? Try crocheting through the crafting experience. The act of crochet is soothing and rhythmic and can help bring your anxiety down so that you can have a calm conversation. It may be important to let the other person know why you are doing this so that they don't think that you're not paying attention!

Giving Back

One of the most common pieces of advice that I have seen again and again in all of my reading about depression is that there is value in helping others. Get yourself out of your own head and do something for someone else in order to help yourself feel better. And while I think that there are some caveats to this advice, in general, I believe that it works. I have certainly heard firsthand many reports of people who have depression that is linked to not feeling useful anymore and who are able to use their crochet to reduce that feeling.

There are so many reasons that we can feel useless, especially in a society that values constant productivity, seemingly endless energy and wealth-earning as signs that we are worthwhile people. Even if we don't believe that ourselves, it is a thought that can seep in and affect our self-worth. Chronic illness, whether physical or mental, often causes us to have to take more downtime than we would like. We have to rest, and sometimes we can't do the things we'd like to do in our work or in our families. An illness or disability may require taking time off of work or ending traditional work all together. Degenerative diseases and aging in general can slowly and steadily take away all of the things that we were once able to do so easily and can make us feel like we no longer hold any value in our society, our community or even our own family. Finding a way to give back to others can significantly reverse this trauma to our self-worth - and crochet can definitely be one way that we give back to others.

Giving back to others through crochet can be very simple and straightforward. It can be as small as making crochet gifts for the people in our lives. But it can be more than this as well. Crocheting for charity can help us heal in our own lives while giving a gift to others, especially when we crochet for a charity that has a cause close to our own hearts. Crocheting for people who have just dealt with tragedy, such as loss in the face of natural disaster, can be a way that we help ourselves to handle the difficult emotions of living in a scary world while also directly helping the people impacted by the tragedy. And crochet can also be used in the form of craftivism to give back to the world in ways that align with our most deeply held philosophies about how we should be living, raising awareness about important issues while we practice what we preach.

The Mandalas for Marinke remembrance project that I started in 2015 has been all of these things for me - a way to heal from my own grief while giving others a place for that healing as well, a way to build community and a way to raise awareness about depression, mental health issues and suicide. In June 2015 crochet designer and author Marinke Slump, who was an online friend of mine, succumbed to suicide after a long battle with depression (related in part to her diagnosis of Asperger's). In the wake of that loss, I was emotionally devastated, adrift with sadness about losing her and confusion about feeling so sad when we were "only" online friends. I was scared about the feelings it brought up in me about my own history of depression and suicidal feelings and I was worried about the many, many other crochet friends I know who cope with these painful feelings. I created the Mandalas for Marinke project, a collaborative art project with a huge depression awareness component, because I felt like I *needed* to do something to channel my own experience, and also because I wanted to give the people in my community something tangible to do with their difficult feelings in the aftermath of the news about Marinke. It was my way of self-healing through giving back, and it is an ongoing process that continues to raise awareness about depression.

Now that sounds like a really big project, and it is, and I'm proud of what it's accomplished already - mostly through the huge generosity of the hundreds of crafters around the world who donated their skills, their yarn creations, their thoughts and their stories to help raise awareness. But don't let that trick you into thinking that it was all a selfless effort easily completed because of a drive to raise awareness. In those early days after hearing about Wink's death, the project was hugely about healing for myself. It was about needing to reach out to my community because I needed their support. I got that support through offering the project as a means of support for everyone but it was as much my own safety net as anyone's. Throughout the summer, there were many, many, many days when I did little that appeared productive, needing to just sit on the couch with a million colors of cozy yarn around me and crochet the same style of mandala over and over again. I practiced some of the meditative crochet techniques here and there and they were helpful but mostly I just needed to have that rhythmic experience of soothing stitching going on beneath my fingertips. And for me, it was helpful that the mandalas had a purpose, rather than just collecting in stacks around me for "no reason".

I actually don't believe that any crochet at all is for "no reason". I believe that even if you make a million granny squares that never become anything or you make, frog and re-make the same blanket ten thousand times, you've done exactly what you needed to do to heal. There is value in that. But I also get tricked by society's messages about needing to be productive, and it can be helpful for me to be able to use my crochet to give back in some way. In this case, the mandalas had a purpose in my project. During other times, I've crocheted blankets and scarves and other items for charity - giving them to projects that donate much-needed items to children, hospitals, the homeless, The Special Olympics and various other populations. It helps me feel like my crochet is not just healing me but can be an ongoing gift that spreads that love throughout the world. And that feeling further heals me.

So this chapter is about ways that you can give back through crochet, whether that's in giving to one other person, giving to charity or giving to the world through craftivism and awareness-raising projects. It is about healing others in our community because doing this heals each of us as well.

Giving Back Exercise #1: Crochet for a Charity

The exercise: Crochet an item for charity.

The purpose: Infuse your work with meaning by making items for people in need.

In depth: There is something really special about setting out at the start of a project with an intention about where that item will go and how it will help someone else. It makes each stitch feel more powerful, transforming the making of a simple item into something hugely special.

Exercise steps:

1. **Identify a charity** that is meaningful for you. (You will find a list of possible charities in the resource section at the end of this book.)
2. **Get familiar** with the rules and regulations of what they accept in terms of handmade donations. Some charities are very open to a wide array of items while others have very strict specifications about sizing, yarn to be used and even patterns. You want what you make to be useful.
3. **Crochet a single item** for that charity. You can always make more later but set your sights small to begin with so that it is a do-able activity.
4. **Prepare the package** to be donated. You might include a special note sharing why you've donated, for example.
5. **Send it off!**

Tips:

- Think about the things in your own life that have been difficult and/ or meaningful and look for charities that are related to that. My dad is an organ transplant survivor, I am a former foster mother and my whole family is concerned about pet welfare so these are the types of charities that I look towards myself but each person has their own interests, causes and concerns, which is what makes this work meaningful.
- Use the skills practiced in making prayer shawls and intentional crafting when crocheting items for charity.
- If you are on social media, don't hesitate to photograph and share what you are donating and why. This helps spread the message about causes that you care about!

Taking it further: Donate locally and in-person! There are plenty of national and even international charities with great causes that you can support. But there is something truly unique about the experience of taking a handcrafted item directly to the hospital, home, school, shelter or other setting and giving it directly to the recipient.

Giving Back Exercise #2: Teach Someone to Crochet

The exercise: Give someone else the basic skills of crochet.

The purpose: Help someone to heal by teaching the craft to them so that they can use it themselves.

In depth: That saying about teaching a man to fish holds true in crafting ... It is certainly wonderful to give a crochet item to an individual in need but the power is magnified when you teach a person to crochet!

Exercise steps:

1. **Identify a person or group** of people you believe could benefit from crafting. This could be one individual that you know or a general population of people; (some examples are provided below).
2. **Gain some basic skills** in teaching crochet to others. You can practice with a family member. (See some resources in the tips below.)

3. **Schedule a teaching session.** Bring all of the supplies that you and the student will need to make it easiest on the student.
4. **Begin to teach crochet.** As you do this, explain why you have found it to be so valuable. This encourages the student to keep at it even if it's not easy at first.

POPULATIONS THAT BENEFIT FROM LEARNING CROCHET

Almost any individual can benefit from learning how to crochet. It is an activity that reduces stress, provides a skill, boosts self-esteem, and helps with a variety of other conditions. Just a few examples of populations you might consider if you're seeking to teach crochet to individuals or groups include:

- At-risk children and teens
- Individuals with learning disabilities
- People in physical therapy, especially for conditions related to hands and arms
- The elderly in nursing homes
- Caregivers
- Mothers-to-be and new mothers
- Substance users in recovery
- Inmates including kids in juvenile detention
- People living in shelters including homeless shelters and domestic violence shelters
- Individuals working in high-stress jobs

Tips:

- Don't worry if you find it a little hard to teach someone else to crochet. Just because you do something well doesn't mean you'll immediately take to teaching it. There are some good resources out there to help you including the Crochet Teaching Guide by the Craft Yarn Council and Teaching a Child to Crochet by The Crochet Guild of America (CGOA). *You'll find links to both of these in the resources at the end of this book.*
- Be liberal with praise and minimal with corrections. This is all about sharing the love of the craft and the way that it heals, not about making perfect products or creating advanced students.

- Don't take it personally if someone doesn't take to the craft right away. You never know what seed you might have planted that the person will remember down the line.

Taking it further: Start your own crochet workshop, regularly teaching others to craft for the joy of the process and the healing it offers!

Giving Back Exercise #3: Donate Supplies

The exercise: Donate yarn, crochet hooks and other craft supplies to groups in need.

The purpose: Help others to be able to heal themselves through crafting with the generosity of your donation.

In depth: There are many people out there who already know how to crochet and who benefit from the craft but who don't have the supplies available to them to make it a regular activity. By gifting them with those supplies, you make it possible for them to heal themselves and perhaps others through crochet.

Exercise steps:

1. **Identify a population** in need of craft supplies; the list above in Exercise Two might give you some ideas.
2. **Contact the individual** who may need the supplies, which is often a coordinator such as a teacher, counselor or house manager. Ask them specifically what they need in terms of supplies.
3. **Put together a care package** of supplies. Make sure that all supplies meet the regulations learned about in Step Two. (For example, you might have to make sure the yarn you send comes from a pet-free, smoke-free home.)
4. **Ship** or take the donation to its new home!

Tips:

- Don't skip the step of finding out exactly what a group needs. Many groups have strict requirements about what they can and can't accept and you don't want this donation to go to waste!

- Donate in person if possible. It helps you to see that your donation is going somewhere that it is really going to be useful to others.
- Choose a population that is related to a cause that you care about. For example, if you are concerned about the rights of the elderly then perhaps you'll want to donate to a nursing home.

Taking it further: Donate your supplies to a group of people who will be using the yarn to crochet items for charity. One example is prison crochet programs. These programs typically use donated yarn, which the inmates use to crochet items for local or national charities. This gives the inmates the benefit of learning a skill, using their time productively, de-stressing, working with others and giving back to the community through their donation. Your donation of yarn goes first to helping this population and then to helping those they donate finished items to after they've made them.

Giving Back Exercise #4: Yarnbombing to Raise Awareness

The exercise: Leave a yarnbomb with a message that matters to you.

The purpose: Use your crochet skills to beautify the world around you while raising awareness about an issue that is close to your heart.

In depth: Yarnbombing is the act of leaving a handmade knit or crochet item in a public place. In this exercise, you attach a tag with a message on it that people can read to learn more about a cause that matters to you. You get their attention with the unexpected beauty of your yarn creation that jumps out at them in a public place and then you focus that attention on your message.

Exercise steps:

- **Crochet a yarnbomb.** This could be as simple as a heart or flower or something larger like a bike rack cozy.
- **Add a tag with a message** about the cause that you care about. You might use your yarnbombing to raise awareness about environmental issues, animal rights, suicide prevention, health care, or even a local issue such as a particular proposition that you care about.

- **Identify the right location** for your yarnbomb. You should place it in a spot where it can be seen by the people you want to target with your message. For example, a positive message about fighting cyberbullying might be well-placed on a stop sign at the crosswalk near a local high school.
- **Hang your yarnbomb**, preferably at eye level.
- **Photograph your yarnbomb** and share it on social media. This spreads the message further than just your local block!

Tips:

- Some people are uncomfortable yarnbombing because it means placing items in public spaces without permission. This fear doesn't have to stop you. A yarnbomb can go on your own property (a mailbox, a bicycle). You can also get permission from homeowners, business owners and city officials to place yarnbombs legally. And you can place small yarn bombs on community bulletin boards where fliers go. You can also get creative - a yarnbomb can be a crocheted bookmark left inside of a library book when you return it.
- Keep your message short and sweet. You don't want to leave paragraphs; slogans have more of an immediate impact. If you want people to have more information, include a website URL where they can get that info.
- Try to phrase your message in a positive way. For example, "Animals smile when you eat veggies" is more likely to jar people into thinking differently about meat-eating than "don't eat meat".

Taking it further: Participate in large scale community yarnbombing activities. These are increasingly popular and can often be found online through social media. The Peyton Heart Project (https://www.facebook.com/ThePeytonHeartProject) is an example from 2015. This project, which is a division of the Sidewalk Smiles Campaign to raise suicide prevention awareness, was created in the name of Peyton James, a 13 year old who was bullied for years and died by suicide in 2014. It encourages people to leave yarnbomb hearts everywhere with inspiring quotes to reduce bullying and raise awareness about teen suicide. The yarnbombs include the #PeytonHeartProject hashtag, helping to spread the word to make it a worldwide project. These types of large-scale yarnbombing activities can have a huge impact, and it can be beneficial to the people who participate to yarnbomb in a way that is bigger than themselves.

Giving Back Exercise #5: Charity Crochet Group

The exercise: Crochet for charity with a group.

The purpose: Amplify your charity crochet efforts by working together with others.

In depth: There are numerous benefits to crocheting in a group, not the least of which is that you provide one another with social support. Crocheting for charity together gives your group a solid sense of purpose, a mission and a reason to come together that strengthens the bonds you share and the benefits you offer, not only to one another but to the community around you.

Exercise steps:

1. **Create a crochet group**. You may already have one. You may be able to access an existing one, such as a group already crafting together at the local yarn store. Or you may need to get a group of crafters together anew.
2. **Brainstorm a list of charities** that you would like to support. Allow everyone to have input as you come together to find common causes that you care about. (The charity list in the resources at the end of this book can provide a starting point.)
3. **Select the first group** that you're going to make items for. Contact that group to find out what items they accept for donation and what, if any, rules they have about those donations.
4. **Set a goal together as a group**. Each person might make one blanket or one square of a blanket, whatever works for your group. You might have a goal of the number of items to complete and a deadline by which you'll send the donation.
5. **Meet regularly** to complete your work and meet your goal. Many groups do some of the work on their own time and some together. Joining motifs is especially popular as a group activity instead of on your own!

6. **Prepare the package** for donation. You might all pitch in for shipping costs or you might all go together to donate the items locally.
7. **Repeat** Steps 3-6!

Tips:

- Groups that can't agree on common charities might allow each person in the group to choose one charity. The whole group might work together on one charity then the next until everyone's charity receives a group donation. Alternatively, each individual in the group might come together physically to craft but work on their own individual donation to the charity of their choosing.
- It is helpful to have a few clear guidelines for the group. Meeting times and frequency, location of the meetings (including whether these rotate or not), amount of commitment required to stay in the group, if and when to allow new members ... each group will have its own rules and some will be stricter than others. Let the group decide this together!
- You can enhance step six by having each person in the group package their own contribution, wrapping it in tissue paper and including a note for the recipient. In some cases, each individual might add an additional donation. For example, each person might include a small handmade or store-bought teddy bear with a prayer shawl donation.

Taking it further: Encourage conversation among the group about the issues related to the charity that you are crafting together for. Each person might do a check-in, sharing why they are happy to give to this specific charity. You might have guest speakers on the topic, such as a NICU nurse if you are donating to preemie babies. Make the whole experience of crafting together fun, meaningful and even educational!

Giving Back Exercise #6: Slow Yarn!

The exercise: Become a part of the Slow Yarn movement.

The purpose: Give back to the world through eco-friendly, simple living practices that are infused into your crafting lifestyle.

In depth: The Slow Movement, as the name suggests, is an intentional shift towards a slower-paced way of life. It is about sustainability, supporting local economy and getting hands-on in every step of a process. Many people know about it because of the Slow Food movement, but it can be applied to crafting as well. Crocheting items yourself is already one step on the Slow Yarn path (because you're engaged in the hands-on making of an item instead of running to the store to purchase it). But crafters can take this to the next level in many ways.

Exercise steps:

NOTE: *In this exercise, unlike most of the exercises in this book, the steps aren't necessarily all required or to be done in order. They are each steps that can be done individually as part of a total Slow Yarn change in your life.*

1. **Sourcing ethical fiber**. The first step in getting yarn is getting the fiber that makes the yarn. If you're really, really into the Slow Yarn movement then this can mean raising your own fiber farm plants and animals. If you can't go that far right now, you can still source your yarn ethically. Slow Yarn is yarn that is raised, spun and dyed locally using sustainable, eco-friendly practices. The book *Knit Local* by Tanis Gray is a great resource for people interested in a better understanding of the history and working philosophies of local yarn sellers.
2. **Spinning your own yarn**. Slow yarn is about doing as much of the yarn process yourself, before you even get to the process of crocheting with it. Turning fiber into yarn through spinning, whether with a drop spindle or a spinning wheel, is one of those steps. You can purchase yarn roving (using the same ethical practices outlined in Step One for sourcing any yarn). Yarn spinning is an entire craft on its own, with a ton of information out there, and it can be a great adjunct craft to your world of crochet.
3. **Dyeing your own yarn**. Likewise, dyeing your own yarn is a great way to slow the process down and be more hands-on with your craftwork. Slow Yarn encourages the use of ethically-sourced natural materials for dyeing, of course. There are some great resources available for using foods and plants for natural dyeing. One good option is *Harvesting Color: How to Find Plants and Make Natural Dyes* by Rebecca Burgess.

4. **Recycling and upcycling.** Slow Yarn can also be about upcycling in your work, making use of existing materials in your crochet. This can be done at any stage of the crochet process. For example, you can recycle old t-shirts, sheets, clothing, plastic bags, wire, bicycle tire tubes and a variety of other materials and make yarn with them, using that yarn to crochet. Alternatively, you can source sustainable Slow Yarn and use it to upcycle other items - turning old pillows into new cushions, making greeting cards into bunting, repurposing Mason Jars into cozy-covered organizers and so much more.

Tips:

- Start anywhere. You don't have to make huge changes to start practicing Slow Yarn, just a few little tweaks to your eco-conscious crafting practices will do. Check labels, take a yarn dyeing class, read more about The Slow Movement.
- Consider each step to be its own craft as well as part of your love of crochet. You may discover that you love spinning or dyeing yarn as much as crocheting with it! Each of these things has its own healing properties - and own communities of enthusiasts!
- Practice slowing down and meditating in every step of the process. Slow Yarn is about total mindful engagement with your craft - and your life!
- You can combine Slow Yarn with the previous exercise on yarnbombing by making a yarnbomb (using earth-friendly bio-degradable materials, of course) with an informative tag on Slow Yarn attached.

Taking it further: There is really no end to how far you can go with your immersion into the Slow Yarn movement. It might start with just being aware of making small changes - purchasing only organic cotton yarn instead of the non-organic kind, for example - and then eventually lead into owning your own fiber farm and doing everything from scratch! A small step can lead big places.

Giving Back Exercise #7: Support Fair Trade Crochet

The exercise: Make purchases from organizations that sell fair trade crochet items.

The purpose: Support others who are engaging in the crochet practices that are better for the world.

In depth: Fair Trade Crochet items are handmade crochet items that are created by people, usually women, in developing nations who are paid a fair, living wage for their work. The companies that are engaged in making Fair Trade Crochet are helping these women to use their artisan skills to gain independence, support their families, improve their quality of life and raise global awareness about the conditions where they live. When you purchase items from these people, you help.

Exercise steps:

1. **Identify an organization** that sells Fair Trade Crochet items. (You'll find a partial list of companies I'm aware of at the back of this book.)
2. **Research the company's mission**, philosophies, practices and history. You want to support organizations that are truly in line with your own beliefs.
3. **Find a product** that they offer that you truly want to own (or gift to someone). Buy items you believe in from businesses that you believe in.
4. **Spread the word**. If this is a gift, include a note about why you've chosen it. If it's for you, take photographs and include information about it on your social media accounts.

Tips:

- Avoid the trap of thinking, "but I can make it myself". It is so important that we support one another in this community, buying items from other crafters including Fair Trade Crochet. It does not take away from what you make yourself; it adds to the entire community of makers. I personally don't like to make amigurumi or wire crochet (even though I can) so I purchase that from other talented makers. And sometimes I purchase crocheted items that I can and do make just because I really love what the person has made or what their business is all about. Really can't bring yourself to buy crochet since you can make it instead? Buy other handmade and Fair Trade items then - knitwear, ceramics, jewelry, etc. Buy what other people are putting their hands and hearts into!

- Send a note of thanks to the maker. Many of the Fair Trade Crochet companies have information about the people who are making the items that you are buying. Feel free to write them an email or send a card thanking them for their efforts. These little gestures mean a lot!
- Pay attention to crowdsourced funding opportunities for Fair Trade artisans. They pop up on sites like Indiegogo and Kickstarter from time to time and this is another way that you can support them.

Taking it further: Engage in the practice of "artistic tithing" in which you commit a certain amount of all of your earnings towards paying it forward by making purchases from other handcrafters and artisans. You can commit to spending that money on Fair Trade Crochet or even just buying it from other individual crafters like yourself. If you needed an excuse to spend more money on things you want on Etsy, artistic tithing is a great reason!

Yarn for Thought: More Musings on Giving Back Through Crochet

- How does helping others help yourself? What are some examples of experiences you've had where your life improved because you were giving to others?
- Make a list of causes and issues that you care about. Consider how crochet can help.
- Who are some of the people who have helped you along the way? How did their generosity improve your life? What can you do to pay it forward?
- One of the creative affirmations that Julia Cameron offers is, "my creativity heals myself and others". What does this mean to you?
- Where do you make most of your purchases? How could you alter your spending habits to be more in line with Slow Living practices and supporting the community of people out there who are making things by hand?

Balance

We are almost at the end of our book (with just one more section after this on taking things further artistically) and it occurs to me that many of the exercises in this book appear to contradict one another. You are asked to be organized and then to be messy, to be logical and then to be whimsical, to let go of things and then to collect things, to make it all yourself and then to buy things other people are making, to create space for crafting in solitude and to join in with crafty groups. That's because life isn't one way or the other. Life isn't about extremes. Life is all about balance.

We need different things at different times in our lives. Heck, we have changing energy levels that mean we need different things at different times on the same day! We need to be alone and we need to be with people, we need to give attention to ourselves and we need to care for others, we need to focus on individual healing and we need to heal our communities, we need to be simple and we need to be complex. Each chapter, and each exercise, in this book is designed to bring out a different element of yourself to meet a different need that you may have at any given time. Sometimes you'll need one type more than the other and sometimes you'll have to repeat the same thing again and again until you get what you need. That's all okay. You can trust yourself in this.

When I think about what my parents gave to me in terms of life skills, I realize that their divergent ways of living actually brought me the thing I needed most - balance. My parents are mostly hugely different from one another. My mom is a busy, busy woman, always on the go, working jobs even after she "retired" and always with a long list of half-started projects in the works. My dad loves to stay busy and never exactly does "nothing" but he does it all slowly and methodically, one project at a time with breaks for reading over coffee. Though they are both usually doing something, I would describe my mom as active and my dad as engaged. When my mom and I sit and talk, the TV is usually on and one or both of us is multi-tasking - crafting or playing a card game or sorting through "junk". When my dad and I sit and talk, the only thing he might be doing besides listening is strumming a guitar. They have a few things in common; I get my voracious appetite for books from both of them - but mostly they are very different. They often have opposite viewpoints and opposite styles of expressing them. And although that was sometimes confusing as a kid, it has been the biggest asset to me as an adult. I always see two points of view to everything and always feel that two opposite ways of doing things can be as completely valid as one another. It has served me well in my work and in my relationships.

My way of growing up has allowed me to see fairly clearly that there is never just one side to a story and that truth usually lies not just in the middle of two different opinions but somewhere in the nuances around each possible version of a truth. Of course, it is a lot easier to see this when I am looking at my parents' stories or the actions of others. It is not as easy to remember in the midst of fighting for my own version of a story - when something I think is so true is really just part of the truth. Not easy ... but so important. The more that I am able to look at a situation and see that what I think may be true isn't the end-all-and-be-all truth of the situation, the better off I am. When I can see the other truths in any given conversation, I feel more at peace. I feel more compassion for everyone's version of events and the roles they played in them. I feel happier.

Crochet can help us learn to meet in the middle. Crochet can remind us that there are two (or more) ways of looking at the same thing. Crochet can show us that one piece of the puzzle is not enough for a whole picture. The exercises in this chapter are all variations on exploring these concepts through yarn.

Balance Exercise #1: Same Item, Different Yarn

The exercise: Crochet any item of your choosing. Crochet the same item again in a different yarn.

The purpose: Make two versions of the same item to acknowledge that neither way is better than the other.

In depth: We often think that there is a "right" way to do things. People who love to follow crochet patterns are especially prone to thinking that the pattern's way is the right way. But really, there are just options, not "right" ways.

Exercise steps:

1. **Choose a pattern** for an item to crochet. Ideally select an item where gauge is not important.
2. **Make the crochet item** to the exact specifications of the pattern, including the yarn that is used. Set it aside.
3. **Make a second version** of the item following the same pattern but using a different yarn. You may choose a yarn of the same

weight or a different weight; a different weight will obviously give more variation to the two items.

4. **Place the two finished items side by side**. Is one really "better" or "more right" than the other? You can challenge this by showing both items to others (in person or online) and asking which they like better; don't tell them which is the "correct" version.

Tips:

- Change the yarn type dramatically to see big differences, change just the color for a small difference.
- Be daring and make a mismatched set to use - one fingerless glove in Yarn A and one in Yarn B - then wear one of each at the same time!
- Notice what comes up for you as you work two versions of the same thing; consider how this relates to maintaining balance.

Taking it further: Work this exercise multiple times, making five or six different versions of the same item. Change the yarn color, weight, fiber and explore all options. You might find that something you make using the "wrong" yarn is actually what you like better. This is great exploration (reminding us of the chapter on adventure) and also shows you a sense of balance in terms of knowing that there's not a "right" way, just a way.

Balance Exercise #2: Holding Your Hook

The exercise: Compare the way you hold your hook to others.

The purpose: This reinforces the notion that there is no "one right way".

In depth: People will tell you that there are only two ways to hold a crochet hook (knife or pencil grip) and some will even tell you that one way is better than the other. Not true! We often think that we do things "wrong" and we criticize ourselves for it. Maintaining balance and offering ourselves reminders that there are "many ways" not "one way" help to counter these mistaken ideas and rebuild our self-esteem. This exercise shows that there are many, many ways to hold a crochet hook.

Exercise steps:

1. Have someone **take photographs** or videos of your hands, close-up, while you crochet.
2. Do an online search to **find images** of the basic "knife grip" vs. "pencil grip" in crochet. Which one are you? (You might have your own style that's not quite either; that's totally okay! - Which are you closest to?)
3. Now do an **online image search** for those in your category (either knife or pencil grip, as determined in Step Two). Look closely at the differences between each image. Is yours similar to any? How is it different? *NOTE: You can see a roundup of some examples on the Moogly blog at* http://www.mooglyblog.com/how-you-hold-your-hook-and-yarn-the-results/.
4. **Ask your craft group** or online friends to all share photos of how they crochet. You may discover that people you respect craft-wise crochet in an entirely different (or the same!) way that you do.
5. **Marvel** at our similarities and differences, at the adaptations people make for various reasons, even in something so simple as how to hold a crochet hook.

Tips:

- Try to stay as natural as possible when crocheting while photos are being taken so you don't alter the images unintentionally.
- Try taking photographs with different types of hooks and while doing different types of projects. You may be surprised to discover that you don't even always hold your own hook the same way!
- Look at both left-handed and right-handed crochet images in your search to see how different people hold their crochet hooks.
- Explore some of the ways that people have adapted to holding a crochet hook when they don't have full use, or even any use, of their hands. There are many inspiring stories online about people crocheting with their feet, with assistive devices and more.

Taking it further: Practice crocheting "the other way". This might mean switching from a basic knife grip to a form of pencil grip. Alternatively it can mean crocheting with the opposite hand (left if you're a rightie). This reinforces that the way you're doing it is perfectly right for you (since this other way is probably going to feel uncomfortable). And it also reminds you that there is balance in the world - many people crochet in a variety of different ways and we all make the same basic things!

Balance Exercise #3: One Item, One Change

<u>The exercise</u>: Crochet the same item as a friend with one minor difference.

<u>The purpose</u>: Everyone can do the same thing, a little bit differently, and produce unique items.

<u>In depth</u>: By making one small tweak to a crochet pattern, you give it your own personal sense of style. When someone else makes their own change, you each have the same item but done a little bit differently, and you can see that there is value in this self-expression. It is another variation on the "no right way" concept.

<u>Exercise steps</u>:

1. **Ask a friend** to participate in this exercise with you.
2. **Select a crochet pattern** that you both want to make (the same pattern will be used by both of you).
3. Agree that you will each **make one small change** to the pattern, but don't tell each other what the change is. (See some options below for changing a pattern.)
4. **Set about making your own items individually**. Come together when you are finished and exchange items. See if you can identify the change that the other person made.
5. **Place the items side by side**. Take turns with each of you saying what you like best about the other person's change and also what you like best about your own.

OPTIONS FOR CHANGING A PATTERN

- Use a different color of yarn. You may make one color change or many. You may make a solid colored project into a multi-colored one or vice versa.
- Use a different type of yarn (weight or fiber).
- Use a different sized hook.

- Make it shorter or longer by changing the number of row increases/repeats.
- Add a border of your own choosing

Tips:

- Make sure to compliment yourself and your partner equally. This is not about someone doing it "better". Maintain balance in this.
- Make sure the change doesn't impact the functionality of the final project. So if gauge matters then make sure that you get the right gauge for the project.

Taking it further: Get an entire craft group to do this exercise together! One option is for everyone to crochet the same square pattern, but with their own change, and for the group to put it all together into a blanket at the end. Each square is unique and "right" in its own way, and it all comes together in a balanced project.

Balance Exercise #4: Four-Handed Crochet Project

The exercise: Work on a crochet project with someone else, each working from the middle outwards.

The purpose: You will each be creating half of the item and will have to establish balance between you to make it work.

In depth: When you and another person work on the same project at the same time, there is a lot to be figured out in terms of balance. There is the logistical balance of how you're going to sit, especially when the project is small at the beginning, to each be able to crochet simultaneously. And there is the balance of growing each side at approximately the same pace.

Exercise steps:

1. **Select a crochet project** that can be grown by working on opposite sides of the same foundation chain. A simple long scarf or blanket is ideal. This works best with projects that simply repeat the same stitch over and over - a V-stitch, a chevron stripe or even a simple half double crochet is a good choice.
2. **One person** should crochet the foundation chain and first row.

3. **Hand the work off** to the second person and they will crochet their first row on the opposite side.
4. **Sit as close together** as possible, knees to knees, and try to crochet your second rows at the same time as each other, with person A working on the "right side" of the foundation chain and person B on the opposite side.
5. **Continue growing your rows**. Make adjustments as necessary to maintain balance throughout the project. This may mean one person has to slow down to adapt to the other's pace. It may mean that you scoot further apart at times. It may mean taking breaks when you don't really want to because the other person needs a break. It's all about maintaining balance between you to the end of the project.

Tips:

- You can truly see the balance (and imbalance) in the process if each person uses a different color of yarn on their side.
- Try to make Step Two above work. If you really can't do it then each person should crochet a few more rows individually on their sides, taking turns, to create a piece wide enough to give you space between each other to be able to work your hands together simultaneously.
- Expect frustration and don't allow it to come between you two. It's irritating when you craft slow and your partner crafts fast, but it can teach you a lot about yourself (and how you handle relationships) if you work towards keeping that balance!

Taking it further: Repeat this exercise with a much more complex pattern. You'll still need a pattern that is symmetrical, of course, but one with more stitch changes, color changes, increasing/decreasing, etc. will add to your challenge level and force you to work even harder on balance.

Balance Exercise #5: Many Hands, One Project

The exercise: Take turns crocheting row by row with one or more other people.

The purpose: Many hands make one final balanced project.

In depth: In this exercise, you will crochet together in a relay fashion, passing the work off to one another to take turns with it. However, during the time when you are not crocheting, you stay engaged in the making process. This challenges you in ways similar to Exercise Four, forcing you to work at someone else's pace, accept their way of doing things, etc., which is a great exercise in balancing your methods with someone else's!

Exercise steps:

1. **Choose an individual or group** to work with you on this collaborative project.
2. Agree on a row-based or round-based **crochet pattern** to follow (as opposed to one where you make motifs).
3. **Agree on an order** for the work. This is easy if it is just two of you but you may need to draw names from a hat to get your order in a group.
4. **Person A crochets** the foundation chain and row or round one. All other individuals watch the work and engage with the process. Engagement may mean talking about the project as it grows or it may mean simply sitting and meditating quietly on your experience of what is happening as others craft.
5. **The work gets passed** to the next person to complete the next row. The engagement/ meditation continues.
6. **Repeat step five** through until each person in the group has done their row. When the final person in the group has completed their row, it goes back to the first person.
7. **Continue repeating** until the work is complete.
8. **Take turns** weaving in ends until the project is completely finished.

Tips:

- Notice any judgments that you have about the way others are crafting. Work with these inside of yourself; it's about you, not them.
- Notice when your mind wanders. How does it feel to sit and do nothing while someone else crochets their row? How does your contribution of sitting there and holding space help with the final project?

- This exercise might bring up insecurities about your crafting. I'm the first to admit that I don't join yarn "right" (I'm fine with putting knots in my yarn) and also that I'm uncomfortable doing that in a group project where people can be picky about such things. This project is about balance - everyone's way of doing things is okay in this exercise - so work with your inner critic to make it okay for yourself too!

Taking it further: Work with a large group and assign one person to keep everyone on task when it's not "their turn". A good way to do this is to have the person who just finished their row be the "leader" when they hand off the work to the next person, so that the leader always changes. This person can lead conversations or meditations about group work, balance, adjusting to each other's styles, etc.

Balance Exercise #6: Convertible Crochet

The exercise: Crochet a convertible item.

The purpose: This is a tangible reminder that there is more than one way of looking at the same thing.

In depth: Convertible crochet items are designed so that they can be used inside out or in some other way on the body for a second look. Everything can be looked at in at least two different ways, which is a great reminder to have in our lives!

Exercise steps:

1. **Select a convertible crochet project**. There are patterns out there for hats that become cowls, cowls that become purses and shawls that become skirts. Search the term "convertible" on a pattern site and find something you like.
2. **Crochet the item**!
3. **Wear or use** the item the first way.
4. **Wear or use the item** the other way! (It may have more than two options; try them all!)

Tips:

- Take the time to make the item something that you really love, using yarn you treasure so that you will want to use the item again and again.
- Notice if you tend to use the item one way more than the other; try to keep a balance in using it both ways.

Taking it further: Make yourself an entire convertible outfit for a great mix-and-match set. For example, you'll find some three-in-one crochet patterns for an item that can be worn as a long skirt, a short dress and as a poncho. Make that same pattern three times and you'll have a layered outfit that you can wear as a dress-top over a skirt with a poncho. Three items really gives you nine items that you can mix and match together in many, many different ways!

Balance Exercise #7: Reversible Crochet

The exercise: Crochet an item using a reversible crochet technique.

The purpose: Make a crochet item that can be looked at two different ways.

In depth: This is a variation on the convertible crochet exercise. You make one item that is always used the same way (as a blanket, for example) but that can be looked at from either side because it's reversible.

Exercise steps:

1. **Explore reversible crochet techniques**. There are several of them; some (like Laurinda Reddig's Reversible Intarsia Crochet) will look the same from either direction while others (like Tanis Galik's Interlocking Crochet) have a different pattern on either side.
2. **Learn the crochet technique** that you've chosen. This may take a little practice.
3. **Make a reversible crochet item**. Find a crochet pattern that you like or freeform your own design utilizing the reversible crochet technique that you have learned.
4. **Wear or use** the reversible crochet item. Make sure to turn it over and use both sides!

Tips:

- For many people, this exercise involves learning a new technique. Remember that you can go back to what you learned in previous exercises to make this experience more adventurous and helpful to you.
- Reversible crochet items that look the same on either side are a way of tangibly showing that you can get the same results different ways. Reversible crochet projects that look different on either side are a tangible way of showing that doing the same thing can produce two beautifully different results. Both are different types of balance. Figure out which you need more right now.

Taking it further: Try using all of your regular crochet items "the wrong way". In crochet there's a "right side" and a "wrong side" to most patterns, but neither is really wrong, is it? There are many crochet patterns that look interesting on both sides. Crocodile stitch, for example, looks totally different on the "wrong side" but I actually like that side better! Wear your cowls inside out for awhile!

Balance Exercise #8: Symmetrical Crochet

The exercise: Crochet a symmetrical item.

The purpose: Embrace balance in the process of the craft.

In depth: Symmetry is naturally appealing to our visual senses; we are instinctively drawn towards it as a thing of beauty. When we work with symmetry, we experience balance. By crocheting a piece that is designed symmetrically, we feel the balance working in our craft.

Exercise steps:

1. **Select a symmetrical crochet pattern**. Ideally your pattern will be one that allows you to crochet the first side then the second side (rather than working continuously across all rows) but any symmetrical pattern will work. (A granny square, for example, is symmetrical, but since it's worked in rounds instead of first-half, second-half, it won't exude the same feeling of balance as it is worked.)

2. **Crochet the pattern**, with attention towards the symmetry of the piece.
3. **Fold the work in half** on the line of symmetry. Explore the texture and visuals of each side to solidify the sense of balance as you wrap up your project.

Tips:

- Choose a crochet pattern that is worked in an increase and decrease where the second half matches the first half perfectly. Many crochet shawls are designed in this manner. Corner to corner crochet is also worked in this way.
- An alternative option is to crochet a motif based project, laying out the motifs symmetrically by both design and color as you work so that you can see the combination of balance and imbalance as it emerges in the work.

Taking it further: A great way to really get the sense of balance that a symmetrical project provides is to crochet an asymmetrical version of the same type of project in order to compare the two. Alternatively, you could make a symmetrical project, with the first half done in one color and the second half done in a contrasting color. Each of these options gives you a sense of the pleasure of balance compared to the discord of imbalance.

Balance Exercise #9: Crochet a Puzzle

The exercise: Make a crochet puzzle.

The purpose: Create and keep a crochet puzzle project to remind yourself that you need all of your "pieces" for the full picture.

In depth: The missing piece of the puzzle is a great metaphor for the feeling of not being in balance in our lives. Everything else is there but that full picture just isn't complete because something is missing. A crochet puzzle is a tangible representation of this.

Exercise steps:

1. **Crochet nine mini granny squares** that are all the same size.
2. Lay the nine squares out **3x3**.

3. **Crochet a chain** long enough to serve as a border around the edge of the 3x3 square.
4. **Glue the chain down** in this square shape, adhering it to cardboard or something similar.
5. **Lay all nine puzzle pieces** loosely into their spots inside of this square. This is your basic crochet puzzle!
6. **Keep your crochet puzzle** out where you can see it, as a reminder of the need to make sure your life has all of its pieces in place.

Tips:

- There are also crochet puzzle patterns out there that you can try for a more advanced project. Check out the book *Amamani Puzzle Balls* by Dedri Uys, for example.
- Create your own advanced crochet puzzle pattern using graphing software. Stitch Fiddle is one example of an online tool that can help you in your design.
- Take one piece of the puzzle out for a period of time. See if this makes you uncomfortable.

Taking it further: Make a list of all of the aspects of your life that need to be fulfilled in order to feel balanced. Mine is a simple six-point list that involves: attention to my health, financial security, creative explorations, artistic expression, connection with others and connection with myself / spirituality. Your list may be long or short. Stitch the words onto each piece of the puzzle. Use the puzzle regularly to determine where your missing pieces are, removing those items that you feel are lacking and replacing them when you get back in balance. This can be a great daily or weekly practice to remind yourself of the ways in which you can maintain balance.

Balance Exercise #10: Crochet The Missing Piece

The exercise: Make a crochet item with a chunk of the pattern missing.

The purpose: Figure out a creative solution to creating the missing piece of a puzzle.

In depth: The balance achieved through creating a full puzzle (as was done in Exercise Nine above) doesn't always come easily. Sometimes we have to find creative solutions to filling in those gaps. That is what this exercise is all about.

Exercise steps:

1. **Select a crochet pattern.** (See tips below.)
2. **Randomly select a chunk of rows** to delete from the pattern. Cross them out so that you can see where they originally were but know not to use the instructions.
3. **Crochet the first part** of the pattern all the way up to where the deleted rows begin.
4. **Pause. Review the work** that you've already done. Look ahead to the rest of the pattern to get a sense of how the project ends.
5. Come up with **your own creative solution** for the missing rows based on your assessment of the "before" and "after" steps. Crochet those rows.
6. **Resume the pattern** and complete the project.
7. **Review the final product** and determine if there are any additions or alterations that you need to make to finalize the piece. If so, make those now.

Tips:

- Choose a crochet pattern that has a lot of variation over many rows/ rounds and doesn't have an easy repeat stitch pattern.
- When you get to the missing chunk, you do not need to crochet the same number of rows as the original pattern. Your own stitches may be taller or shorter than what was called for in the original pattern so just go with your gut and sense of creativity as you work this "missing piece".

Taking it further: Select a crochet pattern that is worked in many parts, such as a sweater pattern where the front, back, sleeves and finishing are all done separately. Remove a chunk of the pattern from each part of the project and fill in those missing pieces with your creative mind.

Balance Exercise #11: The Opposite of What You Want to Make

<u>The exercise</u>: Crochet something that is the opposite of what you planned.

<u>The purpose</u>: Jolt your brain into considering balance by crocheting opposites.

<u>In depth</u>: We often get into creative ruts where we always want to work the same types of projects, over and over. We get out of balance creatively because we're leaning in the direction of the same thing over and over. By crocheting the complete opposite of this type of project, we help restore balance to our artistic lives.

<u>Exercise steps</u>:

1. **Ask yourself** what you want your next project to be.
2. **Review your work** and examine how often you do this type of project; it's likely that it's often.
3. **Ask yourself** what the exact opposite of that type of project would be.
4. **Find a crochet pattern** for the opposite type of project and make that crochet item instead.

<u>Tips:</u>

- Some of the things that you can look at for finding opposites include hook size, yarn weight, color, function, yarn type, and season of use. If you've been making a bunch of Christmas projects, make one for summer, for example.
- Notice the feelings that come up around this exercise. Many people are irritated by it. Explore why.
- Consider whether this exercise in its totality gives you more or less of a sense of balance in your work.

<u>Taking it further</u>: Regularly make it a habit to crochet opposites in your work. After every chunky yarn crochet project, work a thread crochet project. After each detailed crochet garment, work a simple repetitive crochet blanket. At the end of everything that you make, ask yourself what

that project was about and what you can make next to balance out the strongest features of the previous project.

Balance Exercise #12: Crochet a Stone Paperweight

The exercise: Crochet over stones to create paperweights.

The purpose: Paperweights give physical weight to our world.

In depth: A paperweight is physically heavy. Crochet is naturally light so when we crochet over a heavy object to create a paperweight, we are automatically creating an item of balance. The paperweight itself can be used to weight down lighter objects in the home, such as stacks of papers, or even to flatten out crochet projects in the works. Paperweights can also be distributed decoratively around a home to balance out the lighter-weight decor in your space.

Exercise steps:

1. Go on a **nature walk** to select stones. Leave your phone off, go on this walk alone, experience peacefulness in searching for the right stones.
2. Select a **round crochet motif** that is approximately the same diameter as your first stone.
3. **Crochet two** of the same motif.
4. **Sew the motifs** together with the rock in between them. Nature isn't perfect so rocks aren't perfectly round; feel free to freeform and make creative adjustments so it fits.
5. **Repeat** with all of your other rocks.

Tips:

- Look at patterns for flowers, snowflakes, and mandalas to find the right round motif.
- Play with different sizes and colors of stones to find the right balance for you.
- Explore the use of color vs. neutrals when selecting thread / yarn for this exercise. Which option feels more balanced with the stones that you select?

- Try this technique with other materials from nature as well, such as seashells and large leaves. *See crochet artist Susanna Bauer's leaves for amazing examples.*

Taking it further: Crochet a set of stone paperweights and practice the art of rock balancing. This is where you meditatively select one rock after another and stack them into towers. This can be done for an indoor display in your home or outdoors in your yard. You must practice great balance to grow the tower of stones taller and taller.

Balance Crochet Exercise #13: Chakra Crochet

The exercise: Crochet circles for the seven chakras.

The purpose: Balance your mind, body and spirit through chakra crochet.

In-depth: There is a lot that you can learn about chakras and you might find it fun to do so, but for the purpose of this exercise, you just need to know the basics. Your body has seven chakras, running up the spine from its base to the crown of your head. These chakras relate to different sections of your nerve and organ structure as well as different aspects of your emotional, psychological and spiritual life. This is a meditation to work with each of the seven chakras in order to balance yourself.

Exercise steps:

1. Gather the **seven colors of yarn**, one for each chakra (they're the same as the color of the rainbow, see chart below).
2. Begin with your **root chakra color**. Close your eyes before beginning and focus your energy on this part of your body. Notice what you feel there, bring your attention to sending loving energy to the qualities associated with this chakra.
3. Open your eyes and begin the work of **making a crochet circle** using your root chakra color. You can use any simple crochet circle pattern that you desire. I like the granny circle crochet pattern. The instructions for that are:
    a. Ch 4, sl st to close ring
    b. Ch 3 (counts as first dc here and throughout)
    c. Working into the center of the ring: 1 dc, [ch 1, 2 dc] 5 times, ch 1, sl st to top of chain three.

d. Ch 3. Work the following into the same ch1 space next to the chain three: 1 dc, ch 1, dc2tog, ch 1. [Working into the next ch1 space: dc2tog, ch1, dc2tog, ch1.] Repeat [ ] around the round and sl st to top of chain three
e. Ch 3. Work 2dc into same space. Ch 1, 3 dc into next space and repeat all the way around to the end where you will sl st into the top of the first chain three to close the space.
f. Repeat step e.
4. When your circle is complete, set aside and **move on to your next chakra**. Repeat steps two and three for each chakra, moving from your root to the base of your crown.

THE SEVEN CHAKRAS

- Root Chakra (RED). Located at the tailbone, this is the chakra for safety and survival. It gives us a feeling of groundedness. When you're concerned with money and other basic needs, it suffers. When it's in balance, you feel fearless.
- Sacral Chakra (ORANGE). Located about two inches below your belly button, this is our creative and sensual center. It gives us a feeling of abundance. When it is blocked, you feel passionless. When it is in balance, your creative expression flows.
- Gut Chakra (YELLOW). Located in the area of the stomach, this is our region of self-esteem. When blocked, we may feel worthless. When in balance, it is a tremendous source of personal power.
- Heart Chakra (GREEN). Located at the heart, this is all about love, joy and inner peace. It is the center of all of the chakras, connecting the body chakras to the spiritual chakras through the heart. When blocked, we feel lonely and directionless. When open, we feel connected to others.
- Throat Chakra (BLUE). Located in the throat, this chakra is about communicating, especially communicating truth. If you're repressing your highest truth, it is blocked. When in balance, you are able to share your true self with the world.
- Third Eye Chakra (PURPLE). Located in the middle of the forehead, this is the chakra of intuition and inner wisdom. When blocked, you may have trouble making decisions. When in balance, you will have a sense of the bigger picture of all things.

- Crown Chakra (WHITE). Located at the crown of the head, this is our spiritual chakra. When blocked, we feel spiritual uncertainty and doubt. When in balance, we feel connected to all things.

Tips:

- Chakra work is a little too new-agey or different for some people. You can call this color work and just notice how each color can correlate with the different needs and goals of each level. You don't have to specifically focus on chakras if that makes you uncomfortable.
- In some teachings, the third eye chakra is represented by indigo and the crown chakra is represented by violet (rather than the purple/white I've chosen here).

Taking it further: Learn more about the chakras and about working with moving energy through these spaces. Incorporate crochet work with each of the chakra colors to help meet the needs you have at any given time for better balance.

Yarn for Thought: More Musings on Balance

- What does "a balanced life" mean to you?
- Explore the areas of your life that you feel are weighted or exaggerated right now and the areas of life that feel stagnant or under-valued. Where can you make changes to redistribute your time, energy and attention?
- What stories do you tell yourself about the value of crochet? Are these stories the whole truth or only a portion of it? What would be the whole story?
- What myths do you tell yourself about how you crochet, about what other people might think of your crochet work? What is the opposite perspective that you could embrace?
- Draw a pie chart representing how you spend your time.
- Make a list of your ten favorite things to do. Then make a list of your ten least favorite chores. Next to each item, list how long it has been since you did those things. Is one list weighted more recently than the other? How can you adjust that?

Artistic Development

Take a look at yourself in front of the mirror, look yourself in the eye and say aloud, "I am an artist". Turn to a friend or a stranger and say it to them, "I am an artist". Go to an art exhibit, strike up a conversation and when asked about yourself, tell the person, "I am an artist". How does that feel? For most of us, it doesn't feel true. We think of artists as something else, someone with work hanging in a gallery, someone who can paint magnificent landscapes, someone who is creative in a way that we simply can't proclaim ourselves to be. Bollocks.

You crochet, therefore you create, therefore you are an artist. But believe me, I understand the journey it takes to get comfortable with calling yourself that. I went through that journey myself, first in being willing to call myself a writer and then later in calling myself an artist as well. The whole writer thing has been a very winding path. When I was little, I always called myself a writer, because writing was my favorite thing to do. Then there was this whole push and pull thing, where it felt comfortable or didn't, as I went through different phases in my self-identity and my career. I had to answer questions for myself like "am I writer if I'm not getting paid to write?" and "am I writer if I'm not really writing much right now?" and "am I a writer if I'm going to law school or being a foster mom and not sure how much writing I'll ever plan to pursue?" Early in my paid writing career, I called myself "writer" with a sort of fake-it-til-you-make-it bravado. Later it became a matter-of-fact thing.

These days, I absolutely consider myself a writer. It is a crucial part of my identity. It is both what I am and what I do. And in spite of that, or perhaps because of it, when people ask what I do I usually answer something else. There is a reason for that, or many reasons really. I have learned over time that I hate talking about my writing work. When someone asks what you do and you answer, "I'm a writer", one of two questions inevitably follows. The first is, "what do you write?" and the second is "what are you working on?" I've learned never to honestly answer the second question. Something alchemical happens in the writing process and when you talk too much about the work before the work is complete, the life leaks out of it. It damages my writing to talk about what I'm writing.

As for the first question, I just find that more often than not the conversation about what I write is annoying and disinteresting to me. I want to write, not talk about my writing. And often people seem to be expecting a specific answer, so even when I say that I write non-fiction, they start asking about fiction or poetry. They ask where I get published and then I feel forced to explain why I have chosen self-publishing. People are endlessly fascinated by the worlds of writers but the conversations I have about writing are almost never relevant to my actual writing life. Of course there are exceptions. Usually these days I answer that I write and I share an extra something that indicates where I'm willing to go with the conversation. So I'll say, "I write. I'm really interested in craft therapy for mental health" if that's what I'm interested in talking about. Or if I'm not in the mood to talk, I'll say, "Oh, I do a little of this and a little of that".

But knowing all of this about myself, and being able to talk openly about what I'm working on or choosing not to talk about it all, could only come about once I was absolutely comfortable inside of myself with calling myself a writer. It is just a fact now. It's what I do, it's who I am, regardless of what (or if!) I am writing. And I had to reach that level of comfort with calling myself a writer before I could really reap the benefits of being a writer. It is the same with being an artist.

The journey to calling myself an artist was a bit tougher. My drawing skills haven't progressed since the age of four (they've probably devolved, if that's possible). I dislike getting-dirty arts like working with clay. There are a thousand other reasons I might not consider myself an artist. But ultimately, through a journey not that dissimilar to calling myself a writer, I've come to believe in the power of what I create with my hands as a healing force in my life and come to the internal heart-racing conclusion that in my own personal small way, I am indeed an artist. Being able to proclaim that is, I believe, critical to living a full, rich, believe-in-yourself, take-the-best-care-of-yourself-possible kind of lifestyle, which is the only lifestyle I ever want to live. So I encourage you to work with it if you have trouble calling yourself an artist, because learning to say it and believe it about yourself can take you to the next level of creative healing. The journey is a lifelong process in many ways but hopefully the exercises in this final chapter will help you explore new aspects of crochet in an art-minded way that broadens your definition of yourself to "artist".

Art Exercise #1: Frame Your Crochet

The exercise: Frame and hang one of your crochet pieces.

The purpose: Elevate simple crochet into art through its display.

In depth: When we take the time to frame and hang an item, we are giving it a precious place in our spaces. This elevates it from an everyday object into a work of art. Consider, for example, any textile, poster or bowl that has been carefully hung on the wall and how it suddenly differs from its original, ordinary existence. Treat your crochet work with the same care.

Exercise steps:

1. **Select** a favorite existing piece of work that you have already crocheted.
2. **Find a frame** that perfectly compliments the piece. Take your time. The process of working to really finish the piece properly is going to help you to redefine it as art.
3. **Find the right background** for the piece. This might be a mat; a crochet square inside of a mat inside of the right frame is a great example of crochet art. However, it could also be a background that you paint, a fabric that you love, etc. Again, take your time.
4. **Frame the piece**. Are you fully satisfied with it? Adjust if necessary until you are.
5. **Hang the piece** in a prominent display area in your home or workplace. Celebrate the art of crochet!

Tips:

- Squares, flowers and other small motifs are great for framing. However, you can frame scarves and even blankets or clothing if you want to put them on display.
- Shadow boxes are better than flat frames for any crochet art pieces that are thick. Plus, they add interesting dimension to the work!
- Remember that one large frame can hold several small pieces of crochet. A mat with three same-sized squares that each hold smaller crochet motifs inside can be a great display piece, for example.

Taking it further: Dedicate an entire wall of your home to a gallery display of your framed crochet art. Like with your family photos, you can keep the same work up for years or change it out regularly.

Art Exercise #2: Crochet a Frame

The exercise: Crochet a frame to go around another piece of artwork.

The purpose: Use your crochet skills to elevate an ordinary image into a piece of artwork.

In depth: This is the same type of project as an Exercise One except that instead of framing your crochet, you're using crochet to create the frame itself.

Exercise steps:

1. **Select an image** that you want to hang in your home. A photo, a poster, a greeting card or a magazine image will work.
2. **Cut the image** down to the size that you want. Leave enough of a margin around the border to allow yourself stitches that begin the frame.
3. **Use a needle** to poke holes evenly spaced around the edges of the piece where you will begin your crochet.
4. **Use a tapestry needle** to add a blanket stitch around the entire border in a yarn color that complements the image.
5. **Attach yarn** in any corner and crochet around the entire piece, using any edging pattern that you desire, to create your crochet frame.
6. **Hang your framed image**.

Tips:

- Practice crocheting a border on scrap paper until you get the hang of it so you don't ruin your art image.
- Add a backing of the same size as the image to make a thicker piece to work with (before you begin Step Three). Poster board, cardboard or even fabric will work. Carefully adhere the image to the backing and let it dry before proceeding.
- Sometimes you have to play around with different edging styles to find the right one to match your image. Don't be afraid to take time to play! You can create one of your own or find a pattern that you like. One of my favorite reference books for this exercise is Edie Eckman's book *Around the Corner Crochet Borders.*

Taking it further: Crochet frames for an entire set of matching images to create a unique art display for your home.

Art Exercise #3: Crochet Collage on Canvas

The exercise: Adhere crochet motifs to canvas.

The purpose: Canvas is another way to "frame" and hang art.

In depth: Canvas immediately feels like art to most of us. When we work with canvas, we are working with art supplies. By adhering crochet to canvas, we are raising it to the standard of art.

Exercise steps:

1. **Select** a piece of canvas.
2. **Crochet** a set of matching motifs.
3. **Layout the motifs** on the canvas. Find a design that is pleasing to your eye.
4. **Adhere** the motifs to the canvas.
5. After the motifs are dry, **hang the canvas** in a prominent place in your home!

Tips:

- Find the right adhesive for your glue to stick to the canvas. Fabric glue is a top choice. Super glue will also work.
- Use motifs of varying sizes.
- Consider layering some of the motifs over one another, at least partially, to add additional dimension to the canvas.

Taking it further: Paint the canvas with a background design of your choosing before you adhere your crochet motifs. If you don't enjoy painting, create a photo collage of magazine images as the background.

Art Exercise #4: Crochet Painting on Canvas

The exercise: Use crochet motifs to create a painted scene on canvas.

The purpose: This is a non-abstract variation of the previous exercise.

In depth: Sometimes art feels more like "art" to us when it depicts a scene. Crochet yourself a scene to embrace your inner artist.

Exercise steps:

1. **Draw a sketch** of a simple scene comprised of items that you can crochet as appliques. For example, a simple garden scene with grass, a tree, a butterfly and a cloud would work.
2. **Crochet** each of the individual appliques for this scene.
3. **Measure out the size** of your scene and purchase a canvas for the piece.
4. **Adhere your scene** to the canvas.
5. **Are you missing any elements**? If so, crochet them and add them now.
6. **Hang** your beautiful new crochet art!

Tips:

- Keep the scene simple. What do you love to crochet? Base your scene around that.
- Imagine that you are crocheting this piece for a child's room. This can help loosen up the irrational feeling that you must create high art and infuse more of a sense of play into the piece.
- Look at children's storybooks for ideas if you are not sure what to crochet.

Taking it further: Crochet your background instead of using canvas. For example, your garden scene might have a blue crocheted top (for the sky) and a green crocheted bottom (for the grass) with appliques glued on for the clouds, tree and butterfly. (*Shout out to my mom for that particular example, which I stole from a work that she did.*)

Art Exercise #5: Crochet a 3 Dimensional Scene

The exercise: Crochet a full scene using amigurumi techniques.

The purpose: This is a variation on Exercise Six, using amigurumi techniques instead of appliques.

In depth: Crocheting an animal can feel like a craft. Crocheting a set of animals around a tea party in a garden feels more like making crochet art.

Exercise steps:

1. **Daydream a scene** using characters that you can crochet.
2. **Crochet** each of the characters.
3. **Crochet accessories** for each of the characters. Jewelry, weapons, pets ... whatever your characters need to tell their story.
4. **Create a display** that tells the story. This may be on your mantle, on a side table or even in a shadowbox that you hang on the wall.

Tips:

- Many amigurumi crochet books have patterns for characters as well as the items they need to tell their stories in 3d. Check these out for inspiration. *Once Upon a Time in Crochet in Crochet* by Lynne Rowe is a great example.
- Embrace whimsy. This should be a fun, magical, playful art exercise!
- Don't worry about being literal. If you can crochet characters that look exactly like you want them to - great. But if not, just go with abstract versions instead!

Taking it further: Create a diorama. This forces you to fit your story into a specific area and challenges your artistic senses.

Art Exercise #6: Crochet a Self Portrait

The exercise: Crochet a self-portrait

The purpose: Portraits feel so professional! Crochet one to celebrate your skills. Self-portraits honor yourself as the artist.

In depth: Portraits always feel like art. Even the most basic sketch that somewhat resembles the person (or a caricature of the person) rings true as "art" for almost all of us. When you crochet a portrait, even in the abstract, you crochet art, and when you crochet a self-portrait, you are looking at yourself as the artist.

Exercise steps:

1. **Get a large piece of butcher paper**, large enough to spread your whole body out on.
2. Have someone else take a marker and **outline your body** while you are lying on the paper. This is the outline for your crochet self-portrait.
3. **Use your crochet skills** to fill in the outline of yourself in a way that perfectly represents the way that you see yourself. (See tips below for suggestions.)
4. **Title and sign** this piece of artwork. "Self-Portrait of a Crochet Artist" is one possible title.
5. **Frame and hang** this piece of crochet artwork. If it is too large for your space, photograph it and make art cards with the image instead.

Tips:

- Step Three may be literal, figurative or abstract. A literal example would be to crochet your hairstyle, a favorite outfit you always wear and a piece of jewelry you love. A figurative example would be to crochet a large heart, to represent your giving nature, or crochet roots for your feet to represent that you are grounded. An abstract example would utilize colors, shapes and textures to represent your feelings about yourself as they relate to your body.
- You don't have to lie flat on your back for the outline. Curl into fetal position or take your favorite yoga pose if you want to.
- Be gentle with yourself throughout this process. You are the art and the artist!!!

Taking it further: You can use more advanced crochet techniques, such as tapestry crochet, to make realistic-looking portraits and self-portraits. If this feels right to you, explore it. The work of artists Jo Hamilton, Pat Ahern and KatikaArt can inspire you. The techniques offered by Todd Paschall of Crochet by Numbers can be useful. If this is too overwhelming, you might be more inclined to use digital manipulation of crochet images to create your self-portrait; look at the digital portraits from artist Work By Knight to get ideas.

Art Exercise #7: Mixed Media Crochet Art

The exercise: Make a piece of mixed media crochet art.

The purpose: Embrace other art forms through crochet.

In depth: Practice other types of art and combine them with crochet to make a new art piece that you are proud of.

Exercise steps:

1. **Select an art form** that you have wanted to try. Sculpture, drawing, jewelry making, glasswork ... whatever you consider an art form and want to work with.
2. **Take your time** exploring this new art form. When you are ready, select a piece that you have made to incorporate with your crochet work.
3. Come up with a creative way to **combine your two crafts** into a work of art.

Tips:

- Look through the portfolios of mixed media crochet artists for inspiration and ideas.
- Think about ways that you could upcycle existing items using crochet and then consider how you could make that into a piece of art.
- Immerse yourself in the new craft through lessons, classes, practice in order to get the most out of this experience.

Taking it further: Make a large mixed media collage incorporating several different types of craft into one framed piece of art. Alternatively, explore making crochet art installations and using the skill of photography to capture those installations as scenes. Check out the work that artist Slinkachu does creating magnificent tiny scenes that are photographed in intriguing large scale; these aren't crochet but you could make crochet miniatures and explore this type of art.

Art Exercise #8: Crochet a Color Wheel

The exercise: Crochet a color wheel.

The purpose: Learn more about color theory.

In depth: Color theory is so important in art. Colors impact our moods and emotions. Even if you choose not to follow contemporary "rules" about color choice, it is beneficial to know what those standards are. Crochet a color wheel for yourself, researching color theory along the way.

Exercise steps:

1. **Find an image of a color wheel** that you like.
2. **Purchase the yarn** to make each color in your color wheel.
3. **Crochet each color** in the wheel one at a time. As you do, take the time to learn the meaning of each color, with regard to how it impacts the viewer.
4. **Lay out your color wheel in order when it is complete**. As you do this, continue your research into color theory. Why is the color wheel laid out the way that it is? What happens if you lay out the pieces of the color wheel together in an incorrect order? How does this change its impact?
5. **Stitch the pieces** of your color wheel together into a whole piece and place it where you can see it regularly as you work.

Tips:

- There are both simple and complex versions of the color wheel (with some featuring many, many more hues than others). Take your time finding the right inspiration for yours.
- The different shades in a yarn can make a big impact on how true to your color wheel the final project turns out. Make sure that you select the yarn that exactly matches the hue in your color wheel design.
- If you'd prefer, you can glue the pieces of the color wheel to a board instead of stitching them together in Step Five.

Taking it further: Use your color wheel to further explore color theory. Learn about analogous colors and complementary colors. Crochet swatches or motifs based upon these lessons to give you a visual understanding of what you are learning.

Art Exercise #9: Crochet Inspiration Board

The exercise: Create an inspiration board for your crochet.

The purpose: Practice visual brainstorming as a part of the artistic process.

In depth: The inspiration board (or mood board) is a special part of the creative process that can add new layers to your work. Creating an inspiration board for your work will allow you to think about what you create in a new way.

Exercise steps:

1. **Purchase an inspiration board base**. This may be a corkboard, a piece of poster board or a large swath of paper.
2. **Select a theme** for this inspiration board. For example, "everything I'm going to crochet this autumn" or "crochet shawl ideas". *See more examples below.*
3. **Find items** that inspire you and fit the theme. Images from crochet magazines, swatches you crochet, small snippets of yarn you love.
4. **Organize the items** on your inspiration board. Play around with layout until you get a sense of what's really inspiring you.
5. **Hang this in your workspace** to inform your projects. Look at it when deciding what to make next.

EXAMPLES OF INSPIRATION BOARD THEMES

- Art
- Books
- Color
- Destination (vacation, event)
- Fiber inspiration (all alpaca, all novelty yarn)
- Gift recipient (things they love)

- Holidays
- Home design (Scandinavian, nursery rooms)
- Light, dark, shadows
- Musical inspiration
- Opposites (soft and hard, for example)
- Patterns (shapes, motifs, lines)
- Personal style (your ideal outfit)
- Seasons of the year
- Specific items (shawl inspiration, skirt inspiration, jewelry inspiration)
- Texture; textiles

Tips:

- The majority of your inspirational items should be drawn directly from the craft. However, other images and textures can also inspire the work so feel free to add photos, postcards, fabrics, etc.
- You might have one inspiration board that you work from for awhile and then switch it out with another one (seasonally, for example, like fashion designers do) or you may have multiple boards going at once to reflect different themes in your work.
- Make a vision board. This is the same concept as an inspiration board but also keeps certain goals in mind. The idea is that having those goals created in a visual form helps you keep them close to you so that they manifest. So, for example, if a goal of yours is to get a pattern published in a crochet magazine, then your inspiration board would have ideas that inspire the pattern but as a vision board it would also include images of that magazine cover and inspirational quotes to encourage you to work towards that.

Taking it further: Create, maintain and draw from an image file. Keep a file (or several) of images, textiles and other sources of inspiration. Collect them liberally. Periodically go through these files. Throw out anything that no longer speaks to you. Organize some of what is left into a new inspiration board. Keep adding and refreshing your image file. It is good to always have an abundance of inspiration to draw from as an artist!

Art Exercise #10: Write a Story and Crochet the Characters

The exercise: Write your own short story and then illustrate it with crochet.

The purpose: Let your imagination run wild with words and yarn.

In depth: Writing your own story in which you create the characters and the lives that they live is very freeing. It is artistic and creative in a way that many of us just don't play with regularly. Crocheting the story brings it to life.

Exercise steps:

1. **Write a simple short story**. Think in terms of a children's book.
2. Make a list of **all of the characters** in the story.
3. **Sketch out** what each of these characters might look like.
4. Use your sketches to **crochet each of these characters**.
5. **Make a list** of all of the non-character items that might be in your story. Clothing, accessories, houses, landscapes, food, etc.
6. **Crochet** as many of those non-character items as you want.
7. **Tell your story** out loud using your characters! An audience of kids is great for this but even if you just tell it to yourself it's going to feel good!

Tips:

- Stuck for story ideas? A great way to get started is to brainstorm a whole list filling in these blanks: "The (adjective) (noun) of the (adjective) (character)". For example, "The wonderful tree of the silly goose" or "The dancing plant of the creative girl". You can also go to the library and spend an hour looking at children's books for further inspiration.
- You can crochet your characters from scratch, but you don't have to. You could use existing amigurumi patterns as the basis for your characters. You could even purchase dolls and add crochet details if making your own complete characters doesn't feel right for you.

- You don't have to know how to draw well to sketch out ideas. My sketches are basic scratchings that no one else would recognize with lots of words written alongside them because I think in words.

Taking it further: Make a stop motion video sharing your story through the crochet characters! If you've never done this before, embrace being a beginner again!

Art Exercise #11: Submit Your Work to an Art Exhibit

The exercise: Submit your work to an art show or exhibit.

The purpose: Honor yourself as an artist by proclaiming it to the world.

In depth: Once you've gotten comfortable calling yourself an artist in your own mind, it is time to tell it to the world. The best way is to submit your work where other artists submit their work.

Exercise steps:

1. Make a list of **current calls for fiber art** or mixed media art. You will have to do some research to find places that have put out calls for submissions; start in your local area.
2. **Confirm** that they accept crochet work.
3. **Read through all of the rules**, themes and deadlines.
4. **Select one or more calls** to submit your work to.
5. **Submit!**
6. **Continue submissions** until one of your pieces gets accepted.
7. **Tell everyone** when your work is in an art show. It feels so good!

Tips:

- Start with exhibits that are within your reach. Instead of big galleries and museums, go for state fairs and collaborative local art shows.
- Many exhibits require an application fee. It is best to start with those that don't require a fee or that require only a very nominal charge. You shouldn't invest a lot of money right away as this can put the pressure on to "be an artist" which is the opposite of what you want as you begin.

- One similar option is to participate in a large yarnbombing event. Many yarnbombers put out calls for crochet donations, and you can submit your work to these without a formal application process. It is a toe in the door of the art world that can feel less pressured than other art exhibits for some people.

Taking it further: Put on your own exhibit consisting entirely of your crochet art pieces! Rent out a small space for an evening or weekend and invite everyone you know!

Art Exercise #12: Crochet a Dream Catcher

The exercise: Crochet a dream catcher for yourself.

The purpose: Create a symbolic tool to help you realize your dreams.

In-depth: The dream catcher is a web that you place in your home or studio to facilitate the realization of your dreams. The belief is that your bad dreams are caught in the web and the good dreams are allowed to slip through so that you can use them and bring them to life.

Exercise steps:

1. **Select a circular item** for the round portion of your dream catcher. It should be a circular item with a hole in the center, such as a wreath or an embroidery hoop. You can find many items at your local craft store.
2. **Select a doily pattern.** You will crochet a doily that is going to fit inside of the center hole of the circular item that you selected in step one. Openwork, very lacy doily patterns are ideal. Mesh patterns made with thicker yarn also work.
3. **Adhere the doily pattern to the inside of your wreath.** How you do this depends on the materials that you've chosen. For example, you can simply slip it inside of an embroidery hoop but might glue it to a Styrofoam wreath or tie it to a wooden wreath.
4. **Crochet a set of long chains.** You can use any type of yarn for this. Hang them off of the bottom of the wreath. You can choose any length you desire; make them all the same length or create chains that vary in length.
5. **Add additional accessories.** Beads and feathers are two common items that you can add to the chains to finish your dream catcher.

6. **Hang** in your space and let the magic begin!

Tips:

- As an alternative to using a doily pattern in step two, you could opt to simply crochet chains and lay them out strategically inside of your wreath to create the web effect of the dream catcher.
- Carefully consider your color choice. Do you want an organic dream catcher made with a wooden wreath and a hemp twine doily? Do you want a rainbow colored dream catcher with colorful glitter beads? Maybe a pure white dream catcher feels right to you?
- You can make a set of small dream catchers to keep throughout your house rather than one large dream catcher.

Taking it further: There is a lot of interesting history and mythology around the dream catcher. Take the time to learn more about it. Incorporate your work with meditation, affirmations and vision boards into your use of the dream catcher in your home. Write in your journal about the dreams that you have and send them mentally to your dream catcher to let the bad parts get filtered out so

your dreams can come true.

Yarn for Thought: More Musings About Being An Artist

- What does it mean to be an artist?
- How do you know when something is "art?"
- List all of the things that you do that are artistic.
- Write creatively about your crochet. This might be a song, a haiku or other poem about crochet or even a love letter to a favorite yarn or project.
- Stuck while working on a crochet item? Write from the perspective of the piece - what does it want to tell you?
- How does the universe support your creativity? Look for synchronicity and see what you can find.
- What is the difference between creativity and spirituality? What are the similarities?

Conclusion: Back to the Beginning

We are at the end of this book now and I want to take you back to its beginning because the process of getting it completed was long and winding and it accurately represents the truth of what a creative work can look like. This book began as the spark of an idea during the process of writing *Crochet Saved My Life*, back in 2011 and 2012. When the book came out, more and more people contacted me, telling me their stories about how crochet was helping them in their lives, and I became more and more interested in the tangible activities that could be done with the craft to foster a better quality of life for anyone. I began exploring ideas on my own, implementing them, seeing what worked, seeking out insights from other people who were doing creative exercises of any kind.

By January 2013, I had solid notes and an outline for the book. At the time, I had a big vision that *Hook To Heal* would not be just a book but would also be a creativity workshop that people could choose to take as a twelve week online course or through one-on-one creative mentoring with me. So I had notes and a plan, but what I didn't have was the time to finish writing the book because my time was being spent working to pay the bills. I decided to launch an Indiegogo campaign to get support from others who believed in my vision; I am so grateful for those who contributed, and you can find their names in the thanks at the end of this book.

The Initial Vision

Here's an excerpt of how the original campaign read:

Hook to Heal is a multimedia project designed to teach people to use crochet to improve their health, wellness, creativity levels and total quality of life.

Do you have a desire to explore your creativity but also a fear of calling yourself an "artist"? Do you wish you were more creatively fulfilled but fail to take time for yourself to just create? Are there emotional issues blocking your creative side? Crochet can help! This simple and easy-to-learn craft can be used in unique ways to get in touch with your inner artist, explore and eradicate your deepest creative fears and restore balance to your personal life.

Please consider helping me out with my just-launched crowdsourced funding campaign for my next book project, which includes multimedia components like online classes and personalized email coaching. Here are the details ...

About the Project

In my popular book *Crochet Saved My Life* I shared information about the mental and physical health benefits of crochet. Now I want to take it to the next level by helping people learn how to use crochet to heal, improve their daily creativity and enhance their total quality of life. This is going to be done through a new book of creativity exercises as well as the development of online classes and creative email support.

More Details

Hook to Heal with have three core products all coming out in 2013:

1. Creativity Exercises Book. My next book, due out 10/1/2013 is a book of creativity exercises for crocheters. It will show how crochet can be used to achieve mindfulness, release artistic fear, push to the next level of creativity, celebrate life and more. Many topics of creativity will be explored in this book that challenge you to find new ways to craft yourself to wellness.
2. 12 Week Online Creativity Classes. Beginning in Autumn 2013 I will also be launching online creativity classes. These will be weekly classes with chat/ video components that offer detailed lessons and guidance exploring the core ideas presented in the Hook to Heal book.
3. One-on-one Email Support for Crochet Creativity. I am going to take the lessons that I have learned about using crochet to help you get deeper into your creative self. I'll be your personal creative crochet guide armed with hooks to help you get to the next stage of your personal growth.

Hook to Heal is a comprehensive program for people who want to use crafting to better their lives. However, each of the three parts will be available on their own so you don't have to commit to the total plan if you don't want to.

I went on to explain in this campaign what the donations would cover, including the cost of a photographer for what I expected to be an image-rich book, and the cost of video lessons to assist me in the teaching component I expected to do. I explained what "rewards" people would get for assisting me through their funding. I explained the impact that I believed the project would be able to offer.

The Work

Like I said, the above was the original vision for the project. As you can see, I expected to have the book released by the end of 2013, a book filled with photos, and I planned to have a huge online aspect set up shortly thereafter. What I discovered from the funding process was that people were really interested in the book but nobody was interested in taking advantage of the online classes or one-on-one mentoring. Throughout the process, I determined that perhaps this wasn't going to be a part of the project after all, at least initially, since there was so little interest in it. That was okay, I was happy to be writing the book, but it was a sign that the original intentions were already changing, which is something that is normal to the creative process but less easy to swallow when you have already told the world what you plan to do (and asked them for money to do it!) That's okay, though, I would still write the book.

And I did write. A major portion of the book was finished really quickly and I was excited about each exercise that I developed. I couldn't wait to get it into the hands of people that I hoped would be able to benefit and grow from it. I wanted to get the community started using these tools so that I could see what other ideas would emerge.

But it turned out that I was going through deep changes at the same time. January 2013 was a big time for me, and not just because it was when I launched this project. My sister was here visiting that year for the holidays, and while she was here I saw that a small group of people were going to celebrate the new year by doing a Polar Bear Run, where you all dash together into the icy cold chill of the Pacific Ocean. Let me say at this time that I do not go into this ocean, at least not up here in Northern California where it is so, so cold. When I first moved here, I tried to go in and my feet cramped up in pain from the stinging chill. That was the last time I tried to do that ... until New Years Day 2013. The people doing this particular run into the ocean were calling it Dive Fearlessly Into the New Year. It resonated with me. I wanted to be more fearless.

You see, I had pulled myself out of depression a few years previously, through the help of family, friends, therapy, medication, and crochet. I'd slowly cobbled together a life for myself that was richer and more full and generally happier than it had ever been. But in doing so, I had put a ton of safety mechanisms into place, creating a lot of breathing room to protect myself from sliding backwards into that pain again. It was necessary, it was smart, it was right, but after several years of living safely (including having very, very few commitments to anyone or anything), I was feeling ready to start taking a few risks again. So I wanted to dive into that ocean symbolically in order to dive into my life tangibly. And I knew that my sister - my brave, adventurous, wonderfully supportive sister - would have no problem running into that ocean with me. So we did, even though right up until the very last minute I was unsure of whether or not I would do it. I did it mostly because I had to prove to myself that I could do things that were a little bit scary but still basically safe.

And my life changed. The hippie, spiritually-leaning poet in me that believes in synchronicity and symbols and plugging your soul into the electric current of the whole universe is sure that the act of running into that water that day signaled to the larger world that I was ready for more challenges, that I was open to newness. The practical, logical, needs-an-explanation side of me says that by choosing to take that step, I gave myself permission to continue taking next steps. Whatever the "truth" of that, things shifted immediately.

About a week later, I met the man who would become my beaux. For years I'd been slowly allowing the wounds of my previous breakup to heal, learning to move on alone without the person I had loved so much, while also trying to maintain a friendship with him. I had taken a few shaky steps out onto the ledge of bad dates and quickly withdrawn. Then I dove into the ocean, met this new man, and two and a half years later we are still happily together. (Incidentally, my sister met her partner the same week, in a different town, and they are also still happily together as of the writing of this chapter.) Thanks, ocean! (Yes, this was the same man mentioned in a previous chapter who I flaked out on a couple of times because I wanted to learn to swim without getting wet. The irony of the ocean.)

So I started the fundraiser for the book at the same time that I started this new relationship. And at first, there was no conflict. Yes, I was busy falling in love and going on these fabulous dates with this new man, and we spent a lot of hours talking about the past and the present and the glimmerings of a future. But I was also doing a ton of writing, because I was infused with the kind of creative energy that only ever comes at the very beginning stages of falling in love. I had more energy in those months than I'd had in years. I heard music everywhere and the music became words on the page and the book grew before my eyes and I had no doubt at all that it would be released on schedule as I proceeded enthusiastically ahead.

But new love changes you, not right away, but in small twists and turns. You see it later, if you look closely, in the small details of how an everyday life is lived. Most Saturdays of my 2015 life, my partner and I head to the farmer's market closest to me and we stop at the same five or six stands and pick up more or less the same things (depending on the season), which includes the kind of really firm peaches that he prefers and the fresh mint that I've started putting in my water. We get eggs and scallions and broccoli and a loaf of fresh bread and when we get home he usually makes an omelette that we eat together on my couch while I organize my Instagram images for the day. Not every Saturday is like this but most of them are and I can say that no Saturday was like this before him. I didn't usually bother with the farmer's market before him, had cereal for breakfast, wasn't on Instagram, yet, and watched TV at the start of the day. Every Saturday since him is different than every Saturday before him. And of course, the changes are really much deeper than this mundane example, as his world and my world have become our world and belief systems have shifted to accommodate one another.

The point here is that I was changing, so slowly and subtly that I couldn't articulate those changes at the time, couldn't see them myself, yet, could barely tell that they were happening. What it looked like from the outside was writer's block. Laziness. Procrastination. I could no longer complete the ideas in the book that I had started because I was no longer the person who had started that book but I didn't know that was the reason and I blamed everything else under the sun and I mostly blamed myself and felt bad.

A Project Update

In the midst of this, the ocean continued to work its magic, and I decided to apply to a graduate school program to begin that fall. In April 2013, I wrote on my blog:

> I received really exciting news yesterday: I got accepted into the grad school program that I applied for! I'm thrilled for so many

reasons. I wanted to take the time to share some of the details with you, including how it fits into my crochet-loving world (because it does!) and also give you a small blog update.

I am going to be attending a small Masters Program in counseling that is truly unique. It integrates a variety of different approaches including a blend of Eastern spirituality with Western medicine to help students learn a holistic approach to counseling. The core belief of the program is essentially that you need to completely understand yourself in order to be able to help others, something that I wholeheartedly agree with. This basically means that I'll get to spend the next three years immersed in self-development, experiential learning and mental health knowledge exploration. I am so excited!!

It's about the education more than the degree. The truth is that I'm not 100% certain that I want to be a counselor. Psychology is something that I've always been interested in and I can see a lifestyle where becoming a private practice counselor part-time could be satisfying to me and helpful to others. But I'm not placing any expectations on the career path that will come out of this program. What I'm really interested in is deeply immersing myself in the experience. I believe in the value of self-exploration and I think that this amazing program is going to offer me a unique opportunity to use different approaches within a supportive network to learn more and more about myself. I hope that it will make me a more compassionate, more helpful, more well-rounded person also but I'm truly open to seeing what it does for me without placing a lot of judgments on what I think it *should* do for me.

As those of you who are familiar with my writing, particularly *Crochet Saved My Life*, know by now I am someone who believes completely that crafting / creativity are immensely important to total mental health. Crochet played a huge role in my own healing from lifelong depression. Crochet has helped many other people that I know through extremely difficult times in life. It is my every intention to continue exploring, researching and better understanding the ways that crochet can assist people in improving their own mental health and total quality of life.

As I said, I'm not placing any specific expectations on what I'm going to do with school. It is far too soon to be sure what my thesis will be about or where I want to go with this degree. I think assuming that I know that would completely defeat the purpose of the kind of openness this self-exploration curriculum offers to me. That said, I do know that it will remain important to me to keep considering how crafting/ crochet / creativity can play a role in therapy. I fully expect to apply my interest in this to what I'm doing in school and to apply what I'm learning in school to how crafting plays its role in my life. I'll be keeping you posted on that journey! And of course there will be certain stresses with grad school, especially with such an emotionally intense program, so if nothing else I'll certainly be making time to do stress-reducing crochet.

Reading back on that post, I think I knew inside that things were going to change in a way that meant I wouldn't be able to keep working on my crochet work and my writing in the same way I had been. And yet, I only partially acknowledged that to myself, certain that I would still get this book out in the fall. School wasn't starting until August, this was the spring and I was sure that I could write what was left before the summer ended. Logistically I could have, but there was that change thing going on. I got stuck because how can you write from the heart of your experience when your heartbeat has changed and you can't yet dance to its new rhythm?

And although I had hoped school would change me further, I didn't really understand the degree to which it would do so. When I started that program, my world got turned upside down and inside out. It's not that it took up a lot of time really - at least, not time in class and even not that much time reading - but that it took this all-encompassing emotional energy. I would go to classes twelve hours per day one three-day weekend per month and then the entire following week I'd basically sit comatose on my couch because every single iota of energy had been drained from me. Sometimes going to school felt like donating plasma; all the lifeblood was taken out of me, swished around in the machine, and some of it was put back in altered form, with energy slowly coming back into my body. I got monthly transfusions for two years in this way.

I was in denial about the depth of the change, I think, or at least the way that change would impact my creative work. As the deadline I'd set for the book's release drew closer, I began to get immobilized. I felt this huge intense guilt that I would not be able to complete the book on time, a time frame I'd set myself but that other people had expected when they funded this project. I was sure I could still get it done relatively soon, perhaps over the Christmas holidays. In September 2013, I posted on my blog:

> "Earlier this year I announced that I am working on a new book of crochet exercises designed to help people heal and grow. The book, called *Hook to Heal*, has received great early support. I am excited about its progress. However, I feel like it has a little more to go before it is ready for release. Originally slated for an October release, it has now been pushed back to release at the start of the year. This will allow me to incorporate some of the new material I am working with in school as well as to improve the visual layout of the book. *Hook to Heal* will be released in print by the end of January 2014, with a possible earlier digital release coming at the end of this year." I added some authentic appreciation for the patience of my supporters and hit the publish button.

Another Delay

So there it was. The first delay. I felt like I had handled it gracefully and it was received well enough by my supporters and I gained myself some time and I thought (again) that I could finish the book. But there was this huge guilt inside that it wasn't done, yet, and there was still the problem of internal constant change that was preventing it from being finished in the first place even though I completely failed to realize that was what was happening. Eventually, I did realize it, and in February 2014, I shared a blog post titled *Hook to Heal Requires Me To Heal (A Heartfelt Project Update)*:

> "Last year a wonderful group of supporters came together to help fund my next book project, *Hook to Heal*. That project has shifted shape over the past year and the book is almost done but not quite yet. I wanted to share with you the following email I sent as an update to all of my special funders because it shares where I'm at, what my thoughts are on creativity and how being creative is all about process, not product.
>
> *Dear my wonderful supporters of the Hook to Heal book project ...* this is an update about the book and about my own experience of writing it and of working with this material. It's an insight into what's been happening creatively with me over the course of the

past year. And it's information about what's next to come. I hope it reaches you in a good place ...

About a year ago you agreed to fund *Hook To Heal*, my book and creativity project about how to use crochet to heal yourself from a variety of life situations – to improve relationships, to build self-esteem, to expand your own artistic self. I wanted to write these things because I have experienced the power of crochet and craft in this way and I wanted to offer this to others.

Throughout the course of the past year I have been at work on this book. The bulk of the material has been written. The number of pages are there. A lot of exercises are in place. And yet, the book isn't quite done. I originally said that it would be published in September and then I said at the start of this year. And technically, I could publish it and it would be fine, I suppose, but there's something unfinished about it and I'm not ready to release it to the world ...

As most of you know, I started a graduate school program in the fall. It's a degree in Integral Counseling Psychology which is all about approaching psychology and counseling from a holistic perspective that incorporates myriad techniques and worldviews, both east and west (and some north and south). I came to this program out of a deep need for something in my life. It is a program that is designed, I believe, to shake you to your core, to loosen up what is there and then sort of solidify it in a new way so that you can offer it more completely to the world. It is a program that allows you to get so deep inside of yourself that you connect with the umbilical cord of the universe.

This program is changing me. It is changing me in fundamental ways that I simply cannot articulate at this time. And because of these changes, *Hook to Heal* doesn't feel finished. Because through this work I've realized that although I write and create daily, there is a part of my writing that has become more business than creativity. I've lost touch somehow with that deep thing that drives the creative process. I'm reading a book right now by Oriah Mountain Dreamer (*What We Ache For*) where she talks about how creativity cannot be separated from sexuality (what she describes really resonates more with me as sensuality) or with spirituality.

She talks about how spirituality separated from sexuality loses its passion, how spirituality separated from creativity becomes empty, how sexuality separated from spirituality loses the intimacy, how sexuality separated from creativity becomes mechanized, and how creativity separated from the other two "is diminished in its capacity to be a path for the unfolding of the soul". She posits that creativity without spirituality becomes advertising (or what relates to me as the business-ifying of my writing) and that creativity without sexuality loses its aliveness. This is all another way of talking, I think, about the mind-body-spirit connection.

The pages of *Hook to Heal* are written and yet I feel that they are passionless. The right ideas are there and I can stand behind them but somehow they are lifeless. They are cut off from the heart of me. And I just don't feel right putting this book out into the world until the heart of it starts beating. It wouldn't feel right with any book, I suppose, but it especially does not feel right for a book that is all about tapping into the creative through crochet. It needs something else, something more, something that requires me to tap into the depths of the world and then allow the beating of that pulse to come through me into the work. And I'm close. I can feel it. I can sense that I'm on the bleeding edges of something pulsating there. But I'm not there yet. And I can't force myself to be there.

That said, I realize that it has been a year since you gifted me the finances to make this book happen. And I worry that for some of you that is way too long to not see a product. So I am offering this ... I promise that there really is a book and that it is on the way. But I can't say when it will be ready. When it is published, you will be getting your copy if you remain a funder. But if this is too risky and too much of a delay for you and you want to rescind your funding, I do understand. If anyone wants their money back at this stage, please contact me directly via email and we will work something out. I want everyone to be content with their part in this process.

I wish you wellness. I wish you passion. I wish you moments of depth. I wish you laughter. And I wish you lots of creative, healing crochet."

I felt good about this decision. And bad about it, pressuring myself, feeling guilty. But mostly it felt right, and if nothing else it felt necessary.

And On it Goes

I'll spare you the ongoing details of the first year of school but suffice to say I changed and grew and FELT so much and then it was summer 2014 and the book was not written but I thought I could get it done that summer. The thing was that I had finally begun to realize that school had inevitably changed me and that I needed to better understand those changes before I could proceed creatively. The way that I understand myself is always through writing, so I compiled all of my first year of grad school essays into an academic memoir, adding my own thoughts about the experience along the way and published it that summer under the title *Cracked Wide Open*. By the time that book was done, I had a decent grasp of what was going on with me and felt ready to resume the *Hook to Heal* project

In July of 2014, I shared another short announcement, letting people know that the book's text was basically done, but that I wanted to incorporate some of the lessons I'd learned in school and add some images. I said it would be released before the end of the year. You'd think I'd have learned my lesson by now, but apparently I had not.

You see, there is something that happens when you tell the world about a creative project before it is done. It thwarts the work somehow. It changes it, alters its course, sometimes makes it impossible to complete it. A project needs to contain its energy inside of itself, whirling upon itself to generate the friction necessary to properly complete it. When you tell the world about it too early, the energy is released, the friction doesn't build, the work doesn't get done or at least can't get done well.

It didn't help that there was one person who was really nasty about the news. She had promoted the original Indiegogo campaign on her website and felt like I had not only disappointed her by not completing the book but also made her look bad to her readers. Though I'd offered the explanation and the refund, she was angry, although she never told me that directly. She posted about it on her blog and in the comments on other people's blogs, calling me an Internet scammer and other ugly things. I tried multiple times to reach out to her, privately at first and then through public blog comments, and she never responded although she posted several more unhappy things about me on her site. For the most part, I recognized that this was more her problem than mine, that I did what I could and needed to let it go, that I had plenty of amazing people still believing in my vision and more importantly that I really believed in it. But there were days when her voice got into my head and I felt like a fraud, a failure, a disappointment to the world of creative people everywhere. That kind of self-esteem attack isn't exactly conducive to creative confidence; it eats away at it and makes it impossible to move forward.

I tried to move forward anyway. I reorganized the text of the book to get more excited about it again. Every time I re-worked an old exercise, I'd remember why the book meant so much to me. (I worked a lot on the Letting Go and Self-Esteem exercises at that time!) I got freshly interested in the ways that crochet was helping people, launching a survey that summer to discover more about the craft's health benefits. Amazingly, more than ten thousand people responded to that survey, and suddenly I had a wealth of information at my fingertips on the topic. But I wasn't quite sure what to do with the information, yet, wasn't sure how to organize it, wasn't sure if it belonged in this book or its own book or just online or perhaps even just in the back of my head to draw from as I wrote other things. I wasn't sure and I wanted to be sure and then it was time for the second year of grad school to begin.

In December 2014, I finally decided that I was going to make a very clear and firm offer of a refund to everyone who had funded the book, because I absolutely had to release myself from the grips the project had on me, even if those grips were mostly in my own head. I wrote:

> "I've come to the sad decision to refund the generous supporters of my Indiegogo project for my pending book *Hook to Heal*. This has been a long, hard process and a learning lesson for me. The book remains in the final stages and I truly believe that it will have a 2015 release date. However, I seem to just be stuck. The pressure of "owing" this to people seems to be conflicting with the creative process and as much as I hate to do so, I just really need to let that go. The only way I can see to do that is to refund the money, release that pressure valve and put the book out when it's ready to be released into the world. I just don't want to put out sub-par work solely in order to fulfill this commitment.
>
> I offer huge apologies for the long time that you have waited. Each contribution truly has been valued and appreciated. It has gone to complete the work that I've already done on the project. More than that, it has helped me to believe in the value of my work to others. Your belief in me was very special and I'm sorry to have been unable to fulfill this campaign up to this point.

Again, I apologize and hope that you understand that I started this campaign with the best of intentions and that it's been something I've learned a lot from in regards to my own creative process."

I shared the available refund options and a promise to process any refund requests by January 2015.

Here's What Happened

A couple of people immediately asked for a refund and I gave it to them. (Incidentally, I had no trouble meeting that January 2015 deadline of answering all requests.) The nasty person posted my email on her site, never contacting me directly and ignoring all of my requests for information on how to give a refund to her. A handful of people chose to advertise on my site instead of getting a cash refund. But most people just emailed me to say, "hang in there, I still believe in the work, keep at it, don't worry about it". People were generous, not with their money specifically, but with their belief in me. At least a few people said that even if this book never got written, they'd know that their support led to whatever my next project was, and they were happy being a part of that creative process. I got their permission to let this book go because I'd given myself that permission. Then I rested. I knew this book would eventually get done because it was mostly written anyway and I really wanted it out there, but I no longer pressured myself to figure out exactly what that would look like.

Then Marinke died.

It was June 2015 when I opened my blog reader and saw a post on her beautiful website, A Creative Being, from her sister letting the world know that Wink had lost her ongoing battle with depression and succumbed to suicide. I was devastated, in a way that I didn't know I could be devastated by the death of someone I'd never met in person. You see, I knew Wink from our online connection, finding her during the time that I was researching the healing power of crochet for *Crochet Saved My Life*. She shared her story with me then, which I shared in that book, and we connected with each other periodically over the years. A few weeks earlier, I'd seen her post that she was having a hard time, and I knew her depression was back and I'd reached out to her but gotten no response. Then the suicide happened.

Immediately I was compelled into action, starting the Mandalas for Marinke collaborative crochet art project the same day that I heard the news. I mentioned it in a previous chapter here, and you can learn about the project online, but essentially Wink had become known to many of us through her amazing crochet mandala patterns. The mandala is a healing circle and she incorporated color therapy into her mandala designs. It seemed only fitting to create a healing project using her mandalas as inspiration. I put a call out through the Internet letting people know that they could crochet one or more mandalas, preferably using Wink's patterns, and send them to me to be curated into an online collection (and eventually a physical art exhibit) designed to raise awareness about depression and suicide while celebrating Wink's life and creativity. Crochet had brought several extra years of joy, self-esteem, productivity, connection and beauty to Wink's world. Despite the fact that she ultimately didn't make it, her life was improved by the craft.

The mandalas began to pour in, each one filled with the love of handmade color and the intention to brighten the world just a little bit one stitch at a time. I opened each package with focused attention, connecting viscerally with the creator as I held the work in my hands. I shared the work online, allowing each post to tell us more about Marinke, more about depression and more about how craft heals.

I didn't have any intentions about this book when I started the Mandalas to Marinke project – it wasn't even in my mind at all - but life is funny that way. The creative energy that coursed from that project breathed new life into this book. I suddenly felt like it was the right time to finish it, that the passion was there, that the intention was right. I wanted to finish it because of Marinke, because perhaps the ideas in this book could help and inspire someone going through the same things that she was going through. More than that, I needed to finish the book for myself, because I needed to go through and work many of these exercises again to get through grief and heal myself in a new way. In the weeks following the news, I'd worked many, many crochet mandalas myself, just sitting there, processing the information in some deep way. It helped me to heal, and this helped all of the things that had happened before to coalesce.

This Book

That's the story of the book that you're holding in your hands, a book that I hold so close to my heart. This project is so different from my original vision. I let go of the plan for courses and mentoring. Interestingly, I'd forgotten completely that my original vision included a non-profit component but am still at work on a non-profit arm of this type of work in a slightly different form. I originally planned to include examples of my own for each and every exercise, showing how I completed the exercise, and about halfway through I completely scrapped that idea for a number of different reasons.

I had to admit a really difficult truth for me, which is that I didn't care about having photos in this book. I'd said from the beginning that they would be there, and I thought that they "had" to be here, and I realized through some deep, deep work that what I was really reacting to was the complaints of some previous readers that *Crochet Saved My Life* had no images and no patterns, even though that book was all about storytelling. I had to admit that I had insecurities about my image skills, and I wanted to "fix" or resolve those insecurities by including astounding images for all of the exercises, incorporating tutorials, etc. And I had to admit that this doesn't interest me one iota, that in fact I believe that any images of my own use of the exercises could actually limit other people in their imaginations for using the exercises themselves, that almost all of my own personal favorite creativity books (listed in the back of this book) are text-only. I had to accept that some people wouldn't like this decision and I had to get okay with the heart of it.

I also had to completely abandon my hope that the ebook version of *Hook to Heal* could be interactive (with links to online tips for the exercises, etc.) because my technology skills aren't up to par with that yet (someday) and none of the additional post-Indiegogo funding I'd hoped for came through so paying someone to do that part was impossible. I hope that I can do an interactive version of this book someday but I had to be okay with releasing it into the world as is.

That's the whole story of this book.

I share it with you because I want you to know that when I began this book I already had most of the creative tools that you can find within its pages, but they didn't always work for me every step of the way. Creativity is not linear. While I certainly can set out to create an outline and work a book from start to finish and publish it, I can't predict the waves that will come to shift my sands and change it all. I remain open to those changes because that's where true creation lives. And even though I know that truth so deeply in my soul, I still fall prey to self-doubt and guilt and shame and believing that what I'm making isn't enough ... until I remember again that it is. It's a cycle, it's a process. You can work through the exercises from beginning to end one time through and it may or may not change your life. But if you're tuned in to a lifelong process of creativity, you'll probably have to return to these exercises (or create your own) over and over, at different times, to remind yourself of where you've been and to find out where you are going.

I thought I would finish this book. Then I thought I might not. Then I did. I crocheted every step of the way. I engaged in meditative crochet when I needed it, crocheted with affirmations, reminded myself again and again to let go, re-built my flailing self-esteem with crochet … I share the exercises in this book because they are actually what I use in my own life. And I keep a copy of the book for myself because I know that every new project will recreate the (wonderful, fabulous, terrifying, devastating, life-changing, exhilarating, challenging) creative cycle and require me to utilize these exercises again.

It is my deepest hope that you find this book to be helpful in allowing you to heal parts of yourself, accept your inner artist and move forward into a constantly changing creative life. I hope that you'll return again and again to the exercises until the book is dog-eared and underlined and practically falling apart in your hands. I hope that you'll discover your own creative exercises that are different from mine and that you'll not only use them but also share them with others. I hope that you'll trust yourself and love yourself and keep re-inventing yourself. I hope.

References and Resources

Books

Creativity Books:

I work regularly with creativity books of all kinds. I've mentioned a few throughout this book but there are many more that I know have influenced the ideas presented here. Here's a short list of some of my favorite books for exploring creativity:

- All of the books by Julia Cameron, particularly those in The Artist's Way trilogy
- Anything writing by SARK, especially Succulent Wild Woman and Make Your Creative Dreams Real
- Kick-Ass Creativity by Mary Beth Maziarz
- Living Artfully by Sandra Magsamen
- The Creative Habit by Twyla Tharp
- The 52 Lists Project by Moorea Seal
- The Happiness Project and Happier At Home by Gretchen Rubin
- The Zen of Creativity by John Daido Loori
- What We Ache For by Oriah Mountain Dreamer

Crochet and Craft Inspiration Books:

There are tons and tons of great crochet instructional books out there so I'm not going to list them all here. You can search through the "books" category on my blog, Crochet Concupiscence, to find my favorites. What I do want to share here is a short list of books related to crochet and craft that are also inspiring for the creative soul:

- Craftivism by Betsy Greer
- Craft Fail by Heather Mann
- Crafty Girls Talk by Jennifer Forest
- Creative Crochet by Arlene Stimmel and Nicki Hitz Edson
- Crochet Master Class by Jean Leinhauser and Rita Weiss
- Crochet Saved My Life by Kathryn Vercillo
- Dying to Crochet, a mystery novel by Bendy Carter

- Extra/Ordinary: Craft and Contemporary Art by Maria Elena Buszek
- Hooked for Life: Adventures of a Crochet Zelot by Mary Beth Temple
- Love in Every Stitch by Lee Gant
- One Plastic Bag: Isatou Ceesay and the Recycling Women of Gambia, a children's book by Miranda Paul
- The Crochet Woman: A Novel by Ruth Manning Sanders
- The Crocheter's Skill-Building Workshop: Essential Techniques for Becoming a More Versatile, Adventurous Crocheter by Dora Ohrenstein
- The Fine Art of Crochet by Gwen Blakley Kinsler
- Strange Material: Storytelling Through Textiles by Leanne Prain
- Yes! A YA novel by Deborah Burnside
- All crochet mystery novels by Betty Hechtman

Other References and Inspiring Reads:

And here are other titles I referenced throughout the book or believe are good resources on the topic:

- The Art of Asking by Amanda Palmer (which really helped me feel okay about the whole crowdsourced funding journey)
- The Life-Changing Magic of Tidying Up by Marie Kondo
- All About Felted Crochet, an article published in Interweave Crochet Magazine, Fall 2007, by Amy Swensen
- Amamani Puzzle Balls by Dedri Uys
- Around the Corner Crochet Borders by Edie Eckman
- Crochet Teaching Guide by the Craft Yarn Council (http://www.craftyarncouncil.com/crochet_guide.html)
- Teaching a Child to Crochet by The Crochet Guild of America (CGOA) (http://www.crochet.org/?page=ChildLesson)
- Harvesting Color: How to Find Plants and Make Natural Dyes by Rebecca Burgess
- Knit Local by Tanis Gray
- Once Upon a Time in Crochet by Lynne Rowe
- Reversible Color Crochet by Laurinda Reddig
- Uncovering Happiness by Elisha Goldstein

Yarn Clubs:

You can get yarn from monthly subscription services:

- Darn Good Yarn: http://www.darngoodyarn.com
- Yarn Box: https://yarnbox.com
- Yarn Crush: http://www.yarn-crush.com
- FicStitches: http://ficstitchesyarns.com

Or you can get yarn from Fiber CSA's such as:

- Brookfarm: http://www.brookfarmalpaca.com/BROOKFARM/CSA.html
- Sheepshares CSA from Foxfire Fiber: http://www.foxfirefiber.com/special.html

Charities That Accept Crochet Donations

Here is a list of charities that I'm aware of as accepting donations of handmade items, including crochet items, as of late 2015. Please note that the needs of charities change frequently so it is very important to check the websites or contact the coordinator of the program you're interested in to confirm that they still need donations and what they are currently accepting.

For Babies and Children:

- Binky Patrol: http://www.binkypatrol.org
- Caps for Good: http://www.savethechildren.org/atf/cf/%7B9def2ebe-10ae-432c-9bd0-df91d2eba74a%7D/CAPS-FOR-GOOD-KIT-2010.PDF
- Knit a Square: http://www.knit-a-square.com
- Mother Bear Project: http://www.motherbearproject.org
- Project Linus: http://www.projectlinus.org

For the Elderly:

- Adopt a Native Elder: http://www.anelder.org
- SIBOL: http://sunshineinternationalblanketsoflove.blogspot.com

For Homeless, Low-Income, At-Risk, People In Need:

- Bridge and Beyond: http://homelessbridge.blogspot.com
- Friends of Pine Ridge Reservation: http://friendsofpineridgereservation.org/difference/craftforprr.shtml
- From Ewe to You: http://fromewetoyou.webs.com
- Granny Squares of Love: https://grannysol.wordpress.com
- Warm Up America: http://www.warmupamerica.org

For the Military:

- Knit Your Bit: http://www.nationalww2museum.org/learn/knit-your-bit/
- Operation Gratitude, Scarves for Troops: https://opgrat.wordpress.com/2014/01/17/scarves-for-troops/

- Soldiers' Angels: http://soldiersangels.org/Sewing-and-Crafting-Team.html
- The Ships Project: http://www.theshipsproject.com

For People with Cancer:

- Crochet for Cancer: http://www.crochetforcancer.org
- Halos of Hope: http://halosofhope.org
- Knots of Love: http://www.knotsoflove.org

For Pets / Animals:

- Comfort for Critters: http://comfortforcritters.org
- House of Dreams: http://www.kittydreams.org

Two more great resources for finding charities that accept crochet:

- Lion Brand Charity Finder: http://www.lionbrand.com/charityConnection.html
- Handcrafting with Love: http://www.handcraftingwithlove.net/charity/hcharity.html

I'd also like to remind you that you probably have many opportunities to donate locally. You can contact local shelters, community centers, clinics, hospitals, churches, libraries and many other organizations to connect with people and find folks in need.

Fair Trade Crochet Organizations

Fair Trade Crochet is used to describe "first world" companies that purchase crochet from artisans in "developing nations". They pay those artisans a fair wage for their work. They implement ethical practices in working with people in developing nations. These companies sell the crochet piece to first world buyers interested in helping to support these artisans. Fair trade crochet work is usually (but not always) work that is done by women in developing nations for companies based in the United States or Europe. Here's how it helps them:

- Provides women with a means of independently supporting their families. In some cases, such as in war-torn countries, the women may be the only surviving income provider for their children.
- Fair trade crochet allows women to earn a fair wage in a fair treatment environment doing traditional handicrafts.
- Raises awareness among today's consumers of the issues facing women in developing nations today.
- It is worth noting that most, although not all, of these companies are small businesses launched by women, so in addition to helping to support the artisans, consumers are helping to support independent, ethical women business owners in the first world.

The following companies are companies that I am aware of, in late 2015, as Fair Trade Organizations providing a solid livable wage and good working conditions to people crafting for an income in developing nations. Please be aware that I've done as much research as possible before including a company on this list but it's always important for you to do your own research to understand whether or not a company is in line with your own moral and ethical beliefs and practices.

- AHA Bolivia: http://www.ahabolivia.com
- Cambodia Knits: http://cambodiaknits.com
- Coussinet: http://www.coussinet.com.au
- Escama Studio: http://www.escamastudio.com
- Jishike Social Couture: http://www.jishikesocialcouture.com/shop/
- Krochet Kids: http://www.krochetkids.org
- Le Souk: http://www.soukshop.com
- Mar y Sol: http://www.shopmarysol.com/

- Novica: http://www.novica.com
- Pebble: http://www.pebblechild.com
- Same Sky: http://www.samesky.com
- Walleska Ecochicc: http://www.ecochicc.com
- ZemZem Atelier: http://www.zemzematelier.com

Special Thanks

This book was made possible in part thanks to the early contributions from people who supported me through an Indiegogo fundraiser campaign. These wonderful people believed in my work before the book was a book, when it was still notes and an idea, and they put their money where their belief was to help afford me the time to write the book. Thanks from the bottom of my heart:

- Alison68
- Alyssa Crittenden
- Amy Hill
- Anna Fox
- Anne Oldenhuis
- Barbara Cooney
- Bethel of Bethania
- Billy Jack Koncelik
- Carolyn Jarie Getter
- Cheryl Bunch
- Columba Huaraque
- Cre8Tion Crochet
- Crochet Deacon
- CrochetGypsy
- Debi Yorston
- Deborah Hirsch
- Dorothy Hunter Talbot
- Erica Durante
- Eva Maria Martin Arenas
- Gayle Holmes
- Helen Martin
- JD Wolfe
- Jade Singleton
- Jean-Mary Meanyjar
- Jessica Carlos
- Judy Witherby
- Julie Addison
- Julie Marz
- Kara Gunza
- Karen Carino
- Karen Dong
- Katherine Gordon
- Katherine M. Auernheimer
- Ketura of Crochet Savvy
- Kristen Snellings
- Lani Schreibstein
- Lara Finlayson
- Lauren Wiersma
- Laurie Wheeler
- Laurinda Reddig
- Linda Miskowiec
- Lise Solvang
- Lori Sievert
- Lyndi Rivers
- Mags Reid
- Marcia Scarpelli
- Margaret Mills
- Margaret351
- Marinke Slump
- Marjolein Kleinman
- Mary Zeman
- Maureen Hart
- Michael Dore
- Miriam Vercillo
- Oombawka Design (Rhondda)
- Patricia Dille
- Patricia P. Post
- Patrick Ahern
- Patrizia Momigliano
- Patty Stogsdill
- Rachel Hileman
- Sarah Doty
- Sarah Jones
- Sheryl Means
- Sedruola Maruska
- Snarlingbadger (Kristin)
- Sophia Roberts
- Stacy Vaka

Stephanie Broderson
Stephanie Kicks
Suzy Harrison
TerryAnn Porter
Tracy Joyner of CrochetHappy
Wendy McKenney
Wendy Whipple

Additional Thanks

In addition to my gratitude for the Indiegogo supporters (including those not listed above who opted to remain anonymous) I want to give some special thanks to the people in my life who provide the network of support that allows me to practice my crafts of both crochet and writing.

Thank you to my family, who always believe in everything that I do. My mom helped fund the initial stages of this campaign, regularly asking me how it was going yet also knowing when it was better not to ask! More than that, she's the one who initially taught me to crochet, and she's inspired me with her renewed interest in the craft and her participation in art exhibits. She and my dad both always share my work with others and I constantly feel their sense of pride in me. Dad has noticed my steady growth as a writer, which has helped me continue on this path. Watching him change and grow through his own creative career has also helped inspire me. My younger siblings were tirelessly supportive of the development of this project, my sister quietly lending her love and my brother regularly checking on my progress. They look up to me but I also look up to them. Whenever progress was made here, they were the ones I wanted to tell, and whenever it was too hard, they were the ones I turned to. I am only me because I am the daughter and sister of these inspiring people. Thank you.

Thank you to my beaux, Demi, for absolutely everything. I've received a solid kind of love and acceptance in this relationship that provides a platform for my own personal growth and my understanding of the growth of relationships. I have changed endlessly through this relationship while also finding the deepest center of my unchanging, unwavering self. It is through this that I'm able to do the creative work that I do. Thank you.

Thank you to my best friends. Rafael, Kelly, Adam and Jeanette ... I hope you know all of the amazing strength that you offer me. In your own ways, you each know me better than I know myself, you each give me a kind of quiet, endless support that I always know I can rely on, and you each bring out the best in me by being exactly who you are. I can't say thanks enough. There aren't right words.

A special thanks to my CIIS school classmates, particularly my own cohort who traveled the journey with me through my first two years of the program, and especially my small band of text message supporters and close friends (Matt, Courtaney and Pilar). All of you gave me the strength, courage and inspiration to take risks, find and be exactly who I am, honor what makes me different while connecting through what makes me the same and develop the many tools necessary to implement and share the exercises within these pages. You all taught me what it means to be part of a community and this is what I bring forth in all of my creative work. Thank you. I also want to name Megan, Paul and Debbie here – Megan for providing me with the tip to send my inner critic on vacation, Paul for teaching me new things about friendship and Debbie for providing a therapeutic key to the missing piece of the puzzle towards the end of this project.

And finally, endless thanks to my online crochet community. Thanks to the people who read my books, my blogs, my social media posts. Thanks to the people who comment and share and like and those who don't but who continue to come back to my work because something there is inspiring or helpful. Thanks to the crochet designers, authors and artists who share their own work in this world, allowing me to find new sources of inspiration and ideas. Whether or not we've interacted, whether or not I've commented to you directly, your work allows my work to grow and continue. The online network of people who crochet and craft is my wider community, my tribe, my people. This is what encourages me, enlivens me, propels me forward and sometimes saves me in dark times. Each and every single one of you is a light in my life, a sparkling colorful light that creates a world of fairies and fireworks and stars. Each of you is a stitch in the coziest crocheted safety net I could ever imagine, and I am lucky to have that net below me. I mentioned a saying early in this book – leap and the net will appear – and you are that net that allows me to take leaps both creatively and emotionally. Thank you. Endlessly, I thank you.

About the Author

Kathryn Vercillo was born and raised in Tucson, AZ but fell in love with the city of San Francisco the moment that she saw it. She's been living in San Francisco for over a decade, and she thrives on the creativity and celebration of creative expression that this city nurtures, although she still has a bit of the whimsical desert spirit in her heart.

Kathryn is a freelance writer and indie author who has written across a diverse array of mediums and topic areas. She especially loves to write about the intersection between crafting/ creativity (with an emphasis on crochet) and the mental health/ wellness/ personal growth. *Hook to Heal* is an outgrowth of exactly this type of writing.

Kathryn is also the author of:

- Crochet Saved My Life: The Mental and Physical Health Benefits of Crochet
- Cracked Wide Open: Essays, Musings, and Observations from My First Year as a Counseling Psychology Grad Student
- When Grandma Isn't Crocheting, She's Hunting Big Game (a collection of very brief articles about awesome older people who crochet)
- Ghosts of San Francisco and Ghosts of Alcatraz

Most importantly, Kathryn believes in writing from the heart, allowing her work to radiate outward from the center and into the world, where she hopes it can improve lives and affect change. She believes that self-expression is the key to self-realization and also the key to connecting communities.

You can find Kathryn online at www.kathrynvercillo.com, www.crochetconcupiscence.com, and diaryofasmartchick.com. She is active across all social media; links can be found on Crochet Concupiscence.

Printed in Great Britain
by Amazon